U.S. Presidential Elections Trivia Challenge:

1200 questions covering every American presidential election from George Washington to Donald Trump versus Hillary Clinton

Jonathan Ozanne

DEDICATION

For Sarah, Josiah, Gideon, Micah, and Samuel.

CONTENTS

THE WINNERS!

This first category is a warm-up category of sorts. (Can you get them all correct?) Going backwards in time from 2012 to 1789, identify the winner of each presidential election. Each presidential election will be explored in-depth later in the Challenge. Good luck!

1. Who won the 2012 U.S. presidential election?
   A. Barack Obama
   B. Mitt Romney

2. Who won the 2008 U.S. presidential election?
   A. Barack Obama
   B. John McCain
   C. Sarah Palin

3. Who won the 2004 U.S. presidential election?
   A. George W. Bush
   B. Howard Dean
   C. John Kerry

4. Who won the 2000 U.S. presidential election?
   A. Al Gore
   B. George W. Bush
   C. Pat Buchanan

5. Who won the 1996 U.S. presidential election?
   A. Bill Clinton
   B. Bob Dole
   C. Boris Yeltsin

6. Who won the 1992 U.S. presidential election?
   A. Bill Clinton
   B. George H.W. Bush
   C. Ross Perot

7. Who won the 1988 U.S. presidential election?
   A. George H.W. Bush
   B. Michael Dukakis

8. Who won the 1984 U.S. presidential election?
   A. Ronald Reagan
   B. Walter Mondale

9. Who won the 1980 U.S. presidential election?
   A. Jimmy Carter
   B. John Anderson
   C. Ronald Reagan

10. Who won the 1976 U.S. presidential election?
    A. Gerald Ford
    B. Jimmy Carter

11. Who won the 1972 U.S. presidential election?
    A. George McGovern
    B. Gerald Ford
    C. Richard Nixon

12. Who won the 1968 U.S. presidential election?
    A. Hubert Humphrey
    B. Pat Paulsen
    C. Richard Nixon

13. Who won the 1964 U.S. presidential election?
    A. Barry Goldwater
    B. Lyndon Johnson
    C. Nelson Rockefeller

14. Who won the 1960 U.S. presidential election?
    A. John F. Kennedy
    B. Hubert Humphrey
    C. Richard Nixon

15. Who won the 1956 U.S. presidential election?
    A. Adlai Stevenson
    B. Dwight Eisenhower

16. Who won the 1952 U.S. presidential election?
    - A. Adlai Stevenson
    - B. Dwight Eisenhower

17. Who won the 1948 U.S. presidential election?
    - A. Harry Truman
    - B. Thomas Dewey
    - C. Strom Thurmond

18. Who won the 1944 U.S. presidential election?
    - A. Franklin D. Roosevelt
    - B. Harry Truman
    - C. Thomas Dewey

19. Who won the 1940 U.S. presidential election?
    - A. Franklin D. Roosevelt
    - B. Wendell Willkie

20. Who won the 1936 U.S. presidential election?
    - A. Alf Landon
    - B. Franklin D. Roosevelt
    - C. Huey Long

21. Who won the 1932 U.S. presidential election?
    - A. Franklin D. Roosevelt
    - B. Herbert Hoover

22. Who won the 1928 U.S. presidential election?
    - A. Al Smith
    - B. Herbert Hoover

23. Who won the 1924 U.S. presidential election?
    - A. Calvin Coolidge
    - B. John Davis
    - C. Warren Harding

24. Who won the 1920 U.S. presidential election?
    - A. James Cox
    - B. Warren Harding

25. Who won the 1916 U.S. presidential election?
    - A. Charles E. Hughes
    - B. Woodrow Wilson

26. Who won the 1912 U.S. presidential election?
    - A. Theodore "Teddy" Roosevelt
    - B. William Taft
    - C. Woodrow Wilson

27. Who won the 1908 U.S. presidential election?
    - A. William J. Bryan
    - B. William Taft

28. Who won the 1904 U.S. presidential election?
    - A. Alton Parker
    - B. Charlie "Bird" Parker
    - C. Theodore "Teddy" Roosevelt

29. Who won the 1900 U.S. presidential election?
    - A. Theodore "Teddy" Roosevelt
    - B. William J. Bryan
    - C. William McKinley

30. Who won the 1896 U.S. presidential election?
    - A. Theodore "Teddy" Roosevelt
    - B. William J. Bryan
    - C. William McKinley

31. Who won the 1892 U.S. presidential election?
    - A. Benjamin Harrison
    - B. Grover Cleveland
    - C. James Weaver

32. Who won the 1888 U.S. presidential election?
    - A. Benjamin Harrison
    - B. Grover Cleveland
    - C. James Blaine

33. Who won the 1884 U.S. presidential election?
    - A. Benjamin Harrison
    - B. Grover Cleveland
    - C. James Blaine

34. Who won the 1880 U.S. presidential election?
    - A. James Garfield
    - B. Winfield Hancock

35. Who won the 1876 U.S. presidential election?
    - A. Rutherford Hayes
    - B. Samuel Tilden
    - C. Ulysses Grant

36. Who won the 1872 U.S. presidential election?
    - A. Horace Greeley
    - B. Ulysses Grant

37. Who won the 1868 presidential election?
    - A. Horatio Seymour
    - B. Ulysses Grant

38. Who won the 1864 U.S. presidential election?
    - A. Abraham Lincoln
    - B. George McClellan

39. Who won the 1860 U.S. presidential election?
    - A. Abraham Lincoln
    - B. John Breckinridge
    - C. Stephen Douglas

40. Who won the 1856 U.S. presidential election?
    - A. James Buchanan
    - B. John Fremont

41. Who won the 1852 U.S. presidential election?
    - A. Franklin Pierce
    - B. Winfield Scott

42. Who won the 1848 U.S. presidential election?
    - A. Lewis Cass
    - B. Millard Fillmore
    - C. Zachary Taylor

43. Who won the 1844 U.S. presidential election?
    - A. Henry Clay
    - B. James Polk

44. Who won the 1840 U.S. presidential election?
    - A. Martin Van Buren
    - B. William Harrison

45. Who won the 1836 U.S. presidential election?
    - A. Martin Van Buren
    - B. William Harrison

46. Who won the 1832 U.S. presidential election?
    - A. Andrew Jackson
    - B. Henry Clay
    - C. William Wirt

47. Who won the 1828 U.S. presidential election?
    - A. Andrew Jackson
    - B. John Q. Adams
    - C. Wilbur Reynolds

48. Who won the 1824 U.S. presidential election?
    - A. Andrew Jackson
    - B. John Q. Adams
    - C. Marvin Clay

49. Who won the 1820 U.S. presidential election?
   A. James Monroe

Why did the preceding question only have one answer?
   A. Typographical error. Most embarrassing.
   B. There were two candidates running and both were named James Monroe.
   C. James Monroe ran unopposed for re-election in 1820

50. Who won the 1816 U.S. presidential election?
   A. George Clinton
   B. James Monroe
   C. Rufus King

51. Who won the 1812 U.S. presidential election?
   A. Dewitt Clinton
   B. James Madison
   C. Rufus King

52. Who won the 1808 U.S. presidential election?
   A. Charles Pinckney
   B. George Clinton
   C. James Madison
   D. Thomas Jefferson

53. Who won the 1804 U.S. presidential election?
   A. Aaron Burr
   B. Charles Pinckney
   C. Thomas Jefferson

54. Who won the 1800 U.S. presidential election?
   A. Aaron Burr
   B. John Adams
   C. Thomas Jefferson

55. Who won the 1796 U.S. presidential election?
   A. John Adams
   B. Thomas Jefferson

56. Who won the 1792 U.S. presidential election?
   A. George Washington
   B. John Adams
   C. Paul Revere

57. Who won the 1789 U.S. presidential election?
   A. George Washington
   B. John Sullivan
   C. Nathanael Greene

Quick answers (more detailed answers at the back of the book)

1. A. 2. A. 3. A. 4. B. 5. A. 6. A. 7. A.
8. A. 9. C. 10. B. 11. C. 12. C. 13. B.
14. A. 15. B. 16. B. 17. A. 18. A. 19. A.
20. B. 21. A. 22. B. 23. A. 24. B. 25. B.
26. C. 27. B. 28. C. 29. C. 30. C. 31. B.
32. A. 33. B. 34. A. 35. A. 36. B. 37. B.
38. A. 39. A. 40. A. 41. A. 42. B. 43. B.
44. B. 45. A. 46. A. 47. A. 48. A.
49. A., C. 50. B. 51. B. 52. C. 53. C. 54. C.
55. A. 56. A. 57. A.

WHO CAN VOTE FOR THE PRESIDENT AND HOW THE PRESIDENT IS ELECTED

This section covers the major election laws found in the U.S. Constitution its amendments. This section includes questions about election qualifications, voting age, and so on. It also includes questions about the Electoral College.

58. In 1789 roughly what percentage of states had property-ownership requirements for voting?
    A. About half
    B. About three-quarters
    C. All of the original 13 states

59. When did former slaves get the guaranteed right to vote with the passage of the 15th Amendment?
    A. 1840
    B. 1870
    C. 1900

60. Who supplied the election ballots in the 1860s?
    A. Government
    B. Political Parties
    C. No one

61. When was the so-called "Australian ballot" introduced to the United States?
    A. 1888
    B. 1898
    C. 1908

62. What is the difference between the Indiana ballot and the Massachusetts ballot?
    A. One is printed on red paper and the other one is printed on blue paper
    B. One lists only the two major parties and the other lists all of the parties
    C. One sorts the ballot by party and the other sorts it by political office

63. When did women get the guaranteed right to vote?
    A. 1880
    B. 1900
    C. 1920

64. What is the current minimum voting age?
    A. 18 years old
    B. 21 years old
    C. 24 years old

65. Which of the following class of people is generally legally unable to vote?
    A. Convicted felons
    B. Native Americans
    C. People older than 95

66. What day is Election Day?
    A. First Monday in November
    B. First Tuesday in November
    C. First Tuesday after the First Monday in November

67. True or False. The president of the United States is directly elected by the voters?

68. How is the number of electoral votes for each state determined?
    A. Congress decides
    B. It is the same size as the Congressional delegation for the state
    C. Random lottery every 10 years

69. Who appoints the electors who cast the electoral votes?
    A. Congress
    B. President
    C. State legislatures

70. Which method do most states currently use to determine the appointment of electors?
    A. At-large popular vote
    B. Popular vote winner of each congressional district
    C. Legislative election

71. True or False. Until the Twentieth Century most states had the direct election of electors?

72. How were the first presidential elections conducted before any constitutional amendments?
    A. Each elector would get one vote for president and one vote for vice president
    B. Each elector would get two votes and the highest vote getter would be president and the second highest would be vice president
    C. Each elector would get three votes to allocate as he saw fit

73. What was a problem created by the way that the original voting rules in the Constitution worked?
    A. It turned the race into a popularity contest
    B. The president and the vice president could be from different political parties
    C. There were too many ties

74. True or False. The 12th Amendment has an express prohibition on the vice president and the president being from the same state?

75. What happens if no candidate wins a majority in the Electoral College, who decides the winner of the presidency?
    A. U.S. House of Representatives
    B. U.S. Senate
    C. U.S. Supreme Court

76. In the case of no candidate winning a majority in Election Day voting, how many candidates make it to the next round under the current rules?
    A. All of them
    B. Top three
    C. Top five

77. How many votes does each state get in the tie-breaker round?
    A. One
    B. Two
    C. Equal to Electoral College vote
    D. None

78. How many votes does it currently take to win the tie-breaking round?
    A. 18
    B. 26
    C. 37

79. According to the Twelfth Amendment, if no winner of the Electoral College has been determined prior to the expiration of the current president's term, who becomes president?
    A. Outgoing vice president becomes president
    B. Outgoing president remains president
    C. Winner of the popular vote becomes president

80. According to the Twentieth Amendment, if the president elect dies prior to inauguration, what happens?
    A. New election is held to determine who becomes president
    B. Outgoing president remains president
    C. Vice president-elect becomes president

81. What date is the start and end date for presidential terms according to the original articles in the Constitution?
    A. No date is given and the decision is up to Congress
    B. January 20
    C. March 4

82. What date is set for the start and end of presidential terms by the Twentieth Amendment?
    A. No date is given by the Twentieth Amendment
    B. January 20
    C. March 4

83. If no candidate receives a majority in the Electoral College in the votes for vice president, who decides the winner of the vice presidency?
    A. U.S. House of Representatives
    B. U.S. Senate
    C. U.S. Supreme Court

84. How many times has it been necessary for a vice presidential tie to be resolved when there was no question about who had won the presidential election?
    A. Zero
    B. One
    C. Two

85. Since when has Election Day been the same for every state for presidential elections?
    A. 1805
    B. 1845
    C. 1885

86. After serving for one year, President Smith resigns after a scandal and Vice President Jones becomes President of the United States. (Until now Jones has never served as president). How many times can Jones seek election to the presidency?
    A. Zero
    B. One
    C. Two

87. How many votes are needed to win the Electoral College?
    A. 55
    B. 270
    C. 538

88. In 2016 how many states have exactly three electoral votes?
    A. Six
    B. Eight
    C. Ten

89. How many states have 10 or more electoral votes?
    A. 21
    B. 23
    C. 25

90. How many states have 20 or more electoral votes?
    A. Six
    B. Eight
    C. Ten

91. How many states have 30 or more electoral votes?
    A. One
    B. Two
    C. Four

92. How many states have 40 or more electoral votes?
    A. Zero
    B. One
    C. Two

93. How many states have 50 or more electoral votes?
    A. Zero
    B. One
    C. Two

94. How many states have 60 or more electoral votes?
    A. Zero
    B. One
    C. Two

95. Which state has more electoral votes in 2016, Alaska or Hawaii?
    A. Alaska
    B. Hawaii
    C. They both have the same number

96. How many states currently split their electoral votes by congressional district rather than award the whole state as winner-take-all?
    A. Zero
    B. One
    C. Two

THE ELECTIONS (2012 to 1789)

The Elections (2012 to 1789) goes backwards in time starting with the most recent election (2012) and going all the way back to the first election (1789). Questions on the 2016 campaign are in another section altogether. For each election generally there are questions about the results of the popular vote, the results of the electoral vote, the party conventions, and the candidates.

A word about Electoral College questions: Remember that the Electoral College is a closed universe (the size changes from time to time but has not changed recently) and there are a finite number of votes available. If one candidate is getting more votes, another candidate is getting less. The margin is measured not by the total votes but by the number of votes needed to change the result. Starting in 1964 the magic number to win has been 270. The margin is how many votes it takes to get the losing candidate's total to 270.

☆2012 ELECTION☆

97. In 2012 President Barack Obama ran for re-election. Who did he choose as his running mate?
    A. Joe Biden
    B. Joe Lieberman
    C. Hillary Clinton

98. Who won the Republican Party nomination in 2012?
    A. Herman Cain
    B. Mitt Romney
    C. Newt Gingrich

99. In 2012 which party convention featured a well-known actor/director lecturing an empty chair?
    A. Democratic Party
    B. Green Party
    C. Republican Party

100. Support or opposition to what signature piece of legislation from Barack Obama's first term was made into a campaign issue in 2012?
    A. Affordable Care Act
    B. Dodd-Frank Act
    C. Patriot Act Reauthorization

101. Which answer best describes the popular vote result in 2012?
    A. Barack Obama received 60% of the popular vote
    B. Barack Obama received 55% of the popular vote
    C. Barack Obama received 51% of the popular vote

102. Which answer best describes the electoral vote result in 2012?
    A. Barack Obama won by less than 5 electoral votes
    B. Barack Obama won by more than 5 but less than 50 electoral votes
    C. Barack Obama won by more than 50 electoral votes

103. On the campaign trail, Mitt Romney criticized the 47% of Americans who get more money back from the government than they pay in taxes. What percentage of the popular vote did Romney get?
    A. 47%
    B. 48%
    C. 49%

104. What percentage of the Labor vote did Obama win in 2012?
    A. About 40%
    B. About 60%
    C. About 80%

105. How many states plus the District of Columbia did Obama carry in 2012?
    A. 21
    B. 26
    C. 31

106. In what state did Obama win 70% of the popular vote?
    A. Hawaii
    B. Illinois
    C. Vermont

107. What state did Romney win 72% of the popular vote in 2012?
    A. Massachusetts
    B. Ohio
    C. Utah

108. In 2012 if only the 15 largest cities voted for president, who would have won?
    A. Obama
    B. Romney
    C. Tie

109. In 2012 if the winner of the most counties won the White House, who would have won?
    A. Obama
    B. Romney
    C. Tie

Quick answers for the 2012 Election (more detailed answers are at the back of the book)

97. A. 98. B. 99. C. 100. A. 101. C. 102. C.
103. A. 104. B. 105. B. 106. A. 107. C. 108. A.
109. B.

☆2008 ELECTION☆

110. In 2007, where did Barack Obama officially announce his candidacy for president?
    A. Honolulu, Hawaii
    B. Springfield, Illinois
    C. Washington D.C.

111. What early win in the slate of primaries and caucuses validated Obama's candidacy and launched him towards winning the nomination?
    A. Iowa Caucus
    B. Nevada Caucus
    C. New Hampshire Primary

112. Which answer best describes the Obama campaign and technology?
    A. Obama ran a very old-fashioned campaign with less emphasis on using technology
    B. Obama ran an average campaign with no particular focus on technology
    C. Obama ran a very tech-savvy operation that used cutting edge technology to recruit supporters

113. Where did Obama give his acceptance speech when he received the nomination?
    A. At a small indoor venue
    B. At a large indoor venue
    C. At a large outdoor venue

114. What was Barack Obama's slogan when running for president in 2008?
    A. "Yes We Can!"
    B. "Obama is the Man"
    C. "Barack is the One"

115. True or False. Barack Obama raised such prodigious amounts of cash that he became the first candidate to opt-out of accepting federal campaign money for the general election campaign?

116. Who ran against Obama in 2008 in the general election?
    A. John McCain
    B. Mitt Romney
    C. Russ Feingold

117. What diversity milestone did the Republican ticket achieve in 2008?
    A. First African-American won the nomination as a Republican candidate for vice president
    B. First Latino won the nomination as a Republican candidate for vice president
    C. First woman won the nomination as a Republican candidate for vice president

118. True or False. John McCain conceded that he was going to lose Pennsylvania fairly early in the summer and did not spend much time there during the campaign?

119. Which answer best describes voter turnout in 2008?
    A. Below average turnout
    B. Average turnout
    C. Above average turnout

120. Which answer best describes the popular vote result in 2008?
    A. Barack Obama won with 51% of the popular vote
    B. Barack Obama won with 53% of the popular vote
    C. Barack Obama won with 55% of the popular vote

121. Which answer best describes the electoral vote result in 2008?
    A. Barack Obama won by less than 30 electoral votes
    B. Barack Obama won by more than 30 but less than 70 electoral votes
    C. Barack Obama won by more than 70 electoral votes

122. True or False. In 2008 Barack Obama won with the largest electoral vote total for a Democratic candidate since Lyndon Johnson?

123. In 2008, Barack Obama won an electoral vote in one of the two states that currently awards electoral votes by winner of congressional districts. In which state did he win one electoral vote?
    A. Nebraska
    B. Nevada
    C. North Dakota

124. Did the Republican ticket of John McCain and Sarah Palin get more than 200 electoral votes?
    A. Yes
    B. No
    C. It got exactly 200 electoral votes

Quick answers for the 2008 Election (more detailed answers are at the back of the book)

110. B. 111. A. 112. C. 113. C. 114. A.
115. T. 116. A. 117. C. 118. F. 119. C.
120. B. 121. C. 122. F. 123. A. 124. B.

☆2004 ELECTION☆

125. Which candidate gave a war cry to rally his supporters after a disappointing finish in the Iowa Caucus in 2004?
    A. John Edwards
    B. John Kerry
    C. Howard Dean

126. Which former NATO commander and U.S. Army general sought the Democratic Party nomination in 2004?
    A. Al Sharpton
    B. Richard Gephardt
    C. Wesley Clark

127. Which future 2008 presidential candidate gave the keynote address to the 2004 Democratic Convention?
    A. Barack Obama
    B. Hilary Clinton
    C. John Edwards

128. Which city hosted the 2004 Democratic Convention?
    A. Boston
    B. Philadelphia
    C. San Francisco

129. What was a significant source of campaign contributions for the first time?
    A. Foreign donors
    B. Internet
    C. Labor unions

130. What city hosted the 2004 Republican Convention?
    A. Denver
    B. New York City
    C. City of Tampa

131. During the campaign, John Kerry was attacked on his Vietnam War record. Which answer best describes his response?
    A. Slow
    B. Fast

132. Which answer best describes the popular vote result in 2004?
    A. George W. Bush won with only a plurality of the popular vote
    B. George W. Bush won with a slight majority of the popular vote
    C. George W. Bush won with a large majority of the popular vote

133. Which answer best describes the electoral vote result in 2004?
    A. John Kerry needed to flip only Ohio to win
    B. John Kerry needed to flip Ohio and Florida to win
    C. John Kerry needed to flip Ohio, Florida, and Pennsylvania to win

134. Why was John Kerry's electoral vote total one less than would be expected?
    A. One of his electors was sick
    B. One of his electors voted for Edwards instead
    C. One of his electors voted for Bush in a gesture of national unity

135. There was a procedural challenge to George W. Bush's win but the challenge was voted down in the Senate. The challenge questioned the votes from which state?
    A. Florida
    B. Pennsylvania
    C. Ohio

Quick answers for the 2004 Election (more detailed answers are at the back of the book)

125. C. 126. C. 127. A. 128. A. 129. B. 130. B. 131. A. 132. B. 133. A. 134. B. 135. C.

☆2000 ELECTION☆

136. Who was the main challenger to Vice President Al Gore in the 2000 primary season?
    A. Bill Bradley
    B. Joe Lieberman
    C. Kent Conrad

137. Who was the main challenger to Governor George W. Bush in the 2000 primary season?
   A. Fred Thompson
   B. John McCain
   C. George Pataki

138. The 2000 Democratic Convention featured a lengthy kiss between which couple?
   A. Al and Tipper Gore
   B. Bill and Hillary Clinton
   C. Ben Lopez and Jennifer Affleck

139. Where was the Republican Convention held in 2000?
   A. Denver
   B. Los Angeles
   C. Philadelphia

140. Which answer best describes the popular vote result in 2000?
   A. Close (top two candidates within 2% of each other)
   B. Not that close (top two candidates more than 2% but less than 7% apart)
   C. Blowout victory (of the top two candidate, one candidate won by more than 15% of the popular vote)

141. Which answer best describes the electoral vote result in 2000?
   A. Close (change the winner of the three closest states and the winner of the election changes or a tie is created)
   B. Comfortable win (change the winner of the three closest states and the winner of the election does not change. However the election night margin of victory in the electoral college was less than 150)
   C. Blowout victory (the winner won by at least 200 electoral votes on election night)

142. Why did Al Gore receive one less electoral vote than his state total reflected?
   A. One elector abstained to protest the lack of voting representation of Washington D.C.
   B. One elector was sick and unable to vote
   C. One elector switched his vote to George W. Bush in a show of national unity

143. True or False. Vice President Al Gore got approximately half a million more votes than George W. Bush in the 2000 election?

144. True or False. In a much-criticized decision, the U.S. Supreme Court decided the 2000 election by stopping the recounts based on equal protection and due process clause challenges by George W. Bush?

145. What is a "dimpled chad"?
   A. A type of fish
   B. A type of ballot
   C. A type of judge

146. In 2000 the election hinged on disputed votes in which state?
   A. New Mexico
   B. Florida
   C. Texas

147. Did any third party candidates affect the outcome of the 2000 presidential election?
   A. No
   B. Yes

148. A law passed in 1887 governs the procedure for challenging presidential election results. Twenty separate procedural challenges were made in Congress challenging the results of the 2000 Election, all of these procedural challenges were rejected for what reason?
    A. No support from at least one senator as required by law
    B. No support from at least one representative as required by law
    C. No support from the national party chairperson as required by law

> *Quick answers for the 2000 Election (more detailed answers are at the back of the book)*
>
> 136. A. 137. B. 138. A. 139. C. 140. A.
> 141. A. 142. A. 143. T. 144. T. 145. B.
> 146. B. 147. B. 148. A.

☆1996 ELECTION☆

149. Which Republican businessman ran for president on a platform featuring a flat tax in 1996?
    A. Donald Trump
    B. Steve Forbes
    C. Steve Jobs

150. Bob Dole won 46 victories during the primaries (states and territories), his next closest competitor had four wins. Who had four wins?
    A. Lamar Alexander
    B. Pat Buchanan
    C. Steve Forbes

151. How old was Bob Dole when he was nominated for president in 1996?
    A. 67
    B. 70
    C. 73

152. What city hosted the 1996 Democratic Convention?
    A. Baltimore
    B. Chicago
    C. San Antonio

153. Bob Dole served in World War II and was seriously wounded fighting in which country?
    A. France
    B. Italy
    C. Libya

154. Did any third party candidates affect the results of the election in 1996?
    A. No
    B. Yes

155. The presidential election debates between the two candidates required what special accommodation in 1996?
    A. Color blindness
    B. Hearing Impaired
    C. Left-handed

156. Which answer best describes the popular vote result in 1996?
    A. Not that close (top two candidates more than 2% but less than 7% apart)
    B. Big win (top two candidates more than 7% but less than 15% apart)
    C. Blowout victory (of the top two candidate, one candidate won by more than 15% of the popular vote)

157. Which answer best describes the electoral vote result in 1996?
    A. Dole needed about 110 more electoral votes to win
    B. Dole needed about 160 more electoral votes to win
    C. Dole needed about 210 more electoral votes to win

158. True or False. Voter participation in 1996 dropped to a level not seen since the 1920s?

159. Which of the following "red" states did Bill Clinton carry in 1996 that he lost in 1992?
    A. Arizona
    B. Montana
    C. Tennessee

160. True or False. Bill Clinton was the first Democratic president to be elected with a Republican-controlled Congress?

> *Quick answers for the 1996 Election (more detailed answers are at the back of the book).*
> 149. B. 150. B. 151. C. 152. B. 153. B. 154. A. 155. A. 156. B. 157. A. 158. T. 159. A. 160. T.

☆1992 ELECTION☆

161. Which candidate won the 1992 Iowa Caucus?
    A. Paul Tsongas
    B. Jerry Brown
    C. Mario Cuomo

162. In 1992, winning which primary earned Bill Clinton the nickname "comeback kid"?
    A. Florida
    B. New Hampshire
    C. South Carolina

163. True or False. Bill Clinton made a surprise impromptu appearance at the convention in response to delegate cheers?

164. In a 54 minute acceptance speech, Bill Clinton called for a set of programs that he named as what?
    A. New Covenant
    B. New Promise
    C. New Oath

165. Trying to shake his reputation of being gaffe-prone, which answer best describes the new image that Dan Quayle made for himself in his 1992 convention speech?
    A. Family values defender
    B. Fiscal conservative
    C. Foreign policy expert

166. In his acceptance speech, what did George H.W. Bush try to make the election about?
    A. Dreams
    B. Maturity
    C. Trust

167. Bill Clinton was governor of what state when he ran for president?
    A. Arkansas
    B. Missouri
    C. Mississippi

168. Which answer best describes third party candidate Ross Perot's background?
    A. Maverick senator from Texas
    B. Billionaire businessman from Texas
    C. Mayor of a small town in Oklahoma

169. Which answer best describes a major issue during the campaign?
    A. Crime
    B. Economy
    C. National Security

170. Which answer best describes the popular vote result in 1992?
    A. Close (top two candidates within 2% of each other)
    B. Not that close (top two candidates more than 2% but less than 7% apart)
    C. Big win (top two candidates more than 7% but less than 15% apart)

171. Which answer best describes the electoral vote result in 1992?
    A. Bush needed about 50 more electoral votes to win
    B. Bush needed about 100 more electoral votes to win
    C. Bush needed about 150 more electoral votes to win

172. True or False. Bill Clinton was elected in 1992 with more votes for president than any Democrat had received in a single election; but his share of the popular vote at 43% was the fourth lowest share by a winning candidate?

173. True or False. Third party candidate Ross Perot got about 19% of the popular vote in 1992?

174. Generally who would Ross Perot voters have voted for if not for Perot?
    A. George H.W. Bush
    B. Bill Clinton
    C. They would have stayed home and not voted if Perot was not a candidate

Quick answers for the 1992 Election (more detailed answers are at the back of the book).

161. A. 162. B. 163. T. 164. A. 165. A. 166. C. 167. A. 168. B. 169. B. 170. B. 171. B. 172. T. 173. T. 174. A.

☆1988 ELECTION☆

175. Michael Dukakis won the 1988 Democratic primaries. Who was his most successful competitor?
    A. Al Gore
    B. Jesse Jackson
    C. Joe Biden

176. George H.W. Bush won the 1988 Republican primaries. Who was his most successful competitor?
    A. Bob Dole
    B. Jack Kemp
    C. Pat Robertson

177. Who gave an overly lengthy nominating speech at the 1988 Democratic Convention?
    A. Ann Richards
    B. Bill Clinton
    C. Jesse Jackson

178. What famous pledge did George H.W. Bush make at the 1988 Republican Convention?
    A. To get tough on crime
    B. No new taxes
    C. To run an open and transparent administration

179. Before running for president, Michael Dukakis was governor of which state?
    A. Connecticut
    B. Massachusetts
    C. Rhode Island

180. True or False. Ronald Reagan did not endorse any candidate for president in 1988, wanting to be "above the fray"?

181. Michael Dukakis hurt his election chances by giving a poor quality answer to a difficult question about which subject during the 1988 presidential debates?
    A. Crime
    B. Pollution regulations
    C. Taxes

182. True or False. George H.W. Bush overcame a significant deficit in the national polls in 1988?

183. Which answer best describes the popular vote result in 1988?
  - A. Close (top two candidates within 2% of each other)
  - B. Not that close (top two candidates more than 2% but less than 7% apart)
  - C. Big win (top two candidates more than 7% but less than 15% apart)

184. Which answer best describes the electoral vote result in 1988?
  - A. Dukakis needed to win about 100 more electoral votes
  - B. Dukakis needed to win about 150 more electoral votes
  - C. Dukakis needed to win about 200 more electoral votes

185. In 1988 George H.W. Bush held Michael Dukakis to how many states?
  - A. 8
  - B. 11
  - C. 14

186. 1988 was the last year that the Republicans carried which of the following states?
  - A. California
  - B. Florida
  - C. Texas

> *Quick answers for the 1988 Election (more detailed answers are at the back of the book).*
>
> 175. C. 176. A. 177. B. 178. B. 179. B. 180. F. 181. A. 182. T. 183. C. 184. B. 185. B. 186. A.

☆1984 ELECTION☆

187. In addition to Jesse Jackson, who was Walter Mondale's major rival for the Democratic nomination?
  - A. Gary Hart
  - B. George McGovern
  - C. John Glenn

188. What month did Mondale clinch the nomination or have all of his major competitors drop out?
  - A. April
  - B. May
  - C. June

189. Who did Walter Mondale select as his running mate at the 1984 Democratic convention?
  - A. Gary Hart
  - B. Geraldine Ferraro
  - C. Jesse Jackson

190. What was one reason that protests outside at the Republican Convention were relatively sparse?
  - A. Hot weather
  - B. Most protestors had to work during the day and had trouble getting time off from work
  - C. Unusually tight-security for a pre-9/11 convention

191. In 2002, after Paul Wellstone was killed in a tragic plane crash, Walter Mondale served as an emergency substitute candidate for what office?
  - A. Governor of Minnesota
  - B. U.S. House of Representatives
  - C. U.S. Senate

192. True or False. In 1984, Ronald Reagan was the oldest candidate to be nominated for re-election as president?

193. Which of the following subjects was a major campaign issue in 1984, with both major parties taking opposite stands on the issue?
   A. Federal spending
   B. Pollution
   C. Taxes

194. True or False. Walter Mondale thought that any chance of defeating Reagan in the presidential debate disappeared when Reagan made a joke about "not exploiting for political purposes, my opponent's youth and inexperience"?

195. In polling taken during the 1984 campaign, was Mondale ever within 10% of Reagan?
   A. Yes, several times
   B. Yes, just a few times
   C. No, he was never within 10% of Reagan in the polls

196. Which answer best describes the popular vote result in 1984?
   A. Close (top two candidates within 2% of each other)
   B. Not that close (top two candidates more than 2% but less than 7% apart)
   C. Blowout victory (of the top two candidate, one candidate won by more than 15% of the popular vote)

197. Which answer best describes the electoral vote result in 1984?
   A. Mondale needed about 5 more electoral votes to win
   B. Mondale needed about 150 more electoral votes to win
   C. Mondale needed about 250 more electoral votes to win

198. In 1984 how many votes short of a 50 state sweep was Reagan (although he lost the District of Columbia by more than 150,000 votes)?
   A. Less than 5,000
   B. More than 5,000 but less than 10,000
   C. More than 10,000 but less than 15,000

199. In 1984 which of the following electoral milestones did Reagan achieve?
   A. Holding his opponent to Minnesota and the District of Columbia
   B. Getting 525 electoral votes
   C. Winning almost 59% of the popular vote
   D. All of the above

Quick answers for the 1984 Election (more detailed answers are at the back of the book).

187. A. 188. C. 189. B. 190. A. 191. C. 192. T. 193. C. 194. T. 195. C. 196. C. 197. C. 198. A. 199. D.

☆1980 ELECTION☆

200. In 1980, who was Jimmy Carter's most significant rival for the Democratic nomination?
   A. Jesse Jackson
   B. Ted Kennedy
   C. Walter Mondale

201. In 1980 who was Ronald Reagan's most successful rival in the Republican primaries?
   A. George Bush
   B. Howard Baker
   C. John Anderson

202. Which phrase best describes the process of finalizing the 1980 Democratic platform?
    A. Bitter struggle between opposing factions
    B. Harmonious unity
    C. Mild disagreements only

203. Ronald Reagan chose George H.W. Bush to be his running mate. He made his final decision at the convention. Who was the other finalist?
    A. Bob Dole
    B. Gerald Ford
    C. Thomas Kean

204. True or False. Carter's dour pessimism in televised presidential addresses hurt his re-election chances when facing the optimism of Reagan?

205. In what state had Reagan served two terms as governor?
    A. California
    B. Illinois
    C. New York

206. Which of the following was a major issue of the 1980 campaign?
    A. Affirmative action
    B. American prestige
    C. Pollution control

207. True or False. Reagan's victory in 1980 was cemented with a solid debate performance less than one week before Election Day?

208. What percentage of the national popular vote did third party candidate John Anderson achieve?
    A. 6 percent
    B. 10 percent
    C. 11 percent

209. Which candidate did most of Anderson's votes come at the expense of?
    A. Carter
    B. Reagan

210. Which candidate used a cowboy hat as one of his symbols?
    A. Jimmy Carter
    B. John Anderson
    C. Ronald Reagan

211. Which answer best describes the popular vote result in 1980?
    A. Close (top two candidates within 2% of each other)
    B. Not that close (top two candidates more than 2% but less than 7% apart)
    C. Big win (top two candidates more than 7% but less than 15% apart)

212. Which answer best describes the electoral vote result in 1980?
    A. Carter needed about 50 more electoral votes to win
    B. Carter needed about 125 more electoral votes to win
    C. Carter need to win about 200 more electoral votes to win

213. In 1980 Ronald Reagan won big. Carter was held to how many states?
    A. Four
    B. Six
    C. Eight

214. When did Carter concede the election?
    A. Early in the evening
    B. Late at night
    C. Not until the next morning

Quick answers for the 1980 Election (more detailed answers are at the back of the book).

200. B. 201. A. 202. A. 203. B. 204. T. 205. A. 206. B. 207. T. 208. A. 209. B. 210. C. 211. C. 212. C. 213. B. 214. A.

☆1976 ELECTION☆

215. True or False. The 1976 Election was the first one to be governed by significant federal oversight into campaign finances?

216. What distinction does Gerald Ford hold among the presidents?
    A. He was elected interim president by a special senate panel
    B. He was never elected president
    C. So far he has been the only president to lose his home state and still get elected

217. Sometimes conventions are harmonious and sometimes they are bitter, was the Democratic convention harmonious or bitter in 1976?
    A. Bitter
    B. Harmonious

218. When did Carter give his acceptance speech?
    A. 11 pm (local time)
    B. 1 am
    C. 3 am

219. What prior political experience did Ford have besides being vice president?
    A. Governor
    B. State legislator
    C. U.S. Congress

220. Running as an "outsider" what prior political experience did Carter have?
    A. Governor
    B. Mayor
    C. None

221. Which candidate used the slogan "elephants eat peanuts"?
    A. Gerald Ford
    B. Jimmy Carter

222. What year was the slogan "the grin will win"?
    A. Gerald Ford
    B. Jimmy Carter

223. Which candidate won the 1976 presidential debate?
    A. Carter
    B. Ford
    C. Tie

224. Which answer best describes the popular vote result in 1976?
    A. Close (top two candidates within 2% of each other)
    B. Not that close (top two candidates somewhere between 2% and 7% apart)
    C. Big win (top two candidates more than 7% but less than 15% apart)

225. Which answer best describes the electoral vote result in 1976?
    A. Ford needed to win about 20 more electoral votes to win
    B. Ford needed to win about 30 more electoral votes to win
    C. Ford needed to win about 50 more electoral votes to win

226. True or False. Ford almost overcame a significant early deficit in the polls?

227. True or False. Carter won by using a new mix of voters rather than the "New Deal Coalition"?

228. The election of 1976 featured two vice presidential candidates who would later be nominated as presidential candidates in the future. Who was Carter's running mate?
    A. Eugene McCarthy
    B. Hubert Humphrey
    C. Walter Mondale

229. Ford's White House also featured a future vice presidential candidate. Who was Ford's Chief of Staff who later ran for vice president?
   A. Richard Cheney
   B. Donald Rumsfeld
   C. Henry Kissinger

230. The election of 1976 was fairly close. Ford would have won if he had been able to win two more states. He needed to win any state worth at least five electoral votes and this big electoral vote state that is often a crucial part of a candidate's Electoral College path to the White House?
   A. New York
   B. Ohio
   C. Texas

231. What state was Jimmy Carter from?
   A. Arkansas
   B. Georgia
   C. Mississippi

Quick answers for the 1976 Election (more detailed answers are at the back of the book).

215. T. 216. B. 217. B. 218. A. 219. C. 220. A. 221. A. 222. B. 223. A. 224. B. 225. B. 226. T. 227. F. 228. C. 229. A. 230. B. 231. B.

☆1972 ELECTION☆

232. Who was George McGovern's most significant rival for the nomination?
   A. George Wallace
   B. Hubert Humphrey
   C. Tom Connolly

233. True or False. Nixon had no serious opposition to his nomination in the primaries?

234. True or False. Both the Democrats and the Republicans supported the Equal Rights Amendment in their respective party platforms in 1972?

235. True or False. Both the Democrats and the Republicans opposed the legalization of marijuana in their respective party platforms in 1972?

236. Why did Thomas Eagleton withdraw from the Democratic ticket in 1972?
   A. He owed back taxes
   B. He had undergone electric shock treatment for depression
   C. He was seriously injured in a downhill skiing accident

237. Who replaced him?
   A. Hubert Humphrey
   B. Morris Udall
   C. Sargent Shriver

238. Celebrity doctor Benjamin Spock ran for president in 1972. How many votes did he get nationwide?
   A. Less than 100,000 votes
   B. More than 100,000 but less than 500,000 votes
   C. More than 500,000 votes

239. What state did McGovern represent in the Senate?
   A. Idaho
   B. South Dakota
   C. Wyoming

240. True or False. McGovern ran a disorganized campaign in 1972?

241. Which answer best describes the popular vote result in 1972?
   A. Close (top two candidates within 2% of each other)
   B. Not that close (top two candidates more than 2% but less than 7% apart)
   C. Blowout victory (of the top two candidate, one candidate won by more than 15% of the popular vote)

242. Which answer best describes the electoral vote result in 1972?
   A. McGovern needed about 150 more electoral votes to win
   B. McGovern needed about 200 more electoral votes to win
   C. McGovern needed about 250 more electoral votes to win

243. What state did McGovern carry?
   A. Massachusetts
   B. Minnesota
   C. South Dakota

244. How many states did McGovern lose by more than one million votes?
   A. Two
   B. Three
   C. Four

245. True or False. One of the absurdities of the Watergate break-in at Democratic Headquarters in June of 1972 is that it was totally unnecessary. Nixon did not need to order the "plumbers" to steal information to help with his re-election. Nixon absolutely crushed McGovern in the popular vote and the Electoral College?

Quick answers for the 1972 Election (more detailed answers are at the back of the book).

232. A. 233. T. 234. T. 235. F. 236. B. 237. C. 238. A. 239. B. 240. T. 241. C. 242. C. 243. A. 244. C. 245. T.

☆1968 ELECTION☆

246. Who won the most votes in the Democratic Primaries in 1968?
   A. Eugene McCarthy
   B. Hubert Humphrey
   C. Robert Kennedy

247. A very strong finish in New Hampshire Primary by which candidate caused Lyndon Johnson to drop out of the race?
   A. Eugene McCarthy
   B. Hubert Humphrey
   C. Robert Kennedy

248. Who won the most votes in the Republican Primaries in 1968?
   A. Nelson Rockefeller
   B. Richard Nixon
   C. Ronald Reagan

249. Which candidate was assassinated right after giving a speech celebrating that candidate's victory in the California primary?
   A. Eugene McCarthy
   B. Nelson Rockefeller
   C. Robert Kennedy

250. The Democratic convention was marred by violence and arrests that were broadcast live on national television. Approximately how many people were arrested in Chicago for the melee in the streets?
    A. More than 500 but less than 1,000 arrests
    B. More than 1,000 but less than 5,000 arrests
    C. More than 5,000 arrests

251. Nominated at the Democratic Convention in 1968, the Rev. Channing E. Phillips was the first African American nominated for president by either the Democratic or Republican Party. Where was the Rev. Phillips from?
    A. Chicago
    B. Philadelphia
    C. Washington D.C.

252. Who won the Democratic nomination for president?
    A. Eugene McCarthy
    B. Hubert Humphrey
    C. Lyndon Johnson

253. Who won the Republican nomination for president?
    A. Nelson Rockefeller
    B. Richard Nixon
    C. Ronald Reagan

254. At the time of the 1968 campaign, both Nixon and Humphrey had prior experience in what office?
    A. Governor
    B. U.S. House of Representatives
    C. Vice President

255. Edmund Muskie and Spiro Agnew were both from states that start with which letter of the alphabet?
    A. The letter A
    B. The letter M
    C. The letter T

256. Which candidate had a tremendous lead in the polls in the fall of 1968 and then watched that lead evaporate as the election drew near?
    A. Hubert Humphrey
    B. Richard Nixon

257. Which candidate outspent the other one by a 2 to 1 margin in 1968?
    A. Humphrey outspent Nixon
    B. Nixon outspent Humphrey

258. Which of the following candidates had advertisements just using his initials?
    A. George Wallace
    B. Hubert Humphrey
    C. Richard Nixon

259. Which answer best describes the popular vote result in 1968?
    A. Close (top two candidates within 2% of each other)
    B. Not that close (top two candidates more than 2% but less than 7% apart)
    C. Big win (top two candidates more than 7% but less than 15% apart)

260. Roughly what share of the African American vote did Nixon win in 1968?
    A. 5 percent
    B. 10 percent
    C. 15 percent

261. Which answer best describes the electoral vote result in 1968?
    A. Humphrey needed about more 50 electoral votes to win
    B. Humphrey needed about 75 more electoral votes to win
    C. Humphrey needed about 100 more electoral votes to win

262. What fraction of states carried by Goldwater in 1964 did Wallace carry in 1968?
    A. One-half
    B. Two-thirds
    C. Three-quarters

263. Generally speaking, if the U.S. was divided into Northern states, Middle states, and Southern states, which group of states did Nixon carry in 1968?
    A. Northern states
    B. Middle states
    C. Southern states

264. True or False. In 1968 the popular vote for president was close to a tie but the Electoral College showed a clear winner?

Quick answers for the 1968 Election (more detailed answers are at the back of the book).

246. A. 247. A. 248. C. 249. C. 250. A. 251. C. 252. B. 253. B. 254. C. 255. B. 256. B. 257. B. 258. B. 259. A. 260. C. 261. B. 262. B. 263. B. 264. T.

☆1964 ELECTION☆

265. True or False. Johnson essentially ran unopposed for the nomination?

266. True or False. The 1964 Republican convention was marred by feuding between the moderate and conservative wings of the party.

267. What was unusual about the Democratic Convention?
    A. It was very short
    B. It was very long
    C. There were no roll call votes

268. Why was William Miller considered by Goldwater as a possible running mate?
    A. Miller was a moderate to balance Goldwater's extreme conservatism
    B. Miller was good friends with Goldwater
    C. Miller was skilled at irritating Johnson

269. Who was the first Roman Catholic to run on the Republican ticket?
    A. Barry Goldwater
    B. William Miller
    C. William Scranton

270. 1964 marked the beginning of what modern trend?
    A. That the Democratic Convention had considerably more delegates than the Republican one
    B. That the Democratic Convention had considerably fewer delegates than the Republican one
    C. That the Democratic Convention had about the same number of delegates than the Republican one

271. How many presidential debates were there in 1964?
    A. Zero
    B. One
    C. Five

272. How much did Goldwater support the New Deal?
    A. Goldwater was entirely against the New Deal
    B. Goldwater was against about half of the New Deal
    C. Goldwater largely supported the New Deal

273. Which candidate used the slogan "Let us continue"?
    A. Barry Goldwater
    B. Lyndon Johnson

274. Which answer best describes the popular vote result in 1964?
   A. Not that close (top two candidates more than 2% but less than 7% apart)
   B. Big win (top two candidates more than 7% but less than 15% apart)
   C. Blowout victory (of the top two candidate, one candidate won by more than 15% of the popular vote)

275. Which answer best describes the electoral vote result in 1964?
   A. Johnson won more than 270 but less than 300 electoral votes
   B. Johnson won more than 300 but less than 400 electoral votes
   C. Johnson won more than 400 but less than 500 electoral votes

276. Which of the following Deep South states did Johnson win?
   A. Alabama
   B. Florida
   C. Mississippi

277. Did Goldwater win any states in the Midwest or New England?
   A. No
   B. Yes

278. Who could vote in a presidential election for the first time in 1964?
   A. Women
   B. Residents of the District of Columbia
   C. 18 year olds

279. True or False. 1964 marked the last time that several states have been won by the Democratic candidate for president?

☆1960 ELECTION☆

280. Who won the most votes in the 1960 Democratic Party primaries?
   A. Hubert Humphrey
   B. John F. Kennedy
   C. Lyndon Johnson

281. How many years in advance did Kennedy prepare for the West Virginia primary?
   A. Zero
   B. One
   C. Two

282. Who won the most votes in the 1960 Republican Party primaries?
   A. Barry Goldwater
   B. Nelson Rockefeller
   C. Richard Nixon

283. True or False. The Democratic Convention was troubled by the issue that some delegates had signed pledges that repudiated the Civil Rights plank in the Democratic Platform?

284. Who did Kennedy select as his vice president?
   A. Andrew Johnson
   B. Andrew Jackson
   C. Lyndon Johnson

285. Where did Kennedy give his acceptance speech?
    A. At a city park in front of a statue of Woodrow Wilson
    B. At the convention hall
    C. At a crowded stadium

286. In Kennedy's acceptance speech what was the name given to the package of programs and ideas that he outlined?
    A. Great Society
    B. New Deal
    C. New Frontier

287. What lesson does Kennedy's victory in achieving the Democratic nomination offer?
    A. Confront rather than ignore serious issues that voters have about your candidacy even if those issues are unreasonable
    B. Ignore rather than confront serious issues that voters have about your candidacy if those issues are unreasonable

288. Prior to the 1960 Republican Convention, Nixon and Rockefeller met and discussed the Republican Party Platform. Nixon demanded certain changes in the platform. Which of the following was one of the changes that Nixon demanded?
    A. Stronger pro-civil rights plank
    B. Stronger anti-communist plank
    C. Stronger pro-tariff plank

289. How did the Republican Platform urge economic growth to occur?
    A. Corporate tax cut
    B. Free enterprise
    C. Government subsidies

290. Which answer best describes the popular vote result in 1960?
    A. Close (top two candidates within 2% of each other)
    B. Not that close (top two candidates more than 2% but less than 7% apart)
    C. Big win (top two candidates more than 7% but less than 15% apart)

291. Which answer best describes the electoral vote result in 1960?
    A. Nixon needed 20 more electoral votes to win
    B. Nixon needed 50 more electoral votes to win
    C. Nixon needed 70 more electoral votes to win

292. True or False. Kennedy won with the "New Deal Coalition"?

293. The 1960 election featured a famous televised debate between Kennedy and Nixon. Who is widely considered to have won that debate?
    A. Kennedy
    B. Nixon

294. Which candidate made and kept a promise to visit all 50 states while running for president in 1960?
    A. Kennedy
    B. Nixon

295. True or False. On the campaign trail, Kennedy promised to resign if there was a conflict between his religious faith and being president?

296. True or False. The election of 1960 set the 20th century record for voter turnout?

297. Which state was the closest state in 1960?
    A. Arkansas
    B. Hawaii
    C. Missouri

298. What Southern state did Kennedy win by an impressive margin?
    A. Georgia
    B. Florida
    C. Texas

299. Given the closeness of the 1960 election, each major campaign decision by Kennedy or Nixon was important in terms of possibly influencing the election. Which of the following errors did Nixon make?
    A. Not taking advantage of Eisenhower's popularity
    B. Overplaying the issue of Kennedy being Roman Catholic
    C. Spending too much time presiding over the Senate when he should have been out campaigning

300. True or False. President Eisenhower suggested to Nixon that he challenge the election results?

Quick answers for the 1960 Election (more detailed answers are at the back of the book).

280. B. 281. C. 282. C. 283. T. 284. C.
285. C. 286. C. 287. A. 288. A. 289. B.
290. A. 291. B. 292. T. 293. A. 294. B.
295. T. 296. T. 297. B. 298. A. 299. A.
300. T.

☆1956 ELECTION☆

301. Was Eisenhower seriously challenged in the primaries in 1956
    A. No
    B. Yes

302. True or False. Nixon was a very popular vice president and there was no attempt to get him dropped from the ticket in 1956?

303. In 1956, Stevenson won the most delegates of the Democratic candidates. Who finished second?
    A. Estes Kefauver
    B. Harry Truman
    C. John Kennedy

304. What was noteworthy about the timing of the 1956 conventions?
    A. Both conventions ran simultaneously
    B. The Democratic convention was first for the first time in more than 60 years
    C. The Democratic convention was second for the first time in more than 60 years

305. What was unusual about the Democratic vice presidential selection in 1956?
    A. Everyone at the convention knew who the vice presidential candidate would be before the presidential candidate had been selected
    B. The vice presidential selection was decided by a coin toss
    C. Without warning the presidential nominee passed on choosing a running mate and left the selection to the convention

306. Which future president nominated Stevenson at the convention?
    A. John F. Kennedy
    B. Lyndon Johnson
    C. Jimmy Carter

307. Which foreign affairs post did Adlai Stevenson later serve?
    A. Ambassador to the United Nations
    B. Ambassador to France
    C. Secretary of State

308. Was there a significant third party candidate who received any electoral votes and more than 5% of the popular vote in 1956?
    A. Yes
    B. No

309. Which answer best describes the popular vote results in 1956?
    A. Close (top two candidates within 2% of each other)
    B. Big win (top two candidates more than 7% but less than 15% apart)
    C. Blowout victory (of the top two candidate, one candidate won by more than 15% of the popular vote)

310. Which answer best describes the Electoral College results in 1956?
    A. Eisenhower won more states than he did in 1952
    B. Eisenhower won fewer states than he did in 1952
    C. Eisenhower won with the identical states that he carried in 1952

311. Which party won Congress in 1956?
    A. Democrats
    B. Republicans

312. Which state did Stevenson carry in 1956 that he lost in 1952?
    A. California
    B. Illinois
    C. Missouri

313. Which of the following states did Stevenson lose in 1956 that he had won in 1952?
    A. Illinois
    B. Kentucky
    C. Tennessee

Quick answers for the 1956 Election (more detailed answers are at the back of the book).

301. A. 302. F. 303. A. 304. B. 305. C. 306. A. 307. A. 308. B. 309. C. 310. A. 311. A. 312. C. 313. B.

☆1952 ELECTION☆

314. 1952 marked the first time in how many years that there was not an incumbent president on the ballot?
    A. 20 years
    B. 24 years
    C. 28 years

315. Who had the campaign slogan "I like Ike"?
    A. James Buchanan
    B. Grover Cleveland
    C. Dwight Eisenhower

316. Did Adlai Stevenson get the most votes in the 1952 Democratic Primaries?
    A. Yes
    B. No

317. Who was Dwight Eisenhower's main rival for the nomination?
    A. Everett Dirksen
    B. Richard Nixon
    C. Robert Taft

318. What paved the way for Eisenhower's victory at the convention?
   A. Eisenhower won key credentials disputes to open the convention and it gave him enough votes to win
   B. Political operatives worked behind the scenes to discredit Eisenhower's rivals, leaving Eisenhower as the only untainted candidate
   C. Without needing to win any credentials battles, Eisenhower won because so many delegates were World War II veterans who had served under Eisenhower

319. How many ballots did it take for Stevenson to win the nomination?
   A. One
   B. Three
   C. Seven

320. True or False. The Democratic Party instituted loyalty rules at the convention in an effort to prevent a repeat of what happened in 1948?

321. Which answer best describes how Adlai Stevenson won the nomination?
   A. He was a genuinely reluctant candidate and was drafted as an alternative to Estes Kefauver
   B. He actively sought the nomination as a replacement to Estes Kefauver
   C. There was nothing exceptional about how Adlai Stevenson won the nomination. He had the most support in the primaries.

322. True or False. Prior to running for president, Eisenhower was successfully elected and served a term on the Albany, New York, City Council?

323. What was a major issue during the 1952 campaign?
   A. Corruption
   B. Free trade
   C. Immigration

324. Which candidate had the misfortune of being shown on television wearing a worn-out shoe (it had a plainly visible hole in sole) and was attacked in campaign ads with a drawing of the incident and the caption "don't let this happen to you"?
   A. Adlai Stevenson
   B. Dwight Eisenhower

325. Which answer best describes the popular vote result in 1952?
   A. Close (top two candidates within 2% of each other)
   B. Not that close (top two candidates more than 2% but less than 7% apart)
   C. Big win (top two candidates more than 7% but less than 15% apart)

326. Which answer best describes the electoral vote result in 1952?
   A. Eisenhower won by less than 50 electoral votes
   B. Eisenhower won by more than 50 electoral votes but by less than 100 electoral votes
   C. Eisenhower won by more than 100 electoral votes

327. Where did most of Stevenson's support come from?
   A. Midwest
   B. South
   C. West

328. Eisenhower carried Florida in 1952, which party usually won Florida between 1852 and 1952?
   A. Democratic
   B. Republican

329. Did Stevenson carry any states west of the Mississippi River in 1952?
  A. Yes, he carried most of the states west of the Mississippi
  B. Yes, he carried two states that are found west of the Mississippi
  C. No, he carried no states west of the Mississippi

330. True or False. Prior to Dwight Eisenhower running as a Republican in 1952, the Democrats tried to recruit him to run for president?

Quick answers for the 1952 Election (more detailed answers are at the back of the book).

314. B. 315. C. 316. B. 317. C. 318. A.
319. B. 320. T. 321. A. 322. F. 323. A.
324. A. 325. C. 326. C. 327. B. 328. A.
329. B. 330. T.

☆1948 ELECTION☆

331. Who received the most votes for president in the 1948 Republican primaries?
  A. Earl Warren
  B. Robert Taft
  C. Thomas Dewey

332. Who received the most votes for president in the 1948 Democratic primaries?
  A. Harry Truman
  B. Strom Thurmond
  C. Unpledged delegates

333. Early polling showed all of the major potential Republican presidential candidates defeating Truman except who?
  A. Dewey
  B. Stassen
  C. Taft
  D. Warren

334. How many ballots did it take for Thomas Dewey to secure the nomination?
  A. One
  B. Two
  C. Three

335. How many ballots did it take for Harry Truman to secure the nomination?
  A. One
  B. Three
  C. Six

336. At the 1948 Democratic Convention, the mayor of Minneapolis, Hubert Humphrey, gave a powerful speech in favor of what subject?
  A. Civil rights
  B. Poll tax
  C. Recycling

337. What state did Thomas Dewey govern?
  A. Delaware
  B. New Jersey
  C. New York

338. Who was Thomas Dewey's running mate?
  A. Earl Warren
  B. Max Baucus
  C. Robert Taft

339. Who was nominated by acclamation to serve as Truman's vice presidential running mate?
  A. Alben Barkley
  B. Fred Thompson
  C. William Fulbright

340. What baseball stadium did Henry Wallace give his speech, accepting the nomination of the Progressive Party?
  A. Baker Bowl
  B. Ebbets Field
  C. Shibe Park

341. Which of the following ideas, championed by the Progressive Party in 1948, eventually became law?
    A. Direct election of the president
    B. Nationalization of the coal industry
    C. Voting age lowered to 18

342. Which of the following cabinet-level departments, <u>proposed</u> by the Progressive Party in 1948, has yet to come to fruition?
    A. Department of Culture
    B. Department of Propaganda and Truth
    C. Department of Sports and Recreation

343. Upset at the pro-civil rights tone of the 1948 Democratic Convention, a Southern faction of the Democratic Party convened a convention just three days after the end of the official Democratic Convention. How many states were represented at this factional convention?
    A. 7
    B. 11
    C. 13

344. Where was the splinter convention held?
    A. Birmingham
    B. Philadelphia
    C. San Diego

345. Who was the States' Rights Democrats (also known as the Dixiecrats) nominee for president in 1948?
    A. George Wallace
    B. Robert Byrd
    C. Strom Thurmond

346. Which answer best describes the States' Rights Democrats?
    A. Faction of the Democratic Party
    B. New political party
    C. Then-existing political party

347. Unthinkable today, what did many pollsters do after it appeared that Dewey had a large lead early in the race?
    A. They kept polling
    B. They stopped polling

348. Did Dewey campaign effectively in 1948?
    A. Yes
    B. No

349. In 1948 which candidate used a drawing that showed the candidate but the shadow cast by the candidate was that of Franklin D. Roosevelt?
    A. Harry Truman
    B. Henry Wallace
    C. Strom Thurmond
    D. Thomas Dewey

350. How many states did Progressive Party candidate Henry Wallace possibly cost Harry Truman?
    A. Zero
    B. One
    C. Three

351. Did Truman campaign effectively in 1948?
    A. Yes
    B. No

352. Which answer best describes the popular vote result in 1948?
    A. Close (top two candidates within 2% of each other)
    B. Not that close (top two candidates more than 2% but less than 7% apart)
    C. Big win (top two candidates more than 7% but less than 15% apart)

353. Which answer best describes the electoral vote result in 1948?
  - A. Dewey needed 33 more electoral votes to win
  - B. Dewey needed 55 more electoral votes to win
  - C. Dewey needed 77 more electoral votes to win

354. In which of the following groups of states did Dewey do poorly in, meaning that he won none of the states in that region?
  - A. Central Great Plains states
  - B. New England
  - C. The South

355. Which candidate won Ohio in 1948?
  - A. Harry Truman
  - B. Strom Thurmond
  - C. Thomas Dewey

Quick answers for the 1948 Election (more detailed answers are at the back of the book).

331. A. 332. A. 333. C. 334. C. 335. A.
336. A. 337. C. 338. A. 339. A. 340. C.
341. C. 342. A. 343. C. 344. A. 345. C.
346. A. 347. B. 348. B. 349. B. 350. C.
351. A. 352. B. 353. C. 354. C. 355. A.

☆1944 ELECTION☆

356. True or False. 1944 was the first time that the U.S. had been at war for a U.S. presidential election since 1864?

357. Who received the most votes in the 1944 Democratic presidential primaries?
  - A. Franklin Roosevelt
  - B. Harry Truman
  - C. John N. Garner

358. Who received the most votes in the 1944 Republican presidential primaries?
  - A. Douglas McArthur
  - B. Earl Warren
  - C. Thomas Dewey

359. What convention milestone did Dewey achieve in 1944?
  - A. First to accept nomination in person
  - B. First to decline the nomination in person
  - C. Give two speeches accepting the nomination

360. True or False. In 1944 both members of the Republican Ticket had the same first name?

361. At the 1944 Democratic Convention, Henry Wallace was dropped as the vice presidential candidate in favor of which candidate?
  - A. William Douglas
  - B. Hiram Johnson
  - C. Harry Truman

362. Which answer best describes the funds available to the Dewey campaign?
  - A. Frequently low on cash
  - B. Nothing noteworthy about his funds
  - C. Well-supplied with cash

363. Which answer best describes the popular vote result in 1944?
  - A. Close (top two candidates within 2% of each other)
  - B. Not that close (top two candidates more than 2% but less than 7% apart)
  - C. Big win (top two candidates more than 7% but less than 15% apart)

364. In 1944, who won the Central Great Plains states such as Iowa, North Dakota, South Dakota, Kansas, and Nebraska?
    A. Franklin Roosevelt
    B. Thomas Dewey
    C. The candidates split the states with Dewey winning 3 and Roosevelt winning 2

365. 1944 was Franklin Roosevelt's worst re-election. How many electoral votes did he receive?
    A. 292
    B. 332
    C. 432

366. In 1944 did Thomas Dewey (Roosevelt's Republican opponent), get more than 100 electoral votes?
    A. Yes
    B. No

367. Which of the following states did Franklin Roosevelt never win?
    A. Alabama
    B. New Jersey
    C. Vermont

Quick answers for the 1944 Election (more detailed answers are at the back of the book).

356. T. 357. A. 358. A. 359. A. 360. F.
361. C. 362. C. 363. C. 364. B. 365. C.
366. B. 367. C.

☆1940 ELECTION☆

368. Who received the most votes in the 1940 Democratic presidential primaries?
    A. John Garner
    B. Franklin Roosevelt
    C. Henry Wallace

369. Who received the most votes in the 1940 Republican presidential primaries?
    A. Robert Taft
    B. Thomas Dewey
    C. Unpledged

370. True or False. At the 1940 Democratic Convention, Roosevelt issued a statement to the delegates that "he was not a candidate but that they could vote for anyone"?

371. What was unusual about the Republican nominee, Wendell Willkie?
    A. He stood more than 6'6" tall
    B. He was from the Deep South
    C. He had little military and no political experience

372. What occupation did Willkie have immediately prior to running for president?
    A. Member of Congress
    B. 5 Star General
    C. Private Utility Executive

373. True or False. Henry Wallace was not a popular selection as vice president and was reluctantly accepted by the convention?

374. What scandal was a slight drag on Roosevelt's popularity going into the 1940 Election?
    A. Bribery at the Department of the Interior
    B. Court-packing scheme
    C. Corruption at the WPA

375. Which object did Wendell Willkie feature in many of his advertisements?
    A. Banana
    B. Key
    C. Lunch pail

376. True or False. In 1940 Franklin D. Roosevelt used the following slogan "Willkie for the Millionaires, Roosevelt for the Millions"?

377. Which answer best describes the popular vote result in 1940?
   A. Not that close (top two candidates more than 2% but less than 7% apart)
   B. Big win (top two candidates more than 7% but less than 15% apart)
   C. Blowout victory (of the top two candidate, one candidate won by more than 15% of the popular vote)

378. Which answer best describes the electoral vote result in 1940?
   A. Willkie needed about 135 more electoral votes to win
   B. Willkie needed about 155 more electoral votes to win
   C. Willkie needed about 185 more electoral votes to win

379. Which of the following states did Wendell Willkie win in 1940?
   A. Alabama
   B. Iowa
   C. Wyoming

380. Who won in New York in 1940?
   A. Franklin Roosevelt
   B. Wendell Willkie

381. In 1940 Franklin Roosevelt became the first candidate to do what?
   A. Run for a third term as president (including primaries)
   B. Be elected to a third term as president
   C. All of the above

Quick answers for the 1940 Election (more detailed answers are at the back of the book).

368. B. 369. B. 370. T. 371. C. 372. C.
373. T. 374. B. 375. B. 376. T. 377. C.
378. C. 379. B. 380. A. 381. B.

☆1936 ELECTION☆

382. Who received the most votes for president in the 1936 Democratic primaries?
   A. Al Smith
   B. Franklin Roosevelt
   C. Unpledged delegates

383. Who won the most votes for president in the 1936 Republican primaries?
   A. Alf Landon
   B. Earl Warren
   C. William Borah

384. Where did Roosevelt accept his nomination?
   A. Franklin Field at the University of Pennsylvania
   B. At the convention hall
   C. At the White House

385. What major rule change did the Democratic Party make in 1936?
   A. Abolish the two-thirds rule
   B. Abolish the majority rule
   C. Abolish the Westminster rule

386. What was Landon's occupation prior to running for president?
   A. General
   B. Governor
   C. Senator

387. Long before running for president, which administration had Franklin Roosevelt served in the Department of the Navy?
   A. Teddy Roosevelt
   B. William Taft
   C. Woodrow Wilson

388. From which party was a celebrity priest, Father Coughlin, the candidate for president?
    A. Progressive Party
    B. Union Party
    C. Socialist Party

389. What strategy did Landon employ during the 1936 Election?
    A. He attacked all of the New Deal
    B. He attacked parts of the New Deal
    C. He ignored the New Deal

390. Which answer best describes the funding of the Landon campaign?
    A. Poorly-funded
    B. Average funding
    C. Well-funded

391. Since 1936 which demographic has given the majority of its vote to the Democratic Party?
    A. Blacks
    B. Small businesses
    C. Women

392. Which income bracket supported Roosevelt the most heavily?
    A. Poor
    B. Middle Class
    C. Rich

393. Which answer best describes the popular vote result in 1936?
    A. Close (top two candidates within 2% of each other)
    B. Big win (top two candidates more than 7% but less than 15% apart)
    C. Blowout victory (of the top two candidate, one candidate won by more than 15% of the popular vote)

394. Which answer best describes the electoral vote result in 1936?
    A. Landon needed 158 more electoral votes to win
    B. Landon needed 208 more electoral votes to win
    C. Landon needed 258 more electoral votes to win

395. How many states did Roosevelt win in 1936? (out of a possible 48)
    A. 31
    B. 42
    C. 46

396. Which state was the closest one that Landon lost?
    A. Arkansas
    B. Kansas
    C. New Hampshire

Quick answers for the Election (more detailed answers are at the back of the book).

382. B. 383. C. 384. A. 385. A. 386. B. 387. C. 388. B. 389. A. 390. C. 391. A. 392. A. 393. C. 394. C. 395. C. 396.C.

☆1932 ELECTION☆

397. Who won the most votes in the 1932 Democratic presidential primaries?
    A. Franklin Roosevelt
    B. Huey Long
    C. Samuel Houston

398. Who won the most votes in the 1932 Republican presidential primaries?
    A. Herbert Hoover
    B. Joseph France
    C. Charles Dawes

399. Roosevelt's main rival for the nomination was Al Smith. How many times had Roosevelt nominated Smith to be president?
    A. One
    B. Two
    C. Three

400. In the 1932 Republican Party Platform, did Hoover take responsibility for the Great Depression?
    A. No
    B. Yes
    C. Sort of

401. Was Eugene Debs the Socialist Party candidate for president in 1932?
    A. No
    B. Yes

402. Which statement about the significance of the 1932 election for the Socialist Party is true?
    A. 1932 was the best election for the Socialist Party in years
    B. 1932 was the worst election for the Socialist Party in years
    C. The Socialist Party did not participate in the election of 1932

403. Which of the following slogans did Franklin Roosevelt use in 1932?
    A. Roosevelt or Disaster
    B. Roosevelt or Hunger
    C. Roosevelt or Ruin

404. What did Roosevelt do on the campaign trail that Hoover did not do?
    A. Eat local food
    B. Shake hands with people
    C. Smile

405. What relatively new medium was Roosevelt the first candidate to make effective use of on the campaign trail?
    A. Internet
    B. Television
    C. Radio

406. Stricken with polio after his failed run for the vice presidency years earlier, Roosevelt had great difficulty walking. What was his travel schedule like while campaigning for president in 1932?
    A. He only visited eight states
    B. He traveled a fair amount and visited twenty-seven states
    C. He traveled extensively and visited forty-one states

407. True or False. Roosevelt also used the following slogan in 1932 "Roosevelt and Garner = Beer"?

408. What group of people did Roosevelt switch to voting Democratic after decades of mostly Republican dominance in this demographic?
    A. Rich
    B. Rural
    C. Urban

409. Which answer best describes the popular vote result in 1932?
    A. Close (top two candidates within 2% of each other)
    B. Not that close (top two candidates more than 2% but less than 7% apart)
    C. Blowout victory (of the top two candidate, one candidate won by more than 15% of the popular vote)

410. Which answer best describes the electoral vote result in 1932?
    A. Hoover needed about 100 more electoral votes to win
    B. Hoover needed about 150 more electoral votes to win
    C. Hoover needed about 200 more electoral votes to win

411. Who won more states in the West in 1932?
    A. Franklin Roosevelt
    B. Herbert Hoover

412. Generally most of the states that Hoover won were in which area of the country?
    A. The mid-Atlantic states
    B. The Midwest
    C. New England

413. In 1932 what percent of the popular vote did Franklin Roosevelt receive?
    A. 58%
    B. 60%
    C. 70%

Quick answers for the 1932 Election (more detailed answers are at the back of the book).

397. A. 398. A. 399. C. 400. A. 401. A.
402. A. 403. C. 404. C. 405. C. 406. C.
407. T. 408. C. 409. C. 410. C. 411. A.
412. C. 413. A.

☆1928 ELECTION☆

414. Who won the most votes for president in the 1928 Republican primaries?
    A. Calvin Coolidge
    B. Charles Lindbergh (Jr.)
    C. Herbert Hoover

415. Who won the most votes for president in the 1928 Democratic primaries?
    A. Al Smith
    B. Unpledged delegates
    C. William McAdoo

416. Which answer best describes the 1928 Republican Convention?
    A. Hoover was easily nominated on the 1st ballot
    B. Hoover won on the 6th ballot
    C. Hoover prevailed after a bitter struggle, finally winning on the 31st ballot

417. Which answer best describes the 1928 Democratic Convention?
    A. Smith was easily nominated on the 1st ballot
    B. Smith won on the 6th ballot
    C. Smith prevailed after a bitter struggle, finally winning on the 31st ballot

418. The 1928 Democratic Convention was held in Houston, Texas, what was the significance of that choice?
    A. It was the first Southern city to host a major party convention since 1860
    B. The weather was much cooler than it had been in 1924
    C. Smith accepted the nomination in the same state that he had been born

419. What was significant about Sen. Charles Curtis?
    A. First African American vice presidential nominee
    B. First Native American vice presidential nominee
    C. First Southerner on a major party ticket since the Civil War

420. What was significant about Sen. Joseph Robinson?
    A. First African American vice presidential nominee
    B. First Native American vice presidential nominee
    C. First Southerner on a major party ticket since the Civil War

421. 1928 marked the first convention in about 30 years that which Democratic Party luminary was not present due to his recent passing?
   A. Edwin "Boss" Tweed
   B. William Jennings Bryan
   C. Woodrow Wilson

422. Which answer best describes the popular vote result in 1928?
   A. Close (top two candidates within 2% of each other)
   B. Big win (top two candidates more than 7% but less than 15% apart)
   C. Blowout victory (of the top two candidate, one candidate won by more than 15% of the popular vote)

423. Which answer best describes the electoral vote result in 1928?
   A. Smith needed about 30 more electoral votes to win
   B. Smith needed about 160 more electoral votes to win
   C. Smith needed about 180 more electoral votes to win

424. In 1928, Hoover swept most of the electoral map. Most of his few losses were in which region?
   A. The Midwest
   B. The South
   C. The West

425. Which of the following states did Smith win?
   A. Alabama
   B. Massachusetts
   C. Oregon

Quick answers for the 1928 Election (more detailed answers are at the back of the book).

414. C. 415. A. 416. A. 417. A. 418. A.
419. B. 420. C. 421. B. 422. C. 423. C.
424. B. 425. A.

☆1924 ELECTION☆

426. Who won the most votes in the 1924 Republican presidential primaries?
   A. Calvin Coolidge
   B. Hiram Johnson
   C. Robert La Follette

427. Who won the most votes in the 1924 Democratic presidential primaries?
   A. Henry Ford
   B. James Cox
   C. William McAdoo

428. Which answer best describes the 1924 Republican Convention?
   A. Coolidge was easily nominated
   B. Coolidge had to make several secret deals to secure the nomination
   C. Coolidge agreed to serve again only after the convention was unable to agree on his replacement

429. Which answer best describes the 1924 Democratic Convention
   A. Short and pleasant; Davis was easily nominated
   B. Long and pleasant; the delegates spent a long time carefully crafting the party platform but overall the convention was harmonious
   C. Long and bitter; the urban and rural factions of the party battled for more than two weeks before settling on a compromise candidate.

430. In addition to fighting about civil rights, and prohibition, what else did the 1924 Democratic Convention delegates fight about?
    A. Civil service reform
    B. League of Nations
    C. Tariff reform

431. The 1924 marked the first time that what media was used to broadcast from a convention?
    A. Internet
    B. Television
    C. Radio

432. Which answer best describes the popular vote result in 1924?
    A. Not that close (top two candidates more than 2% but less than 7% apart)
    B. Big win (top two candidates more than 7% but less than 15% apart)
    C. Blowout victory (of the top two candidate, one candidate won by more than 15% of the popular vote)

433. What percentage of the national popular vote did Progressive Party candidate, Robert La Follette receive?
    A. About 7 percent
    B. About 12 percent
    C. About 17 percent

434. Which of the following statements about the 1924 Progressive Party platform is true?
    A. Opposed cuts in military spending
    B. Supported nationalization of certain industries
    C. Supported repeal of the Sherman Anti-Trust Act

435. True or False. The Socialist Party did not run a candidate in 1924 but instead endorsed La Follette?

436. Which answer best describes the electoral vote result in 1924?
    A. Davis needed 30 more electoral votes to win
    B. Davis needed 100 more electoral votes to win
    C. Davis needed 130 more electoral votes to win

437. Davis primarily won states from which group of states?
    A. Former Confederacy states
    B. Former original thirteen colony states
    C. There is no readily-identifiable pattern to the states that Davis managed to win

438. Which state did Coolidge win by the greatest percentage of the vote?
    A. Florida
    B. Massachusetts
    C. Vermont

439. What was Calvin Coolidge's slogan when running for president in 1924?
    A. "Silent Cal is Your Pal"
    B. "Keep Cool with Coolidge"
    C. "Coolidge for America"

440. In 1924 what state did Progressive Party candidate Robert La Follette win?
    A. Texas
    B. Washington
    C. Wisconsin

Quick answers for the 1924 Election (more detailed answers are at the back of the book).

426. A. 427. C. 428. A. 429. C. 430. B.
431. C. 432. C. 433. C. 434. B. 435. T.
436. C. 437. A. 438. C. 439. B. 440. C.

☆1920 ELECTION☆

441. Who won the most votes for president in the 1920 Republican primaries?
   A. Hiram Johnson
   B. Herbert Hoover
   C. Warren Harding

442. Who won the most votes for president in the 1920 Democratic primaries?
   A. James Cox
   B. Mitchell Palmer
   C. Unpledged delegates

443. True or False. In 1920 there was no clear front runner when the Republican Convention convened?

444. On what ballot did Harding win the Republican nomination?
   A. Easily on the 1st ballot
   B. Slowly but surely on the 10th ballot after backroom deals were made
   C. After four days and 43 ballots, Harding prevailed

445. True or False. In 1920 there was no clear front runner when the Democratic Convention convened?

446. In what city was the Democratic Convention held in 1920?
   A. Denver
   B. Philadelphia
   C. San Francisco

447. Which answer best describes how Cox won the Democratic nomination in 1920?
   A. Easily on the 1st ballot
   B. Blew an early lead and came back from behind to win on the 44th ballot
   C. Triumphed on the 52nd ballot after cutting a deal to end the deadlock

448. True or False. 1920 marked the first election since 1824 where both vice presidential candidates would later be elected president?

449. Where was Eugene Debs when he received his fifth nomination to be the Socialist Party candidate for president?
   A. At the convention hall
   B. At home
   C. In prison

450. Which of the following statements was not part of the 1920 Socialist Party platform?
   A. Legal protections for migratory workers
   B. Recognition of the U.S.S.R.
   C. Tax cuts for factory owners

451. Which candidate had campaign buttons endorsing "For President convict No. 9653"?
   A. Eugene Debs
   B. James Cox
   C. Warren Harding

452. Which answer best describes the popular vote result in 1920?
   A. Not that close (top two candidates more than 2% but less than 7% apart)
   B. Big win (top two candidates more than 7% but less than 15% apart)
   C. Blowout victory (of the top two candidate, one candidate won by more than 15% of the popular vote)

453. Which answer best describes the electoral vote result in 1920?
   A. Cox needed about 40 more electoral votes to win
   B. Cox needed about 70 more electoral votes to win
   C. Cox needed about 140 more electoral votes to win

454. True or False. Despite Harding winning the White House, the Democrats retained control of Congress?

455. Which of the following states did Harding win in 1920, which Coolidge lost in 1924?
   A. Delaware
   B. Maine
   C. Tennessee

456. Which of the following states gave Harding the largest margin of victory?
   A. California
   B. Ohio
   C. West Virginia

457. In 1920 for the first time since the popular votes began to be counted in 1824, what popular vote feat was achieved by winner Warren Harding?
   A. He won with 55% of the popular vote
   B. He won with 57% of the popular vote
   C. He won with 60% of the popular vote

458. 1920 also marked another more important milestone. Who could vote for the first time in the 1920 election?
   A. Women
   B. Slaves
   C. 18 year olds

459. What future president lost as a vice presidential candidate in 1920?
   A. Calvin Coolidge
   B. Herbert Hoover
   C. Franklin Roosevelt

Quick answers for the 1920 Election (more detailed answers are at the back of the book).

441. A. 442. C. 443. T. 444. B. 445. T.
446. C. 447. B. 448. T. 449. C. 450. C.
451. A. 452. C. 453. C. 454. F. 455. C.
456. A. 457. C. 458. A. 459. C.

☆1916 ELECTION☆

460. Who won the most votes for president in the 1916 Democratic primaries?
   A. Judson Harmon
   B. Mitchell Palmer
   C. Woodrow Wilson

461. Who won the most votes for president in the 1916 Republican primaries?
   A. Charles Hughes
   B. Robert La Follette
   C. Unpledged delegates

462. Who provided the keynote speech at the 1916 Democratic convention?
   A. Alton Parker
   B. Grover Cleveland
   C. William Bryan

463. Which future president chaired the 1916 Republican convention?
   A. Coolidge
   B. Harding
   C. Hoover

464. True or False. The 1916 Democratic Convention was one of the most contentious in party history for a year when a sitting president was seeking re-election?

465. What branch of government had Charles Hughes served in before running for president and which branch would he serve in after running for president?
    A. Executive branch before and Executive branch after
    B. Judicial branch before and Judicial branch after
    C. Judicial branch before and Executive branch after

466. True or False. In 1916 both members of the Republican Ticket had the same first name?

467. True or False. The tariff disappeared as a major campaign issue in 1916 after being an enduring issue for decades?

468. Wilson's support for Women's Voting Rights helped him win in which region of the country?
    A. North
    B. South
    C. West

469. Which of the following helped Wilson win in 1916?
    A. Campaigning in the right states
    B. Doubling down on patriotism
    C. Vilifying his opponent

470. Which of the following candidates did not use the slogan "America First" in 1916?
    A. Charles Hughes
    B. Eugene Debs
    C. Woodrow Wilson

471. Which answer best describes the popular vote result in 1916?
    A. Close (top two candidates within 2% of each other)
    B. Not that close (top two candidates more than 2% but less than 7% apart)
    C. Big win (top two candidates more than 7% but less than 15% apart)

472. Which answer best describes the electoral vote result in 1916?
    A. Hughes needed 12 more electoral votes to win
    B. Hughes needed 22 more electoral votes to win
    C. Hughes needed 42 more electoral votes to win

473. Which state did Hughes and Wilson split in 1916
    A. New Jersey
    B. New York
    C. West Virginia

474. In addition to the South, which other region of the country did Wilson generally get most of his victories in?
    A. The Midwest
    B. New England
    C. The West

475. The 1916 election was one of the closest elections of all time. Republican Charles Evans Hughes would have won the Electoral College by winning any one of ten states that the Democratic incumbent Woodrow Wilson carried. Many of these states were not close but which pivotal state was decided by fewer than 5,000 votes – thus deciding the election?
    A. California
    B. Indiana
    C. Minnesota

Quick answers for the 1916 Election (more detailed answers are at the back of the book).

460. C. 461. C. 462. C. 463. B. 464. F.
465. B. 466. T. 467. T. 468. C. 469. A.
470. B. 471. B. 472. A. 473. C. 474. C.
475. A.

☆1912 ELECTION☆

476. Who won the most votes in the 1912 Democratic presidential primaries?
    A. James "Champ" Clark
    B. John Burke
    C. Woodrow Wilson

477. Who won the most votes in the 1912 Republican presidential primaries?
    A. Theodore Roosevelt
    B. Unpledged delegates
    C. William Taft

478. What degree did Woodrow Wilson have that was a first for presidential candidates?
    A. Doctorate in Political Science
    B. Law Degree (J. D.)
    C. Medical Degree (M.D.)

479. Which of the following ideas was included in the 1912 Socialist Party platform?
    A. Opposition to the Sherman Anti-trust Act
    B. Support for a minimum wage
    C. Support for privatization of railroads

480. Who was Wilson's major rival for the nomination?
    A. Alton Parker
    B. James "Champ" Clark
    C. William J. Bryan

481. How many ballots did it take for Wilson to win the nomination at the 1912 Democratic Convention?
    A. He won easily on the 1st ballot
    B. He won on the 6th ballot after a brief struggle
    C. He won a protracted fight on the 46th ballot

482. True or False. The 1912 Democratic Party platform supported a graduated income tax?

483. Which answer best describes the 1912 Republican Convention?
    A. Placid
    B. Robust
    C. Tumultuous

484. What happened when Taft won a procedural vote that effectively guaranteed him the nomination?
    A. Roosevelt's supporters quietly staged a walk-out protest
    B. Roosevelt's supporters began chanting "We want Teddy!"
    C. Roosevelt's supporters at the convention made noises like steamrollers with sandpaper and horns

485. The Progressive Party convention met almost immediately after the Republican Convention adjourned; delegates were present from every state but which one?
    A. New Jersey
    B. South Carolina
    C. South Dakota

486. Who did the Progressive Party nominate for president?
    A. Eugene Debs
    B. Teddy Roosevelt
    C. William J. Bryan

487. Which candidate ran using the following slogan "social and industrial justice"?
    A. Theodore Roosevelt
    B. William Taft
    C. Woodrow Wilson

488. Which answer best describes the popular vote result in 1912?
- A. Close (top two candidates within 2% of each other)
- B. Not that close (top two candidates more than 2% but less than 7% apart)
- C. Big win (top two candidates more than 7% but less than 15% apart)

489. Which answer best describes the electoral vote result in 1912?
- A. Roosevelt needed about 100 more electoral votes to win
- B. Roosevelt needed about 150 more electoral votes to win
- C. Roosevelt needed about 175 more electoral votes to win.

490. With Roosevelt and Taft splitting the Republican vote, did that translate into Republican gains in Congress in 1912?
- A. Yes
- B. No

491. In 1912, William Taft became the first president to finish third in a presidential election. Although he was competitive in many states, he only carried two. Which two states did he carry?
- A. Vermont and Utah
- B. Maryland and Delaware
- C. Maryland and Connecticut

492. The 1912 election marked the first time that which two states participated in a presidential election?
- A. Alaska and Hawaii
- B. Arizona and New Mexico
- C. Idaho and Utah

493. What electoral milestone did third-party candidate Teddy Roosevelt set in the 1912 election?
- A. He was the first ex-president to run as a third party candidate
- B. He won more than 80 electoral votes, the most in a single election for a third party candidate
- C. He won more than 100 electoral votes, the most in a single election for a third party candidate

494. In the 1912 election Woodrow Wilson became the first candidate to do what?
- A. Win 30 states and 300 electoral votes
- B. Win 35 states and more than 350 electoral votes
- C. Win 40 states and more than 400 electoral votes

Quick answers for the 1912 Election (more detailed answers are at the back of the book).

476. C. 477. A. 478. A. 479. B. 480. B. 481. C. 482. T. 483. C. 484. C. 485. B. 486. B. 487. B. 488. C. 489. C. 490. B. 491. A. 492. B. 493. B. 494. C.

☆1908 ELECTION☆

495. True or False. In 1908, the Socialist Party nominated Eugene Debs for president?

496. Which of the following ideas was in the 1908 Socialist Party platform?
- A. Privatization of public utilities
- B. End child labor
- C. Workhouses for debtors

497. How many ballots did it take for William Taft to secure the nomination in 1908?
    A. One
    B. Two
    C. Three

498. True or False. With the nomination of the conservative William Taft in 1908, the Republican platform was radically changed from 1904?

499. Where was the 1908 Democratic Convention held?
    A. Denver
    B. Kansas City
    C. New York City

500. How many ballots did it take for Bryan to secure the nomination in 1908?
    A. One
    B. Two
    C. Three

501. True or False. The major differences between the Republican and Democratic parties in 1908 revolved around foreign policy and foreign trade?

502. Which answer best describes the popular vote result in 1908?
    A. Close (top two candidates within 2% of each other)
    B. Not that close (top two candidates more than 2% but less than 7% apart)
    C. Big win (top two candidates more than 7% but less than 15% apart)

503. Which answer best describes the electoral vote result in 1908?
    A. Bryan needed 20 more electoral votes to win
    B. Bryan needed 40 more electoral votes to win
    C. Bryan needed 80 more electoral votes to win

504. The 1908 election marked the first time that which state, often known as Indian Territory, participated in a presidential election?
    A. Arizona
    B. North Dakota
    C. Oklahoma

505. In 1908, Taft generally won which geographic area?
    A. North
    B. South
    C. Neither; the split between Taft and Bryan was east/west

Quick answers for the 1908 Election (more detailed answers are at the back of the book).

495. T. 496. B. 497. A. 498. F. 499. A. 500. A. 501. T. 502. C. 503. C. 504. C. 505. A.

☆1904 ELECTION☆

506. Which of the following candidates made his first run for president in 1904?
    A. Eugene Debs
    B. William Taft
    C. Woodrow Wilson

507. Which answer best describes Republican candidate Theodore Roosevelt?
    A. Personally conservative and advocated conservative policies
    B. Personally conservative and advocated liberal policies
    C. Personally liberal and advocated conservative policies

508. What was the most contentious issue that the 1904 Republican Convention considered?
   A. Adjournment
   B. Hawaii
   C. President

509. A telegram containing what message was read to the Republican delegates after the platform had been adopted?
   A. That they would have to start over again on the platform
   B. That President Roosevelt sends his congratulations
   C. That a rescue mission was underway in Morocco

510. Who was eventual Democratic Party nominee, Alton Parker's major rival for the nomination?
   A. William Bryan
   B. William Heart
   C. Woodrow Wilson

511. What was noteworthy about vice presidential candidate Henry Davis of West Virginia?
   A. Less than a year earlier he had been a Republican
   B. Oldest vice presidential nominee of a major party
   C. Youngest vice presidential nominee of a major party

512. Which party was opposed to providing federal subsidies for American shipping firms?
   A. Democratic
   B. Republican
   C. Both parties were opposed

513. Which answer best describes the popular vote result in 1904?
   A. Close (top two candidates within 2% of each other)
   B. Big win (top two candidates more than 7% but less than 15% apart)
   C. Landslide victory (of the top two candidate, one candidate won by more than 15% of the popular vote)

514. Which answer best describes the electoral vote result in 1904?
   A. Parker needed 39 more electoral votes to win
   B. Parker needed 69 more electoral votes to win
   C. Parker needed 99 more electoral votes to win

515. Generally speaking, Parker's state wins were confined to which geographic area of the country?
   A. East
   B. South
   C. West

516. Both Parker and Roosevelt had strong ties to New York, which candidate carried the state?
   A. Parker
   B. Roosevelt

517. In Teddy Roosevelt's landslide win in 1904, what election record was set?
   A. He was the first to win more than 25 states
   B. He was the first to win more than 27 states
   C. He was the first to win more than 30 states

☆1900 ELECTION☆

518. In 1900 on what ballot did William McKinley win the Republican Party nomination?
    A. First ballot
    B. Third ballot
    C. Fifth ballot

519. In 1900 on what ballot did William J. Bryan win the Democratic Party nomination?
    A. First ballot
    B. Fifth ballot
    C. Tenth ballot

520. True or False. In 1900 both major party candidates ran unopposed for the nomination?

521. In 1900 which major party proposed creating a Department of Labor?
    A. Democratic
    B. Republican

522. How many ballots did it take for Teddy Roosevelt to win the vice presidential nomination?
    A. One
    B. Two
    C. Four

523. In 1900 who won the Democratic Party nomination for vice president?
    A. Adlai Stevenson
    B. Alton Parker
    C. William Hearst

524. True or False. In 1900 both major parties favored a canal through present-day Panama?

525. Which answer best describes the popular vote result in 1900?
    A. Close (top two candidates within 2% of each other)
    B. Not that close (top two candidates more than 2% but less than 7% apart)
    C. Big win (top two candidates more than 7% but less than 15% apart)

526. Which answer best describes the electoral vote result in 1900?
    A. Bryan was short by about 20 electoral votes
    B. Bryan was short by about 50 electoral votes
    C. Bryan was short by about 70 electoral votes

527. What was unusual about the 1900 election?
    A. Bryan failed to carry Mississippi
    B. Bryan failed to carry Nebraska
    C. McKinley failed to carry Ohio

528. In terms of the total number of votes won, (not percentage of the vote) which state was Socialist Party candidate Eugene Debs's best state?
    A. New York
    B. Washington
    C. Wisconsin

529. What Electoral College milestone was set in the 1900 election which saw William McKinley cruise to an easy re-election?
   A. He was the first candidate since the popular vote was counted to hold his opponent to single digits in the Electoral College.
   B. He was the first candidate to get more than 290 electoral votes.
   C. His election saw a record number of "faithless electors" (electors who do not vote for the candidate they are pledged to).

Quick answers for the 1900 Election (more detailed answers are at the back of the book).

518. A. 519. A. 520. T. 521. A. 522. A. 523. A. 524. F. 525. B. 526. C. 527. B. 528. A. 529. B.

☆1896 ELECTION☆

530. What ballot did William McKinley win the nomination?
   A. First
   B. Third
   C. Fifth

531. What ballot did William Jennings Bryan win the nomination?
   A. First
   B. Third
   C. Fifth

532. What issue did Bryan give a speech on at the convention during the platform debate that ultimately propelled him to the nomination?
   A. Currency
   B. Railroad regulations
   C. Tariffs

533. In 1896 which party favored the gold standard?
   A. Democratic
   B. Republican
   C. Both parties

534. In 1896 which party platform took a strong stand against lynching?
   A. Democratic
   B. Republican
   C. Both parties took a strong stand against lynching

535. In 1896 which party platform favored presidential term limits?
   A. Democratic
   B. Republican
   C. Neither party favored presidential term limits in 1896

536. What state was William McKinley from?
   A. Nebraska
   B. Ohio
   C. Pennsylvania

537. What state was William J. Bryan from?
   A. Nebraska
   B. Ohio
   C. Pennsylvania

538. Which party was stronger in urban areas in 1896?
   A. Democratic
   B. Populist
   C. Republican

539. Bryan tried and failed to get which group to support him?
   A. Doctors
   B. Government workers
   C. Labor

540. True or False. By 1896 geographic fault lines had re-emerged with Republicans being stronger in the North and Democrats being stronger in the South?

541. In 1896 if you wore a gold beetle on your lapel pin, who did you support?
   A. William J. Bryan
   B. William McKinley

542. In 1896 if you wore a silver beetle on your lapel pin, who did you support?
   A. William J. Bryan
   B. William McKinley

543. Which candidate had an advertisement showing an analog clock that showed the time 12:44?
   A. William J. Bryan
   B. William McKinley

544. Which answer best describes the popular vote result in 1896?
   A. Not that close (top two candidates more than 2% but less than 7% apart)
   B. Big win (top two candidates more than 7% but less than 15% apart)
   C. Blowout victory (of the top two candidate, one candidate won by more than 15% of the popular vote)

545. Which answer best describes the electoral vote result in 1896?
   A. Bryan was short by about 20 electoral votes
   B. Bryan was short by about 50 electoral votes
   C. Bryan was short by about 100 electoral votes

546. Which two states were very closely contested and awarded a split of electoral votes?
   A. California and Kentucky
   B. North Carolina and South Carolina
   C. Wisconsin and Wyoming

547. 1896 was the first year that which of the following states participated in presidential elections?
   A. Idaho
   B. Oklahoma
   C. Utah

Quick answers for the 1896 Election (more detailed answers are at the back of the book).

530. A. 531. C. 532. A. 533. B. 534. B.
535. A. 536. B. 537. A. 538. C. 539. C.
540. T. 541. B. 542. A. 543. B. 544. A.
545. B. 546. A. 547. C.

☆1892 ELECTION☆

548. Where was the 1892 Republican convention held?
   A. Chicago
   B. Minneapolis
   C. Richmond

549. What future Republican president was chair of the convention?
   A. McKinley
   B. Roosevelt
   C. Taft

550. In 1892 how many ballots did it take to nominate Benjamin Harrison?
   A. One
   B. Two
   C. Three

551. Where was the 1892 Democratic convention held?
   A. Chicago
   B. Minneapolis
   C. Richmond

552. What problem plagued the 1892 Democratic convention?
   A. Leaky convention hall roof
   B. Noisy crowds in the street
   C. Unbearably hot weather

553. In 1892 how many ballots did it take to nominate Grover Cleveland?
   A. One
   B. Three
   C. Five

554. Both Cleveland and Harrison had a reputation for which trait?
   A. Honesty
   B. Tact
   C. Vice

555. Which party favored prohibition?
   A. Democratic
   B. Republican

556. In 1892 one state switched to award electoral votes by congressional district (it switched back to winner-take-all before the next election), which state made such a switch in 1892?
   A. Arkansas
   B. Michigan
   C. Tennessee

557. True or False. Third party candidates did particularly poorly in 1892 and none of them managed to get more than 2% of the national popular vote?

558. Which party's vice presidential candidate was the grandfather of a future presidential candidate?
   A. Democratic
   B. Populist
   C. Republican

559. Did the corrupt political organization known as Tammany Hall support or oppose Grover Cleveland for president?
   A. Oppose
   B. Support

560. What animal was the symbol of the Populist Party in the 1890s?
   A. Goose
   B. Ox
   C. Pig

561. Which answer best describes the popular vote result in 1892?
   A. Close (top two candidates within 2% of each other)
   B. Not that close (top two candidates more than 2% but less than 7% apart)
   C. Big win (top two candidates more than 7% but less than 15% apart)

562. Which answer best describes the electoral vote result in 1892?
   A. Harrison needed about 25 more electoral votes to change the result
   B. Harrison needed about 50 more electoral votes to change the result
   C. Harrison needed about 75 more electoral votes to change the result.

563. How many new states voted in a presidential election for the first time in 1892?
   A. 2
   B. 4
   C. 6

564. What unusual election result happened in North Dakota in the 1892 election?
- A. 3-way split of the electoral vote
- B. Cleveland and Harrison received the same number of popular votes, and Cleveland was declared the winner after a coin toss
- C. Loss of an electoral vote due to the last minute incapacity of an elector

565. True or False. In 1892, Harrison became the first sitting president to lose an election for president to an ex-president?

Quick answers for the 1892 Election (more detailed answers are at the back of the book).

548. B. 549. A. 550. A. 551. A. 552. A. 553. A. 554. A. 555. B. 556. B. 557. F. 558. A. 559. A. 560. A. 561. B. 562. C. 563. C. 564. A. 565. T.

☆1888 ELECTION☆

566. True or False. Grover Cleveland was unopposed for the Democratic Party nomination?

567. Benjamin Harrison won the nomination on the eighth ballot, how many days did it take to conduct those ballots, including any days off from balloting?
- A. Two
- B. Four
- C. Six

568. What was noteworthy about Allen Thurman, the Democratic Party nominee for vice president in 1888?
- A. He was 75 years old
- B. He was 35 years old
- C. He had six fingers on his right hand

569. What was the symbol of 1888 Democratic Party vice presidential nominee Allen Thurman?
- A. A red bandana
- B. A silver cane
- C. A black glove

570. Which party wanted to reduce the import tariff in 1888?
- A. Democratic Party
- B. Republican Party

571. In addition to opposing alcoholic beverages, what else was the Prohibition Party against in 1888?
- A. Immigration quotas
- B. Polygamy
- C. Protectionism

572. Which party strongly supported pensions for veterans in 1888?
- A. Democratic Party
- B. Republican Party

573. Which answer best describes the popular vote result in 1888?
- A. Close (top two candidates within 2% of each other)
- B. Not that close (top two candidates more than 2% but less than 7% apart)
- C. Blowout victory (of the top two candidate, one candidate won by more than 15% of the popular vote)

574. Which answer best describes the electoral vote result in 1888?
- A. Cleveland needed about 15 more electoral votes to change the result
- B. Cleveland needed about 30 more electoral votes to change the result
- C. Cleveland needed about 45 more electoral votes to change the result

575. In addition to New York, what other state did Harrison win that Cleveland had won four years earlier?
   A. Indiana
   B. Ohio
   C. Pennsylvania

Quick answers for the 1888 Election (more detailed answers are at the back of the book).

566. T. 567. B. 568. A. 569. A. 570. A.
571. B. 572. B. 573. A. 574. B. 575. B.

☆1884 ELECTION☆

576. Which short-lived diversity milestone was achieved in 1884 at the Republican Convention?
   A. First African American as a temporary chair of the convention
   B. First woman as temporary chair of the convention

577. How many ballots did it take for Cleveland to win the nomination?
   A. One
   B. Two
   C. Seven

578. What type of candidate was Cleveland the first of?
   A. First president from Maryland
   B. First Roman Catholic
   C. First urban progressive

579. What state was James Blaine from?
   A. Indiana
   B. Maine
   C. New Hampshire

580. Which best describes the party platforms of 1884?
   A. Closer together on the issues than usual
   B. Further apart on the issues than usual

581. Which answer best describes the popular vote result in 1884?
   A. Close (top two candidates within 2% of each other)
   B. Big win (top two candidates more than 7% but less than 15% apart)
   C. Blowout victory (of the top two candidate, one candidate won by more than 15% of the popular vote)

582. Which answer best describes the electoral vote result in 1884?
   A. Blaine needed about 20 more electoral votes to win
   B. Blaine needed about 40 more electoral votes to win
   C. Blaine needed about 80 more electoral votes to win

583. True or False. A series of gaffes the week before the election cost Blaine dearly?

584. Again in 1884 the election came down to New York, with the winner claiming the presidency. About how many votes was New York Governor Grover Cleveland's margin of victory in the Empire State?
   A. Less than 2,000
   B. More than 2,000 but less than 10,000
   C. More than 10,000 but less than 17,000

585. What New England state did Cleveland win in three consecutive elections starting in 1884?
   A. Connecticut
   B. Massachusetts
   C. Rhode Island

☆1880 ELECTION☆

586. True or False. Ulysses Grant sought the nomination for a third term in 1880?

587. Was James Garfield actively seeking the nomination for president?
    A. No
    B. Yes

588. How many ballots did it take for the Republicans to choose a nominee in 1880?
    A. 5
    B. 15
    C. 35

589. How many days did it the Republican balloting for president take in 1880?
    A. Two
    B. Four
    C. Six

590. What state was Chester Arthur put on the Republican ticket to help win?
    A. New York
    B. Pennsylvania
    C. Ohio

591. Which of the following statements about the Republican Convention of 1880 is true?
    A. It was the last convention when Democrats and Independents could participate
    B. It was the first convention that only Republicans could participate

592. Which answer best describes the attitude of the Democratic Party in 1880 towards the federal government?
    A. It favored centralization with more power flowing to the federal government
    B. It favored decentralization with more power flowing to the states

593. How many ballots did it take for Winfield Hancock to win the Democratic nomination?
    A. Two
    B. Four
    C. Six

594. Both the Democrats and the Republicans ran popular Civil War generals for president in 1880, did the two parties also have similar platforms?
    A. Yes
    B. No

595. Which answer best describes the monetary policy of the Greenback Party?
    A. Hard currency backed by metallic reserves
    B. Inflationary currency with unlimited coinage of gold and silver

596. Which answer best describes the popular vote result in 1880?
    A. Close (top two candidates within 2% of each other)
    B. Not that close (top two candidates more than 2% but less than 7% apart)
    C. Big win (top two candidates more than 7% but less than 15% apart)

597. Which answer best describes the electoral vote result in 1880?
    A. Hancock needed 15 more electoral votes to win
    B. Hancock needed 30 more electoral votes to win
    C. Hancock needed 70 more electoral votes to win

598. About how many votes was the important swing state of New York decided by?
  A. 21,000
  B. 51,000
  C. 76,000

Quick answers for the 1880 Election (more detailed answers are at the back of the book).

586. T. 587. A. 588. C. 589. A. 590. A. 591. B. 592. B. 593. A. 594. A. 595. B. 596. A. 597. B. 598. A.

☆1876 ELECTION☆

599. Which prominent African American gave a speech at the 1876 Republican Convention?
  A. Frederick Douglas
  B. George Washington Carver
  C. Harriet Tubman

600. Which of the following was not a name of one of the three factions of the Republican Party in 1876?
  A. Half-breeds
  B. Reformers
  C. Tories

601. What happened during the speech nominating James Blaine?
  A. Bleacher collapse
  B. Electrical power failure
  C. Loud protest

602. How many ballots did it take to determine a winner at the 1876 Republican Convention?
  A. Two
  B. Seven
  C. Twelve

603. Where did the 1876 Democratic Convention take place?
  A. Chicago
  B. Philadelphia
  C. St. Louis

604. How many ballots did it take to determine a winner at the 1876 Democratic Convention?
  A. Two
  B. Seven
  C. Twelve

605. True or False. Samuel Tilden was a reformer?

606. Which answer best describes the popular vote result in 1876?
  A. Close (top two candidates within 2% of each other)
  B. Not that close (top two candidates more than 2% but less than 7% apart)
  C. Big win (top two candidates more than 7% but less than 15% apart)

607. Which answer best describes the electoral vote result in 1876?
  A. Tilden needed one more electoral vote to win
  B. Tilden needed three more electoral votes to win
  C. Tilden needed twenty more electoral votes to win

608. The election returns from which four states were disputed and the winner was decided by a special commission?
  A. Alabama, Florida, Mississippi, North Carolina
  B. Florida, Louisiana, Oregon, South Carolina
  C. Florida, North Carolina, South Carolina, Texas

609. How many of the disputed states did the special commission award to Hayes?
    A. Two
    B. Three
    C. Four

610. Democrats threatened to filibuster the election certification unless what concessions were made?
    A. An end to both the Reconstruction and the federal occupation of former confederate states.
    B. That Hayes formed a coalition government and governed as a centrist.
    C. That Hayes named Tilden as secretary of state.

Quick answers for the 1876 Election (more detailed answers are at the back of the book).

599. A. 600. C. 601. B. 602. B. 603. C. 604. A. 605. T. 606. B. 607. A. 608. B. 609. C. 610. A.

☆1872 ELECTION☆

611. True or False. Ulysses Grant was nominated after a brief but vigorous convention challenge from fellow Civil War veteran General William T. Sherman?

612. What did the major change to the Republican platform involve?
    A. Civil rights
    B. Free speech
    C. Term limits

613. What was the major issue uniting the Liberal Republican Party?
    A. Civil Rights
    B. Corruption
    C. Free trade

614. What major scandal tarnished Grant's re-election bid in 1872?
    A. Coffee Sands
    B. Credit Mobilier
    C. Huntingdon Hall

615. How many ballots did it take Horace Greeley to win the Liberal Republican nomination?
    A. 6
    B. 12
    C. 17

616. True or False. In an unprecedented move, the Democratic Party did not run its own candidate in 1872 but instead endorsed a rival Republican candidate?

617. Was Horace Greeley able to capitalize on the major scandal around Grant?
    A. Yes
    B. No

618. Which candidate was known as the "Galena Tanner" in campaign literature that attempted to focus on his humble origins and working class ties?
    A. Horace Greeley
    B. Ulysses Grant

619. Which answer best describes the popular vote result in 1872?
    A. Not that close (top two candidates more than 2% but less than 7% apart)
    B. Big win (top two candidates more than 7% but less than 15% apart)
    C. Blowout victory (of the top two candidate, one candidate won by more than 15% of the popular vote)

620. Which answer best describes the electoral vote result in 1872?
- A. Greeley needed about 25 more electoral votes to win
- B. Greeley needed about 50 more electoral votes to win
- C. Greeley needed about 115 more electoral votes to win

621. How many states had results disqualified due to ballot integrity issues in 1872?
- A. Zero
- B. One
- C. Two

622. Where were the most allegations of vote fraud and vote suppression in 1872?
- A. Reconstructed Southern states
- B. War-torn Northern states
- C. Wild Western states

623. What significant event happened after Election Day 1872 but before the Electoral College results were certified that influenced but did not change the ultimate result of the election?
- A. Horace Greeley died after the election but before the Electoral College had met.
- B. Horace Greeley was scandalously arrested after the election and many of his electors switched their votes to the winner Ulysses Grant.
- C. The electoral results in Alabama were contested with allegations of voter fraud on both sides. However Alabama's 10 electoral votes did not matter to decide the election because Grant had won in a landslide. In the end the investigation was dropped and each candidate was awarded half of Alabama's electoral votes.

Quick answers for the 1872 Election (more detailed answers are at the back of the book).

611. F. 612. A. 613. B. 614. B. 615. A. 616. T. 617. B. 618. B. 619. B. 620. C. 621. C. 622. A. 623. A.

☆1868 ELECTION☆

624. True or False. The former Confederate states were represented at both major party conventions in 1868?

625. How many candidates besides Ulysses Grant were running for the Republican Party nomination in 1868?
- A. Zero
- B. One
- C. Two

626. How many candidates received votes for vice president on the first ballot at the 1868 Republican Convention?
- A. 0
- B. 1
- C. 11

627. What was odd about the Republican civil rights plank in 1868?
- A. Nothing
- B. It only called for voting rights for former slaves in the South and it left voting rights for former slaves in the North up to those states
- C. It called for turning enforcement of civil rights laws over to local governments

628. True or False. The Democratic Party voted to renew the two-thirds rule at the 1868 Democratic Convention?

629. True or False. Like Eisenhower nearly 85 years later, Ulysses Grant had been sought as a possible candidate by the Democratic Party in 1868?

630. What happened to break the gridlock after the 22nd ballot at the Democratic Convention?
   A. Nothing in particular
   B. The chairman of the convention was reluctantly nominated
   C. A coin was flipped to determine whether Colfax or Johnson would drop out

631. Which answer best describes the popular vote result in 1868?
   A. Not that close (top two candidates more than 2% but less than 7% apart)
   B. Big win (top two candidates more than 7% but less than 15% apart)
   C. Blowout victory (of the top two candidate, one candidate won by more than 15% of the popular vote)

632. True or False. New black voters voted for Grant in significant numbers in 1868?

633. Which answer best describes the electoral vote result in 1868?
   A. Seymour needed about 20 more electoral votes to win
   B. Seymour needed about 50 more electoral votes to win
   C. Seymour needed about 70 more electoral votes to win

634. After the Civil War, how many states did not participate in the 1868 presidential election due to the Reconstruction?
   A. 3
   B. 8
   C. 11

635. Which state voted for the first time in 1868?
   A. Alaska
   B. Montana
   C. Nebraska

> Quick answers for the 1868 Election (more detailed answers are at the back of the book).
>
> 624. T. 625. A. 626. C. 627. B. 628. T. 629. T. 630. B. 631. A. 632. T. 633. C. 634. A. 635. C.

☆1864 ELECTION☆

636. True or False? The Republicans invited Democrats to the 1864 Republican Convention?

637. Some states from the Confederacy sent delegates to the Republican Convention, and most of these delegates were not allowed to vote, except the delegates from Tennessee and which other state?
   A. Arkansas
   B. Kentucky
   C. South Carolina

638. Lincoln was nominated without issue on the first ballot; did he choose his vice president or did he let the convention choose?
   A. Convention chose the vice presidential nominee
   B. Lincoln chose the vice presidential nominee

639. True or False. Like the Republican Convention, delegates from some of the states in the Confederacy attended the 1864 Democratic Convention?

640. True or False. Both members of the 1864 Democratic ticket had the same first name?

641. Which party supported unconditional surrender as a term for ending the Civil War?
    A. Democratic
    B. Republican
    C. Both parties

642. Which answer best describes the popular vote result in 1864?
    A. Close (top two candidates within 2% of each other)
    B. Big win (top two candidates more than 7% but less than 15% apart)
    C. Blowout victory (of the top two candidate, one candidate won by more than 15% of the popular vote)

643. Which answer best describes the electoral vote result in 1864?
    A. McClellan needed about 50 more electoral votes to win
    B. McClellan needed about 75 more electoral votes to win
    C. McClellan needed about 100 more electoral votes to win

644. How many states did McClellan win?
    A. Three
    B. Five
    C. Seven

645. Maryland had a history of being hostile to Lincoln. Did Lincoln carry Maryland in 1864?
    A. No
    B. Yes

646. How many states participated in a presidential election for the first time in 1864?
    A. One
    B. Two
    C. Three

647. How many states were under Union occupation but did not vote in 1864?
    A. Zero
    B. One
    C. Two

648. What was noteworthy about the 1864 election between George McClellan and Abraham Lincoln?
    A. It marked the first time that a general had run for president
    B. It marked the first time that a man fired by a president became the opposing party nominee for president
    C. It marked the first time that two candidates from the same home state ran against each other

Quick answers for the 1864 Election (more detailed answers are at the back of the book).

636. T. 637. C. 638. A. 639. F. 640. T. 641. B. 642. B. 643. C. 644. A. 645. B. 646. C. 647. C. 648. B.

☆1860 ELECTION☆

649. Where was the Democratic Convention in April of 1860 held?
    A. Baltimore, Maryland
    B. Charleston, South Carolina
    C. Richmond, Virginia

650. Due to the intra-party rift on slavery, the Democratic Party was unable to choose a presidential nominee when it met for the convention in April and adjourned until June and reconvened in which city?
    A. Baltimore, Maryland
    B. Charleston, South Carolina
    C. Richmond, Virginia

651. Who was finally selected as the Democratic Party nominee in 1860?
   A. Franklin Pierce
   B. James Buchanan
   C. Stephen Douglas

652. The Democratic Party platform was pro-slavery but it also maintained the status quo, this was insufficient for some members of the Democratic Party who split and ran on an even more pro-slavery platform that favored expanding slavery further, who did these Southern Democrats nominate as their candidate for president?
   A. John Breckenridge
   B. John Calhoun
   C. Millard Fillmore

653. Concerned about the split over slavery, another third-party arose, this party sought national unity, what was the name of this unity party?
   A. Constitutional Union Party
   B. Democratic-Republican Party
   C. Stars and Stripes Forever Party

654. Which party favored unlimited immigration to the United States?
   A. Democratic Party
   B. Republican Party
   C. Both

655. True or False. Both the main Democratic Party and the Republican Party favored federal spending to subsidize a transcontinental railroad?

656. Which party favored federal subsidies for harbor improvements?
   A. Democratic Party
   B. Republican Party

657. In 1860 which party campaigned with slogan "vote yourself a home"?
   A. Democrats
   B. Republicans
   C. Southern Democrats

658. True or False. Lincoln used slavery as a wedge issue to split the Democrats?

659. Which candidate gave out a "rail splitters badge" to supporters?
   A. Abraham Lincoln
   B. John Bell
   C. John Breckinridge
   D. Steven Douglas

660. Which answer best describes the popular vote result in 1860?
   A. Close (top two candidates within 2% of each other)
   B. Not that close (top two candidates more than 2% but less than 7% apart)
   C. Big win (top two candidates more than 7% but less than 15% apart)

661. To deny Lincoln an outright victory in the Electoral College, the non-winning candidates needed to win how many more electoral votes (that Lincoln won)?
   A. 9
   B. 19
   C. 29

662. How many new states participated in their first presidential election?
   A. Zero
   B. One
   C. Two

663. Which of the following candidates received the second highest electoral vote total in 1860?
   A. John Bell
   B. John Breckinridge
   C. Steven Douglas

664. Who carried California in 1860?
    A. John Breckinridge
    B. Steven Douglas
    C. Abraham Lincoln

665. Which candidate was on the ballot in the most states?
    A. John Breckenridge
    B. Steven Douglas
    C. Abraham Lincoln

Quick answers for the 1860 Election (more detailed answers are at the back of the book).

649. B. 650. A. 651. C. 652. A. 653. A. 654. C. 655. T. 656. B. 657. B. 658. T. 659. A. 660. C. 661. C. 662. C. 663. B. 664. A. 665. B.

☆1856 ELECTION☆

666. Where was the first national Republican Convention held?
    A. Baltimore, Maryland
    B. Madison, Wisconsin
    C. Philadelphia, Pennsylvania

667. Among the procedural rules established at that first convention was the amount of delegate support needed to win the nomination, what level of support was required to win?
    A. Simple majority
    B. Two-thirds majority
    C. Three-quarters majority

668. What issue unified the Republican Party?
    A. Federalism
    B. Opposition to slavery
    C. Transcontinental railroad

669. What issue unified the Whig American Party (better known by their nickname as the Know Nothing Party)?
    A. Immigration
    B. Slavery
    C. Transcontinental railroad

670. Who was the presidential candidate of the Know Nothing Party?
    A. John Tyler
    B. Martin Van Buren
    C. Millard Fillmore

671. How many ballots did it take for James Buchanan to win the Democratic nomination?
    A. 5
    B. 13
    C. 17

672. What best describes the foreign policy advocated by the Democratic Party in 1856?
    A. Expansionist
    B. Isolationist

673. Which answer best describes the popular vote result in 1856?
    A. Close (top two candidates within 2% of each other)
    B. Not that close (top two candidates more than 2% but less than 7% apart)
    C. Big win (top two candidates more than 7% but less than 15% apart)

674. Which answer best describes the electoral vote result in 1856?
    A. Fremont needed 14 more electoral votes to win
    B. Fremont needed 34 more electoral votes to win
    C. Fremont needed 54 more electoral votes to win

675. Who won California in 1856?
- A. James Buchanan
- B. John Fremont
- C. Millard Fillmore

676. Most Fremont's electoral votes came from which region?
- A. Midwest
- B. New England
- C. South

677. In 1856, former president Millard Fillmore ran as a third party candidate for the notoriously anti-immigrant, Whig-American party. How many states did he carry?
- A. Zero
- B. One
- C. Two

Quick answers for the 1856 Election (more detailed answers are at the back of the book).

666. C. 667. A. 668. B. 669. A. 670. C.
671. C. 672. A. 673. C. 674. B. 675. A.
676. B. 677. B.

☆1852 ELECTION☆

678. True or False. In 1852 the first permanent national chairman of the Democratic National Committee was selected?

679. What rule change was made to make Democratic Convention sizes more manageable?
- A. Each state was given the same number of delegates
- B. Each state was given a number of delegates based on the size of the state
- C. States with delegations of over twenty members were required to give advance notice

680. True or False. Franklin Pierce actively campaigned for the Democratic presidential nomination?

681. Pierce won on the 49th ballot. How many days did the balloting take?
- A. Two
- B. Five
- C. Seven

682. How many ballots did it take Winfield Scott to win the Whig Party nomination?
- A. 46
- B. 50
- C. 53

683. True or False. The first few Whig Party vice presidential nominees refused the nomination in 1852 and eventually a choice was made and it was declared to be unanimous without an actual vote?

684. True or False. The Free Soil Party opposed the Compromise of 1850?

685. In addition to slavery, the other major difference between the two parties was the issue of federal spending for internal improvements, which party favored greater federal spending on internal improvements that might only benefit a few states?
- A. Democratic Party
- B. Whig Party

686. True or False. By 1852 both the Whigs and the Democrats had turned against the Compromise of 1850 and condemned it in their respective party platforms?

687. Which answer best describes the popular vote result in 1852?
   A. Close (top two candidates within 2% of each other)
   B. Not that close (top two candidates more than 2% but less than 7% apart)
   C. Big win (top two candidates more than 7% but less than 15% apart)

688. Which answer best describes the electoral vote result in 1852?
   A. Scott needed to win about 10 more electoral votes to win
   B. Scott needed to win about 50 more electoral votes to win
   C. Scott needed to win about 100 more electoral votes to win

689. In the 2010s, California with 55 electoral votes is the biggest Electoral College prize. In 1852 which state was the biggest Electoral College prize (with 35 electoral votes)?
   A. New York
   B. California
   C. Ohio

690. How many electoral votes did California have in 1852?
   A. Two
   B. Three
   C. Four

691. How many states did Scott win?
   A. Two
   B. Three
   C. Four

Quick answers for the 1852 Election (more detailed answers are at the back of the book).

678. T. 679. B. 680. F. 681. A. 682. C. 683. T. 684. T. 685. B. 686. F. 687. B. 688. C. 689. A. 690. C. 691. C.

☆1848 ELECTION☆

692. Which state had two rival groups of delegates at the 1848 Democratic Convention and neither delegation ended up voting?
   A. Massachusetts
   B. New York
   C. South Carolina

693. Who was Lewis Cass's main rival for the nomination?
   A. James Buchanan
   B. James Madison
   C. James Polk

694. Which answer best describes the Democratic Party position on slavery in 1848?
   A. Federal government decides slavery questions
   B. The people of states and territories decide slavery questions

695. Which party had an agrarian, populist-leaning, base?
   A. Democrats
   B. Whigs

696. True or False. At the Whig Convention, Texas did not send delegates but let Louisiana vote on its behalf?

697. Which of the following people was not one of Zachary Taylor's rivals for the Whig Party nomination?
   A. Henry Clay
   B. John Calhoun
   C. Winfield Scott

698. Did the Whig Party have an official platform in 1848?
   A. Yes
   B. No

699. Who did the Free Soil Party nominate for president?
- A. John Quincy Adams
- B. Martin Van Buren
- C. William Retslowe

700. Most of the Free Soil Party Platform of 1848 is devoted to denouncing slavery. Which of the following other positions did the Free Soil Party take?
- A. Against federal spending for harbor improvements
- B. For cheap postage
- C. For transcontinental railroad

701. Which answer best describes the popular vote result in 1848?
- A. Close (top two candidates within 2% of each other)
- B. Not that close (top two candidates more than 2% but less than 7% apart)
- C. Big win (top two candidates more than 7% but less than 15% apart)

702. Which answer best describes the electoral vote result in 1848?
- A. Cass needed 19 more electoral votes to win
- B. Cass needed 39 more electoral votes to win
- C. Cass needed 69 more electoral votes to win

703. In 1848 the election came down to Pennsylvania. By how many votes did Taylor win Pennsylvania (and with it the presidency)?
- A. About 1,000
- B. About 16,000
- C. About 26,000

704. In what state might the Free Soil Party have influenced the outcome of the election?
- A. Connecticut
- B. New Jersey
- C. New York

705. How many new states participated in the 1848 presidential election?
- A. Zero
- B. Two
- C. Four

706. Generally (with a few exceptions) did Taylor do better with states that bordered the seacoast or interior states?
- A. Taylor did better with coastal states
- B. Taylor did better with interior states

Quick answers for the 1848 Election (more detailed answers are at the back of the book).

692. C. 693. A. 694. B. 695. A. 696. T.
697. B. 698. B. 699. B. 700. B. 701. B.
702. A. 703. B. 704. C. 705. B. 706. A.

☆1844 ELECTION☆

707. True or False. The Whig and Democratic Party platforms had so few words that they could have each fit onto their own postcard in 1844?

708. In 1844, what did the Whig Party propose to do with the revenue from the sale of federal land?
- A. Remit the revenue from the sale to the states
- B. Keep the revenue in the federal treasury

709. The Liberty Party held its second convention in August of 1843. What was the main focus of the Liberty Party?
- A. Abolition of slavery
- B. Free trade
- C. Western expansion

710. Who did the Whig Party nominate for president in 1844?
    A. Henry Clay
    B. John Tyler
    C. Daniel Webster

711. Who did the Democratic Party nominate for president in 1844?
    A. Lewis Cass
    B. James Polk
    C. Martin Van Buren

712. Why did the Democratic Party nominee get to select his own vice president rather than the convention?
    A. Convention nominee was ineligible
    B. Convention nominee got sick
    C. Convention nominee refused

713. What proved to be a significant campaign issue in 1844?
    A. Annexation
    B. Puerto Rico
    C. Slavery

714. Which candidate used a folksy raccoon character in an effort to appear folksier?
    A. Henry Clay
    B. James Polk

715. Which answer best describes the popular vote result in 1844?
    A. Polk won the popular vote 50% to 48%
    B. Pierce won the popular vote 53% to 44%
    C. Clay won the popular vote 51% to 47%

716. Which answer best describes the electoral vote result in 1844?
    A. Clay needed to win 33 more electoral votes to win
    B. Clay needed to win 66 more electoral votes to win
    C. Clay needed to win 99 more electoral votes to win

717. In 1844 the election was remarkably close and close everywhere. It is the only election since the popular vote began to be counted where the winner did not win any states by more than how many votes?
    A. 5,000
    B. 15,000
    C. 25,000

718. True or False. The Liberty Party may have influenced the outcome of the election in New York?

719. Looking at a map of the 1844 election results, is there a clear geographic pattern to the map?
    A. No
    B. Yes

Quick answers for the 1844 Election (more detailed answers are at the back of the book).

707. T. 708. A. 709. A. 710. A. 711. B. 712. C. 713. A. 714. A. 715. A. 716. A. 717. B. 718. T. 719. A.

☆1840 ELECTION☆

720. True or False. In 1840, the Whig Party had a lengthy platform with a long essay about the importance of preserving liberty through law?

721. True or False. Secret ballot rules at the Whig Convention helped William Harrison defeat Henry Clay?

722. True or False. The Democratic Party Platform of 1840 favored an unlimited federal government?

723. Which answer best describes the popular vote result in 1840?
- A. Close (top two candidates within 2% of each other)
- B. Not that close (top two candidates more than 2% but less than 7% apart)
- C. Big win (top two candidates more than 7% but less than 15% apart)

724. Which answer best describes the electoral vote result in 1840?
- A. Van Buren needed 22 more electoral votes to win
- B. Van Buren needed 44 more electoral votes to win
- C. Van Buren needed 88 more electoral votes to win

725. Looking at a map of the 1840 election results, is there a clear geographic pattern to the map?
- A. No
- B. Yes

726. How many new states participated in the 1840 election?
- A. Zero
- B. One
- C. Two

727. Who had the slogan "Tippecanoe and Tyler Too"?
- A. John Adams
- B. William Henry Harrison
- C. Millard Fillmore

728. True or False. William Harrison's "Log Cabin and Hard Cider" campaign captivated the imagination of the electorate?

Quick answers for the 1840 Election (more detailed answers are at the back of the book).

720. F. 721. T. 722. F. 723. B. 724. C. 725. A. 726. A. 727. B. 728. T.

☆1836 ELECTION☆

729. The first credential dispute in American national political convention history occurred this year when rival delegations from which state both showed up at the Democratic Convention?
- A. Maryland
- B. Pennsylvania
- C. Virginia

730. How many ballots did it take to nominate Martin Van Buren in 1836?
- A. One
- B. Three
- C. Seven

731. What was unusual about the timing of the Democratic Convention for the 1836 election?
- A. Nothing
- B. It was earlier than usual
- C. It was much later than usual

732. Did the Democratic Party have a platform in 1836?
- A. Yes
- B. No

733. Did the Whig Party have a platform in 1836?
- A. Yes
- B. No

734. Which answer best describes the popular vote result in 1836?
- A. Close (top two candidates within 2% of each other)
- B. Not that close (top two candidates more than 2% but less than 7% apart)
- C. Big win (top two candidates more than 7% but less than 15% apart)

735. Which answer best describes the electoral vote result in 1836?
- A. The Whigs needed to win 23 more electoral votes for a tie
- B. The Whigs needed to win 53 more electoral votes for a tie
- C. Whigs needed to win 83 more electoral votes to cause a tie

736. What rare feat did Martin Van Buren accomplish in 1836?
- A. He was a sitting vice president and he was elected president.
- B. He was one of two Democrat presidents to carry Massachusetts in the 19th century.
- C. He campaigned in all 30 states.

737. In 1836 the Whig party attempted to win by running three regional candidates for president to deny the Democrat, Martin Van Buren, a win in the Electoral College. According to the strategy this lack of an Electoral College winner would cause the election to go to the House of Representatives where a Whig candidate was sure to win. The strategy almost worked but it failed when Van Buren won which state by about 5,000 votes and with it outright victory in the Electoral College?
- A. New York
- B. Pennsylvania
- C. South Carolina

738. How many new states participated in the election of 1836?
- A. Zero
- B. One
- C. Two

Quick answers for the 1836 Election (more detailed answers are at the back of the book).

729. B. 730. A. 731. B. 732. B. 733. B. 734. C. 735. A. 736. A. 737. B. 738. B.

☆1832 ELECTION☆

739. In what city did the first presidential nominating convention take place?
- A. Baltimore
- B. New York
- C. Philadelphia

740. Who was the first person nominated by a political convention for president?
- A. Henry Clay
- B. Martin Van Buren
- C. William Wirt

741. Who was the first candidate nominated by the Democratic Party for vice president?
- A. Andrew Jackson
- B. Martin Van Buren
- C. Roger Taney

742. True or False. In contrast to the Democratic Party which stood for continuing past policies, the other political parties of 1832 were formed by their opposition to certain people and ideas?

743. What was the main focus of the National Republican Party? (this party is not related to the current Republican Party)
   A. Opposition to Andrew Jackson
   B. Opposition to recent Supreme Court decisions
   C. Support for harbor improvements

744. Which answer best describes the popular vote result in 1832?
   A. Not that close (top two candidates more than 2% but less than 7% apart)
   B. Big win (top two candidates more than 7% but less than 15% apart)
   C. Blowout victory (of the top two candidate, one candidate won by more than 15% of the popular vote)

745. Which answer best describes the electoral vote result in 1832?
   A. Clay needed to win about 10 more electoral votes to win
   B. Clay needed to win about 30 more electoral votes to win
   C. Clay needed to win about 100 more electoral votes to win

746. How many states did the anti-Mason candidate, Wirt, carry?
   A. Zero
   B. One
   C. Three

747. In addition to winning Kentucky, what region did Henry Clay do well in?
   A. Coastal states
   B. Frontier boundary states
   C. New England

☆ 1828 ELECTION ☆

748. How was Andrew Jackson nominated for president in 1828?
   A. Congress
   B. Convention
   C. State Legislature

749. How was John Q. Adams nominated for president in 1828?
   A. Congress
   B. Convention
   C. State Legislature

750. Which answer best describes the popular vote result in 1828?
   A. Not that close (top two candidates more than 2% but less than 7% apart)
   B. Big win (top two candidates more than 7% but less than 15% apart)
   C. Blowout victory (of the top two candidate, one candidate won by more than 15% of the popular vote)

751. Which answer best describes the electoral vote result in 1828?
   A. Adams needed about 25 more electoral votes to win
   B. Adams needed about 50 more electoral votes to win
   C. Adams needed about 75 more electoral votes to win

752. In 1828 who won the states and electoral votes won by Crawford and Clay four years earlier?
   A. Generally went to Adams
   B. Generally went to Jackson
   C. Split fairly evenly between Adams and Jackson

753. How many states split their electoral votes between Jackson and Adams in 1828?
   A. Zero
   B. Three
   C. Six

Quick answers for the 1828 Election (more detailed answers are at the back of the book).

748. C. 749. C. 750. B. 751. B. 752. A. 753. B.

☆1824 ELECTION☆

754. Who did the Congressional Caucus choose to nominate for president in 1824?
   A. Andrew Jackson
   B. John Q. Adams
   C. William Crawford

755. What derisive nickname had the Congressional Caucus process received by 1824?
   A. King Caucus
   B. Prince Caucus
   C. Tyrant Caucus

756. True or False. In 1824 there was only one national political party but there were factions within that party?

757. Who received the most electoral votes for vice president in 1824?
   A. Andrew Jackson
   B. John Q. Adams
   C. John Calhoun

758. Which answer best describes the popular vote result in 1824?
   A. Close (top two candidates within 2% of each other)
   B. Big win (top two candidates more than 7% but less than 15% apart)
   C. The winner of the popular vote was not elected president

759. Which answer best describes the electoral vote result in 1824?
   A. Small win
   B. Medium win
   C. Big win
   D. Tie

760. True or False. 1824 was the first year that the popular vote for president was counted?

761. Generally where was John Q. Adams electoral strength?
   A. Midwest
   B. New England
   C. South

762. Who decided the winner of the 1824 election?
   A. Electoral College
   B. U.S. House of Representatives
   C. U.S. Senate

763. Which answer best describes John Q. Adams victory in Congress?
   A. Small win
   B. Big win

764. Who won the popular vote in 1824?
   A. John Q. Adams
   B. Henry Clay
   C. Andrew Jackson

765. True or False. Andrew Jackson was upset at his defeat in 1824?

766. What percentage of the population of the United States participated in the 1824 election?
   A. About 5%
   B. About 25%
   C. About 50%

Quick answers for the 1824 Election (more detailed answers are at the back of the book).

754. C. 755. A. 756. T. 757. C. 758. C. 759. D. 760. T. 761. B. 762. B. 763. A. 764. C. 765. T. 766. A.

☆1820 ELECTION☆

767. True or False. James Monroe was highly popular when he ran for re-election?

768. True or False. James Monroe was not formally nominated for president in 1820?

769. How many new states voted in 1820 for the first time?
   A. Two
   B. Five
   C. Eight

770. True or False. In 1820 James Monroe became the first and only president since George Washington to run unopposed for re-election?

771. True or False. An elector from New Hampshire deliberately voted for John Adams to deny James Monroe a unanimous win in the Electoral College?

Quick answers for the 1820 Election (more detailed answers are at the back of the book).

767. T. 768. T. 769. B. 770. T. 771. T.

☆1816 ELECTION☆

772. Who was James Monroe's major rival for the Democratic-Republican nomination for the presidency?
   A. DeWitt Clinton
   B. Elbridge Gerry
   C. William Crawford

773. Which answer best describes the attendance at the first Democratic-Republican caucus held to determine the 1816 nominee?
   A. Low attendance
   B. Average attendance
   C. High attendance

774. Supporters of which candidate were most numerous at the first caucus?
   A. Elbridge Gerry
   B. James Monroe
   C. William Crawford

775. True or False. James Madison and James Monroe used to be friends but Madison refused to endorse Monroe for president after Monroe complained about the "dull parties" that Madison hosted?

776. What state was the Federalist Party candidate, Rufus King, from?
   A. New York
   B. Pennsylvania
   C. Rhode Island

777. True or False. James Monroe had a long and successful career serving in important posts for the Washington, Jefferson, and Madison administrations prior to running for president?

778. How many states did King win in 1816?
    A. Three
    B. Four
    C. Seven

779. How many new states voted for the first time in the 1816 election?
    A. Zero
    B. One
    C. Two

780. True or False. The embarrassment of Washington D.C. being sacked in the War of 1812 cost James Monroe the election in 1816?

Quick answers for the 1816 Election (more detailed answers are at the back of the book).

772. C. 773. A. 774. C. 775. F. 776. A. 777. T. 778. A. 779. B. 780. F.

☆1812 ELECTION☆

781. True or False. The Federalist Party nominated Francis Marion to run against James Madison?

782. Who from Madison's own party ran against him in 1812?
    A. DeWitt Clinton
    B. Israel Putnam
    C. William Harrison

783. Madison's vice president from his first term had died and he needed a new running mate as he sought re-election. Why did John Langdon of New Hampshire decline the nomination to be Madison's vice president?
    A. Langdon thought himself to be too old
    B. Langdon thought that Madison would lose
    C. Langdon intensely disliked Madison

784. Did the outbreak of war in June of 1812 hurt Madison's re-election bid?
    A. No, the war made him more popular
    B. Yes, the war made him less popular but he still won re-election
    C. Yes, the war made him so unpopular that it cost him re-election

785. Geographically, where did much of Madison's support come from in 1812?
    A. All over
    B. New England
    C. South

786. How many new states voted for the first time in the 1812 election?
    A. One
    B. Two
    C. Three

787. True or False. The war with Great Britain cost James Madison electoral votes in New England in 1812?

Quick answers for the 1812 Election (more detailed answers are at the back of the book).

781. F. 782. A. 783. A. 784. B. 785. C. 786. A. 787. T.

☆1808 ELECTION☆

788. How was James Madison nominated?
   A. Convention
   B. Congress
   C. Secret Meeting

789. How was Charles C. Pinckney nominated?
   A. Convention
   B. Congress
   C. Secret Meeting

790. Who was Madison's running mate?
   A. Israel Putnam
   B. George Clinton
   C. Roger Sherman

791. What did Pinckney and Madison have in common?
   A. Both helped draft the Declaration of Independence
   B. Both were major participants at the Constitutional Convention
   C. Both fought together in the Battle of Brandywine Creek

792. True or False. Thomas Jefferson withheld his endorsement of Madison, preferring to see his protégé sink or swim on his own merits?

793. What post had Madison held for all eight years of Jefferson's presidency prior to seeking the nomination?
   A. Attorney General
   B. Secretary of State
   C. Vice President

794. How many new states voted for the first time in 1808?
   A. Zero
   B. One
   C. Two

795. What small state was a Federalist bastion, and was never carried by a Democratic-Republican candidate until after the Federalist Party ceased to exist?
   A. Delaware
   B. Rhode Island
   C. Vermont

Quick answers for the 1808 Election (more detailed answers are at the back of the book).

788. B. 789. C. 790. B. 791. B. 792. F. 793. B. 794. A. 795. A.

☆1804 ELECTION☆

796. In 1804 how did each party nominate its respective choices for president and vice president?
   A. Caucus
   B. Convention
   C. State legislature

797. True or False. Thomas Jefferson was easily re-elected in 1804?

798. Which Federalist ran against Jefferson in 1804?
   A. Charles C. Pinckney
   B. Elbridge Gerry
   C. John Adams

799. Which answer best describes the electoral vote result in 1804?
   A. Pinckney needed 25 more electoral votes to win
   B. Pinckney needed 50 more electoral votes to win
   C. Pinckney needed 75 more electoral votes to win

800. How many new states voted for the first time in 1804?
   A. Zero
   B. One
   C. Two

Quick answers for the 1804 Election (more detailed answers are at the back of the book).

796. A. 797. T. 798. A. 799. C. 800. B.

☆1800 ELECTION☆

801. How did both political parties select their respective tickets in 1800?
   A. Caucus
   B. Convention
   C. State legislatures

802. What pattern of president and vice president home state was set in 1800 and was true in four out of five elections from 1800 to 1820?
   A. President from New York, vice president from New Jersey
   B. President from New York, vice president from Virginia
   C. President from Virginia, vice president from New York

803. True or False. The election result in 1800 triggered the passage of a constitutional amendment that changed the way that the electors voted for president and vice president?

804. Where was John Adams's electoral strength?
   A. Frontier
   B. New England
   C. South

805. Where was Thomas Jefferson's electoral strength?
   A. Frontier
   B. New England
   C. South

806. Which two candidates tied in the Electoral College?
   A. Adams and Burr
   B. Adams and Jefferson
   C. Burr and Jefferson

807. Which state did Jefferson carry in 1800 that he had not carried in 1796?
   A. Pennsylvania
   B. New York
   C. Virginia

808. What historic first in the history of presidential elections happened in the election of 1800?
   A. Two electors were killed in a duel.
   B. No candidate received half of the votes plus one in the Electoral College and the House of Representatives decided the election.
   C. Women voted in the election.

Quick answers for the 1800 Election (more detailed answers are at the back of the book).

801. A. 802. C. 803. T. 804. B. 805. A. 806. C. 807. B. 808. B.

☆1796 ELECTION☆

809. How many new states voted for the first time in 1796?
- A. Zero
- B. One
- C. Two

810. Who finished second in 1796?
- A. Aaron Burr
- B. Alexander Hamilton
- C. Thomas Jefferson

811. How was Jefferson nominated in 1796?
- A. Convention
- B. Congress
- C. Secret Meeting

812. What was unusual about Thomas Jefferson's run for president in 1796?
- A. He ran while out of the country
- B. He ran without a running mate
- C. He ran because of a bet with Benjamin Franklin

813. How was John Adams nominated?
- A. George Washington nominated him in a speech before Congress
- B. Some Federalist members of Congress met and nominated Adams
- C. He was not formally nominated

814. What happened in the election of 1796 that prompted a constitutional amendment?
- A. Slaves were allowed to vote.
- B. There were too many "faithless electors" (electors who do not vote for the candidate they are pledged to).
- C. The president and the vice president were elected from different political parties.

815. Who helped create the election result in 1796 because of his underhanded scheming?
- A. Alexander Hamilton
- B. James Monroe
- C. John Jay

Quick answers for the 1796 Election (more detailed answers are at the back of the book).

809. B. 810. C. 811. B. 812. B. 813. B. 814. C. 815. A.

☆1792 ELECTION☆

816. Which of the following changes was made to presidential election laws in 1792?
- A. Campaign finance reform
- B. Greater flexibility on the election date was ratified by Congress
- C. No significant changes were made

817. Was any attempt made to replace George Washington in 1792?
- A. Yes
- B. No

818. Was George Washington formally nominated for president in 1792?
- A. Yes
- B. No

819. Did Thomas Jefferson run for president in 1792?
- A. Yes
- B. No

820. True or False. George Washington unanimously re-elected in 1792?

821. True or False. John Adams was formally nominated for vice president in 1792?

822. Which of the following two new states were not part of the United States in 1788 but had joined by 1792?
    A.   New York and New Jersey
    B.   Vermont and Kentucky
    C.   Maine and Georgia

Quick answers for the 1792 Election (more detailed answers are at the back of the book).

816. B. 817. A. 818. B. 819. B. 820. T. 821. F. 822. B.

☆1789 ELECTION☆

823. If the presidents of the United States are elected for four year terms and all other elections are known by even-numbered years (for example the Election of 1792), why is the first election known as the election of 1789?
    A.   The election in 1789 was for a 3 year term
    B.   Due to bad weather the election was delayed until early 1789
    C.   The election and inauguration were in the same year in 1789

824. True or False. There was a national election day in 1789 and on this day all of the electors were chosen?

825. Who received the most votes for president?
    A.   George Washington
    B.   John Adams
    C.   John Jay

826. How many electoral votes did George Washington receive in 1789?
    A.   13
    B.   26
    C.   69

827. True or False. George Washington was unanimously elected?

828. True or False. In the first presidential election not all of the states voted because some of them had not yet ratified the Constitution?

829. Although there were not yet political parties, who became the opposition leader in Congress?
    A.   Aaron Burr
    B.   James Madison
    C.   Thomas Jefferson

Quick answers for the 1789 Election (more detailed answers are at the back of the book).

823. C. 824. F. 825. A. 826. C. 827. T. 828. T. 829. B.

CLINTON, TRUMP, AND 2016

This category deals with some trivia about the respective backgrounds of the Democratic and Republican Party nominees. It also has some questions about the 2016 campaign through July of 2016.

830. What day is Hillary Clinton's birthday?
  A. June 14
  B. August 4
  C. October 26

831. What year was Clinton born?
  A. 1945
  B. 1947
  C. 1949

832. What day is Donald Trump's birthday?
  A. June 14
  B. August 27
  C. October 26

833. What year was Donald Trump born?
  A. 1944
  B. 1946
  C. 1948

834. In what major metropolitan area did Hillary Clinton live while growing up?
  A. Chicago
  B. Little Rock
  C. Washington D.C.

835. In what major metropolitan area did Donald Trump live while growing up?
  A. Boston
  B. New York City
  C. Philadelphia

836. In what industry did Hillary Clinton's father work?
  A. Construction
  B. Finance
  C. Textiles

837. In what industry did Donald Trump's father work?
  A. Construction
  B. Finance
  C. Textiles

838. Both Clinton and Trump have family ties to the United Kingdom. Clinton's ancestors in the United Kingdom included?
  A. Cornish tin miners
  B. Scottish farmers
  C. Welsh coal miners

839. Both Clinton and Trump have family ties to the United Kingdom. Trump's ancestors in the United Kingdom included?
  A. Cornish tin miners
  B. Scottish farmers
  C. Welsh coal miners

840. Which candidate's grandmother forcibly intervened to prevent doctors from amputating the candidate's father's leg when the father was involved in a serious accident with an ice delivery truck in 1920?
  A. Donald Trump
  B. Hillary Clinton
  C. Neither candidate

841. Which candidate's grandfather was the owner of a saloon in the Yukon?
  A. Donald Trump
  B. Hillary Clinton
  C. Neither candidate

842. Where did Hillary Clinton attend college?
    A. Smith
    B. Vassar
    C. Wellesley

843. Where did Donald Trump attend college?
    A. Brooklyn
    B. Rutgers
    C. Pennsylvania

844. Which type of spiritual leader made a difference for Clinton?
    A. Celebrity pastor
    B. Guru
    C. Youth pastor

845. Which type of spiritual leader made a difference for Trump?
    A. Celebrity pastor
    B. Guru
    C. Youth pastor

846. How many times has Clinton been married
    A. One
    B. Two
    C. Three

847. How many times has Trump been married?
    A. Two
    B. Three
    C. Four

848. What is the name of the Trump's second wife?
    A. Marla
    B. Melania
    C. Michelle

849. True or False. Clinton attended one of Trump's weddings?

850. How many children does Clinton have?
    A. One
    B. Three
    C. Five

851. How many children does Trump have?
    A. Three
    B. Four
    C. Five

852. Where did Clinton get her law degree?
    A. Harvard
    B. Stanford
    C. Yale

853. Are Bill and Hillary Clinton related to 18th and 19th century presidential candidates George and DeWitt Clinton?
    A. Yes
    B. No

854. What area of law did Clinton specialize in?
    A. Children
    B. Corporate
    C. Criminal

855. What hotel did Trump successfully renovate as one of his first major deal-making accomplishments?
    A. The Commodore
    B. The Grand Luxor
    C. The Waldorf

856. What policy reform did Hillary Clinton participate in during her husband's first term?
    A. Federal deficit
    B. Healthcare
    C. Welfare

857. What business venture has generally not been successful at turning a long-term profit for Donald Trump?
    A. Casinos
    B. Hotels
    C. Merchandizing

858. How many candidates were in the Republican field at the start of the contest?
   A. 8
   B. 9
   C. 17

859. True or False. Determining who won delegates in a particular primary or caucus is often more complicated than simply winner-take-all?

860. In 2016 which party had more delegates at its convention?
   A. Democratic
   B. Republican

861. How many states did Donald Trump win in the Republican Primary?
   A. 26
   B. 30
   C. 38

862. Who finished second to Trump in the Republican Primaries?
   A. John Kasich
   B. Marco Rubio
   C. Ted Cruz

863. How many candidates were at the first Democratic Party debate?
   A. 4
   B. 8
   C. 12

864. How many states did Hillary Clinton win in the Democratic Primaries?
   A. 24
   B. 27
   C. 33

865. Which party was lamenting superdelegates during the 2016 primaries?
   A. Democratic
   B. Republican
   C. Both

866. If you had to predict the election outcome based only knowing the winner of two states, which two states would be most helpful in 2016 in predicting whether Clinton or Trump had won?
   A. Alabama and Mississippi
   B. Florida and Pennsylvania
   C. Oregon and New Hampshire

867. Throughout the primary campaign what happened to Trump's standing in the polls after he made a controversial statement?
   A. It went up
   B. It went down
   C. It stayed the same

868. What issue did Donald Trump make a signature issue of his campaign?
   A. Expanding free trade
   B. Immigration
   C. Healthcare reform

869. 2016 is likely to feature a historic gap between which category of voters
   A. Gender
   B. Income
   C. Race

870. Hilary Clinton is the first woman to win the nomination for president of the United States from any major political party in the United States. Her winning the nomination is a major accomplishment. Who was the first woman to be nominated for president?
   A. Clara Barton
   B. Susan B. Anthony
   C. Victoria C. Woodhull

871. What year was the first woman nominated for president of the United States?
   A. 1872
   B. 1904
   C. 1920

872. What year was the first woman nominated for president by the Republican Party?
   A. 1920
   B. 1964
   C. 1976

873. What year was the first woman nominated for president by the Democratic Party?
   A. 1916
   B. 1960
   C. 1972

874. What office was Hillary Clinton elected to in 2000?
   A. Governor
   B. Representative
   C. Senator

875. What state was Hillary Clinton elected from?
   A. Arkansas
   B. Illinois
   C. New York

876. What office did Donald Trump run for in 2000?
   A. Governor
   B. President
   C. Senator

877. What cabinet post was Hillary Clinton appointed to by Barack Obama?
   A. Chief of Staff
   B. National Security Advisor
   C. Secretary of State

878. True or False. In the cabinet Hillary Clinton largely stayed in Washington D.C. and conducted most business by telephone?

879. The same night as the Bin Laden raid in Abbottabad, Pakistan, Barack Obama attended the White House Correspondents Dinner. Who did Obama roast at the Dinner?
   A. Donald Trump
   B. Hillary Clinton
   C. Osama Bin Laden

880. In a famous picture taken in the White House Situation Room, why is Hillary Clinton covering her mouth?
   A. She has just seen something horrific
   B. She is trying to avoid blurting out a secret with so many people in the room
   C. She is trying not to sneeze

881. Who did Hillary Clinton choose as her running mate?
   A. Bill Clinton
   B. Julian Castro
   C. Tim Kaine

882. Who did Donald Trump choose as his running mate?
   A. Mike Pence
   B. Scott Walker
   C. Ted Cruz

883. How many current states are considered to be likely Democratic states based only on Barack Obama winning by at least 5% of the vote in 2012?
   A. 21
   B. 23
   C. 25

884. How many current states are considered to be likely Republican states based only on Mitt Romney winning by at least 5% of the vote in 2012?
   A. 21
   B. 23
   C. 25

885. Based on the same analysis how many states were won by less than 5% in 2012 and so are considered to be swing states?
- A. 4
- B. 8
- C. 12

886. Based on the polling in August 2016, what year might the election results resemble?
- A. 1960
- B. 1996
- C. 2004

U.S. PRESIDENTIAL ELECTIONS' GREATEST HITS

This section is about lopsided victories and has questions that compare one election to another and therefore were not included in a particular presidential election year. (Based on the organization of the book it would either be too great a hint or too sneaky a trick to ask such questions in a particular year category).

887. True or False. No election map has ever duplicated another one with candidates from the same parties winning the exact same states?

888. Which president was elected to the most terms in office?
    A. Franklin D. Roosevelt
    B. George Washington
    C. Teddy Roosevelt

889. Who received the highest percentage of the popular vote?
    A. Franklin Roosevelt
    B. Lyndon Johnson
    C. Ronald Reagan

890. Who received the smallest share of the popular vote and still won the election?
    A. Abraham Lincoln
    B. Bill Clinton
    C. John Quincy Adams

891. Who won a unanimous election in the Electoral College?
    A. George Washington
    B. John Tyler
    C. Harry Truman

892. Who won the popular vote by the fewest votes?
    A. James Garfield
    B. William McKinley
    C. William Taft

893. How many elections were won by a candidate who received less than 50% of the popular vote?
    A. 9
    B. 10
    C. 18

894. Who received the second highest percentage of the popular vote?
    A. Franklin Roosevelt
    B. Lyndon Johnson
    C. Richard Nixon

895. Who won the popular vote by the greatest margin in terms of number of votes?
    A. Lyndon Johnson
    B. Richard Nixon
    C. Ronald Reagan

896. Who won the popular vote by the second greatest margin in terms of number of votes?
    A. Lyndon Johnson
    B. Richard Nixon
    C. Ronald Reagan

897. Who won the popular vote by the third greatest margin in terms of number of votes?
    A. Lyndon Johnson
    B. Richard Nixon
    C. Ronald Reagan

898. Considering 1900 to be part of the nineteenth century, who had the largest margin of victory in the popular vote 19th century by total number of votes?
    A. Andrew Jackson
    B. Ulysses Grant
    C. William McKinley

899. Considering 1900 to be part of the nineteenth century, who had the second largest margin of victory in the popular vote 19th century by total number of votes?
    A. Andrew Jackson
    B. Ulysses Grant
    C. William McKinley

900. Considering 1900 to be part of the nineteenth century, who had the third largest margin of victory in the popular vote 19th century by total number of votes?
    A. Andrew Jackson
    B. Franklin Pierce
    C. James Buchanan

901. Considering 1900 to be part of the nineteenth century, who had the largest margin of victory in the popular vote 19th century by percentage of the vote?
    A. Andrew Jackson
    B. Ulysses Grant
    C. William McKinley

902. Considering 1900 to be part of the nineteenth century, who had the second largest margin of victory in the popular vote 19th century by percentage of the vote?
    A. Andrew Jackson
    B. Ulysses Grant
    C. William McKinley

903. Considering 1900 to be part of the nineteenth century, who had the third largest margin of victory in the popular vote 19th century by percentage of the vote?
    A. Abraham Lincoln
    B. Ulysses Grant
    C. William McKinley

904. Since 1912 who won the most states in an election by total number of states won?
    A. Richard Nixon
    B. Ronald Reagan
    C. Tie between Richard Nixon and Ronald Reagan

905. Who won the second most states in an election by total number of states won?
    A. Franklin Roosevelt
    B. Lyndon Johnson
    C. Woodrow Wilson

906. Who won the third most states in an election by total number of states won?
    A. Franklin Roosevelt
    B. Lyndon Johnson
    C. Another tie involving Ronald Reagan

907. Who won the fourth most states in an election by total number of states won?
    A. Franklin Roosevelt
    B. Herbert Hoover
    C. Woodrow Wilson

908. Who won the fifth most states in an election by total number of states won?
    A. Dwight Eisenhower
    B. Herbert Hoover
    C. Woodrow Wilson

909. Since 1912 who won the fewest states in a victory, measured by total number of states won?
    A. Calvin Coolidge
    B. Jimmy Carter
    C. John F. Kennedy

910. Who won the second fewest states in a victory, measured by total number of states won?
    A. Harry Truman
    B. Jimmy Carter
    C. John F. Kennedy

911. Who won the fewest states all-time in an election but was still elected to the presidency?
    A. Herbert Hoover
    B. John Quincy Adams
    C. Millard Fillmore

912. Who won the most states in a single election in the 19th century?
    A. Lincoln in 1864
    B. Grant in 1872
    C. McKinley in 1900

913. Through all U.S. presidential elections how many times did both candidates win the same number of states?
    A. Two
    B. Four
    C. Nine

914. Which answer best describes the slogan "In gold we trust"?
    A. Catchy slogan for McKinley and gold-backed currency
    B. Edgy slogan from Reform Party candidate Pat Buchanan meant as a social critique
    C. Failed slogan from McGovern in 1972, criticizing Nixon for taking the U.S. off the gold standard

915. Which general ran under the slogan "hero of many battles"?
    A. Dwight Eisenhower
    B. Ulysses Grant
    C. Winfield Scott

916. What year did Republicans try the slogan "It's an elephant's job no time for donkey business"?
    A. 1896
    B. 1932
    C. 1960

917. Some analysts think that 2016 could be a huge landslide. When was the last election that a candidate won 40 or more states?
    A. 2008
    B. 1988
    C. 1984

918. How many times has a candidate won 40 or more states?
    A. 7
    B. 10
    C. 16

919. What was the last year that a candidate won fewer than 20 states in a victory?
    A. 1880
    B. 1884
    C. 1888

920. What was the greatest number of states that a Democrat switched from Republican to Democratic in a single election?
    A. 30
    B. 34
    C. 36

921. What is the greatest number of states that a Republican switched from Democratic to Republican in a single election?
    A. 26
    B. 30
    C. 34

922. What candidate won the closest election in the Electoral College without needing the House of Representatives to resolve a tie?
    A. Thomas Jefferson
    B. John Quincy Adams
    C. George W. Bush

923. How many times has the candidate who lost the popular vote still won based on the Electoral College vote?
   A. Two
   B. Three
   C. Four

924. The closest election of the 20th century was in 2000 (closest in terms of fewest votes needed to change the outcome). What year was the second closest election in the 20th century?
   A. 1916
   B. 1920
   C. 1944

925. Starting with the 1804 election, how many presidential elections hinged on the winner of a single state if the winner of the state is reversed, the winner of the election is reversed or a tie is created?
   A. Five
   B. Nine
   C. Thirteen

926. How many presidential elections have gone to tie-breakers in the House of Representatives or needed an outside decision by a committee or a court to resolve questions of ballots?
   A. Three
   B. Four
   C. Five

927. How many exact ties in the Electoral College?
   A. Zero
   B. One
   C. Two

928. What is the only election that the U.S. Senate has had to decide the vice presidential winner?
   A. 1824
   B. 1836
   C. 1976

929. What year did two presidential candidates run with the same vice presidential candidate?
   A. 1824
   B. 1844
   C. 1888

930. What 19th century election most resembled the election held in the year 2000? (Hotly contested election results involving problems with ballots in states, with the election winner not known until close to inauguration day)
   A. 1860
   B. 1868
   C. 1876

931. Who has received more popular votes for president than any other candidate?
   A. Ronald Reagan
   B. Barack Obama
   C. George W. Bush

932. The 1956 election was noteworthy because it featured the most recent time that the loser of the previous election (in this case Adlai Stevenson) ran in a rematch against the winner. Since 1824 how many times has the loser won the rematch?
   A. Zero
   B. One
   C. Three

933. Since 1824 in presidential general election rematches how many times has the loser of the first election lost the rematch?
   A. Zero
   B. Two
   C. Three

934. How many presidents have won over 500 votes in the Electoral College in a single election?
   A. Zero
   B. Three
   C. Five

935. Who is the lowest all-time scorer in the popular vote among the Republican candidates, receiving the lowest percentage in a single election?
    A. William Taft in 1912
    B. Alf Landon in 1936
    C. Barry Goldwater in 1964

936. Who is the lowest all-time scorer in the popular vote among Democratic candidates, receiving the lowest percentage in a single election?
    A. John Davis in 1924
    B. George McGovern in 1972
    C. Walter Mondale in 1984

937. Which state has not been carried by the Republican candidate since 1972?
    A. Massachusetts
    B. Minnesota
    C. Vermont

938. How many states have not been carried by the Democratic candidate since 1964?
    A. Five
    B. Seven
    C. Nine

939. Which state has only backed the loser of the popular vote a single time?
    A. Alabama
    B. New Mexico
    C. Washington

940. Which state has done the worst job of backing a winning candidate in the last 100 years of presidential elections (1912 through 2012)?
    A. Alabama
    B. Tennessee
    C. Vermont

941. How many states have supported the non-winning candidate 5 or fewer times?
    A. 11
    B. 13
    C. 15

Quick answers for U.S. Presidential Elections' Greatest Hits (more detailed answers are at the back of the book).

887. T. 888. A. 889. B. 890. C. 891. A.
892. A. 893. C. 894. A. 895. B. 896. C.
897. A. 898. C. 899. B. 900. C. 901. A.
902. B. 903. A. 904. C. 905. A. 906. C.
907. A. 908. A. 909. C. 910. B. 911. B.
912. B. 913. B. 914. A. 915. C. 916. B.
917. B. 918. B. 919. A. 920. B. 921. A.
922. C. 923. C. 924. A. 925. C. 926. B.
927. B. 928. B. 929. A. 930. C. 931. B.
932. C. 933. B. 934. B. 935. A. 936. A.
937. B. 938. C. 939. B. 940. A. 941. C.

FIFTY STATE CHALLENGE

This section looks at the voting habits of each state in terms of which party has won the particular state more often. There is also a question about how many electoral votes that particular state is worth. Some states are bellwether states and tend to vote for the winner more often. Other states consistently vote for the same party each election. The states are listed in the order that they joined the United States. When there is a question about whether a third party has ever won the state, the question clarifies which past and present parties are not considered third parties. This book consider the Democratic Party to have begun starting in 1832 (Andrew Jackson's re-election campaign year) because the first national Democratic Party Convention was held after the 1828 Election. Unfamiliar states may be rather challenging. Throughout the category there are ten questions about various pairs of states, for example North and South Dakota. To someone not from the region those states might seem to be interchangeable. When was the last time that those two voted for different candidates? Some of these pairs have recently diverged other have been voting together for a long time. Do you know which is which?

DELAWARE

942. In presidential elections from 1789 through 2012 which party has won Delaware the most times?
    A. Democratic Party
    B. Republican Party
    C. Tie

943. In how many presidential elections did the Federalist Party win Delaware?
    A. Four
    B. Six
    C. Eight

944. How many times has a third party candidate carried Delaware? (Any party except the Federalist, Democratic-Republican, National Republican, Democratic, Whig, and Republican Parties)
    A. Zero
    B. One
    C. Two

945. How many electoral votes is Delaware worth in the 2016 election?
    A. Three
    B. Four
    C. Five

946. From 1912 through 2012 how many times has Delaware been carried by a losing candidate?
    A. Three
    B. Five
    C. Seven

PENNSYLVANIA

947. In presidential elections from 1789 through 2012 which party carried Pennsylvania the most times?
    A. Democratic Party
    B. Republican Party
    C. Tie

948. How many times has a third party candidate carried Pennsylvania? (Any party except the Federalist, Democratic-Republican, National Republican, Democratic, Whig, and Republican Parties)
    A. Zero
    B. One
    C. Two

949. How many electoral votes is Pennsylvania worth in the 2016 election?
    A. 18
    B. 20
    C. 22

950. From the 1912 election through the 2012 election how many times has Pennsylvania been won by a non-winning candidate?
    A. Three
    B. Five
    C. Seven

NEW JERSEY

951. In presidential elections from 1789 through 2012 which party carried New Jersey the most times?
    A. Democratic Party
    B. Republican Party
    C. Tie

952. How many times did the Whig Party win New Jersey?
    A. Two
    B. Four
    C. Eight

953. How many times has a third party candidate carried New Jersey? (Any party except the Federalist, Democratic-Republican, National Republican, Democratic, Whig, and Republican Parties)
    A. Zero
    B. One
    C. Two

954. How many electoral votes is New Jersey worth in the 2016 election?
    A. 13
    B. 14
    C. 15

955. From the 1912 through 2012 how many times has New Jersey been won by a candidate who lost the overall election?
    A. Three
    B. Five
    C. Seven

GEORGIA

956. In presidential elections from 1789 through the 2012 which party carried Georgia the most times?
    A. Democratic Party
    B. Republican Party
    C. Tie

957. How many times has a third party candidate carried Georgia? (Any party except the Federalist, Democratic-Republican, National Republican, Democratic, Whig, and Republican Parties)
    A. Zero
    B. One
    C. Two

958. How many electoral votes is Georgia worth in the 2016 election?
    A. 16
    B. 17
    C. 18

959. Has a single party dominated and won Georgia 25 or more times in presidential elections?
    A. Yes
    B. No

960. From the 1912 election through the 2012 election did Georgia back the election winner in all but three or fewer elections?
    A. Yes
    B. No

CONNECTICUT

961. In presidential elections from 1789 through 2012 which party carried Connecticut the most times?
    A. Democratic Party
    B. Republican Party
    C. Tie

962. How many times did the Federalist Party win Connecticut?
    A. Two
    B. Four
    C. Eight

963. How many times has a third party candidate carried Connecticut? (Any party except the Federalist, Democratic-Republican, National Republican, Democratic, Whig, and Republican Parties)
    A. Zero
    B. One
    C. Two

964. How many electoral votes is Connecticut worth in the 2016 election?
    A. Six
    B. Seven
    C. Eight

965. From the 1912 election through the 2012 election has Connecticut backed the winner in all but three or fewer elections?
    A. Yes
    B. No

MASSACHUSETTS

966. In presidential elections from 1789 through 2012 which party carried Massachusetts the most times?
    A. Democratic Party
    B. Republican Party
    C. Tie

967. How many times has a third party candidate carried Massachusetts? (Any party except the Federalist, Democratic-Republican, National Republican, Democratic, Whig, and Republican Parties)
    A. Zero
    B. Two
    C. Three

968. How many electoral votes is Massachusetts worth in the 2016 election?
    A. 11
    B. 13
    C. 15

969. From the 1912 election through the 2012 election has Massachusetts backed the winner in all but three or fewer elections?
    A. Yes
    B. No

Delaware through Massachusetts:
(More detailed answers at the back of the book)
942. A. 943. C. 944. B. 945. A. 946. B.
947. B. 948. B. 949. B. 950. C. 951. A.
952. B. 953. A. 954. B. 955. B. 956. A.
957. C. 958. A. 959. A. 960. B. 961. B.
962. C. 963. A. 964. B. 965. B. 966. B.
967. A. 968. A. 969. B.

MARYLAND

970. In presidential elections from 1789 through 2012 which party carried Maryland the most times?
    A. Democratic Party
    B. Republican Party
    C. Tie

971. How many times has a third party candidate carried Maryland? (Any party except the Federalist, Democratic-Republican, National Republican, Democratic, Whig, and Republican Parties)
    A. One
    B. Two
    C. Three

972. How many electoral votes is Maryland worth in the 2016 election?
    A. Six
    B. Eight
    C. Ten

973. From the 1912 election through the 2012 election has Maryland backed the winner in all but three or fewer elections?
    A. Yes
    B. No

SOUTH CAROLINA

974. In presidential elections from 1789 through 2012 which party carried South Carolina the most times?
    A. Democratic Party
    B. Republican Party
    C. Tie

975. How many times has a third party candidate carried South Carolina? (Any party except the Federalist, Democratic-Republican, National Republican, Democratic, Whig, and Republican Parties)
    A. Two
    B. Three
    C. Four

976. How many electoral votes is South Carolina worth in the 2016 election?
    A. Six
    B. Nine
    C. Twelve

977. From the 1912 election through the 2012 election has South Carolina backed the winner in all but three or fewer elections?
    A. Yes
    B. No

978. When did South Carolina adopt the direct election of presidential electors?
    A. 1832
    B. 1868
    C. 1916

NEW HAMPSHIRE

979. In presidential elections from 1789 through 2012 which party carried New Hampshire the most times?
    A. Democratic Party
    B. Republican Party
    C. Tie

980. How many times has a third party candidate carried New Hampshire? (Any party except the Federalist, Democratic-Republican, National Republican, Democratic, Whig, and Republican Parties)
    A. Zero
    B. One
    C. Three

981. How many electoral votes is New Hampshire worth in the 2016 election?
    A. Three
    B. Four
    C. Five

982. What year did New Hampshire set the all-time record for the closest margin of victory ever when a Democratic candidate for president carried the state by only 56 votes?
    A. 1916
    B. 1936
    C. 1980

983. Starting in 1912, how many times has a candidate who failed to win the election won New Hampshire?
    A. Four
    B. Six
    C. Eight

VIRGINIA

984. In presidential elections from 1789 through 2012 which party carried Virginia the most times?
    A. Democratic Party
    B. Republican Party
    C. Tie

985. From 1904 through the 2012 election which party carried Virginia the most times?
    A. Democratic Party
    B. Republican Party
    C. Tie

986. How many times has a third party candidate carried Virginia? (Any party except the Federalist, Democratic-Republican, National Republican, Democratic, Whig, and Republican Parties)
    A. Zero
    B. One
    C. Two

987. How many electoral votes is Virginia worth in the 2016 election?
    A. 11
    B. 13
    C. 15

988. How many times from 1912 through 2012 has Virginia backed the non-winner in the presidential election?
    A. Two
    B. Four
    C. Six

989. Is Virginia just East Virginia? When did West Virginia and Virginia most recently vote for different candidates for president?
    A. 2004
    B. 2008
    C. 2012

NEW YORK

990. In presidential elections from 1792 through 2012 which party carried New York the most times?
    A. Democratic Party
    B. Republican Party
    C. Tie

991. How many times has a third party candidate carried New York? (Any party except the Federalist, Democratic-Republican, National Republican, Democratic, Whig, and Republican Parties)
    A. Zero
    B. One
    C. Two

992. How many electoral votes is New York worth in the 2016 election?
    A. 29
    B. 32
    C. 35

993. How many times from 1912 through 2012 has New York backed the non-winner in the presidential election?
    A. Six
    B. Eight
    C. Ten

NORTH CAROLINA

994. From 1792 through 2012 which party carried North Carolina the most times?
    A. Democratic Party
    B. Republican Party
    C. Tie

995. How many times has a third party candidate carried North Carolina? (Any party except the Federalist, Democratic-Republican, National Republican, Democratic, Whig, and Republican Parties)
    A. Zero
    B. One
    C. Two

996. How many electoral votes is North Carolina worth in the 2016 election?
    A. 11
    B. 13
    C. 15

997. From 1912 through 2012 how many times has North Carolina backed the non-winner in presidential elections?
    A. Five
    B. Seven
    C. Nine

998. Many people think of North Carolina and South Carolina as basically being the same state, when was the last time that North and South Carolina voted for different presidential candidates?
    A. 1912
    B. 1960
    C. 2008

RHODE ISLAND

999. From 1792 through 2012 which party carried Rhode Island the most times?
    A. Democratic Party
    B. Republican Party
    C. Tie

1000. How many times has a third party candidate carried Rhode Island? (Any party except the Federalist, Democratic-Republican, National Republican, Democratic, Whig, and Republican Parties)
    A. Zero
    B. One
    C. Two

1001. How many electoral votes is Rhode Island worth in the 2016 election?
    A. Three
    B. Four
    C. Five

1002. From 1912 election through 2012 how many times has Rhode Island backed the non-winner of the presidential election?
    A. Three
    B. Five
    C. Seven

1003. To some people Rhode Island and Delaware are identical small states forget the fact that they had very different founders. When was the last time that they voted for different candidates for president?
    A. 1988
    B. 1992
    C. 1996

VERMONT

1004. From 1792 through 2012 which party carried Vermont the most times?
    A. Democratic Party
    B. Republican Party
    C. Tie

1005. Prior to 1992 who was the only Democratic president to win Vermont?
    A. Franklin Pierce in 1852
    B. John F. Kennedy in 1960
    C. Lyndon Johnson in 1964

1006. How many times has a third party candidate carried Vermont? (Any party except the Federalist, Democratic-Republican, National Republican, Democratic, Whig, and Republican Parties)
   A. Zero
   B. One
   C. Two

1007. How many electoral votes is Vermont worth in the 2016 election?
   A. Three
   B. Four
   C. Five

1008. How many times has the Republican Party won the presidential election in Vermont?
   A. 25
   B. 30
   C. 33

1009. In how many presidential elections from 1912 through 2012 election has Vermont backed the non-winner?
   A. Four
   B. Nine
   C. Eleven

1010. When was the last time that Vermont and New Hampshire voted for different candidates?
   A. 1988
   B. 2000
   C. 2004

KENTUCKY

1011. From 1792 through 2012 which party carried Kentucky the most times?
   A. Democratic Party
   B. Republican Party
   C. Tie

1012. How many times has a third party candidate carried Kentucky? (Any party except the Federalist, Democratic-Republican, National Republican, Democratic, Whig, and Republican Parties)
   A. Zero
   B. One
   C. Two

1013. How many electoral votes is Kentucky worth in the 2016 election?
   A. Six
   B. Eight
   C. Ten

1014. In presidential elections from 1912 through 2012 how many times has Kentucky backed the non-winner?
   A. Three
   B. Five
   C. Seven

TENNESSEE

1015. From 1796 through 2012 which party carried Tennessee the most times?
   A. Democratic Party
   B. Republican Party
   C. Tie

1016. Prior to Harding winning Tennessee in 1920, who was the only Republican to win Tennessee?
   A. Lincoln in 1860
   B. Grant in 1868
   C. Roosevelt in 1904

1017. How many times has a third party candidate carried Tennessee? (Any party except the Federalist, Democratic-Republican, National Republican, Democratic, Whig, and Republican Parties)
   A. Zero
   B. One
   C. Five

1018. How many electoral votes is Tennessee worth in the 2016 election?
   A. 11
   B. 13
   C. 15

1019. From 1912 through 2012 how many times has Tennessee backed the non-winner in presidential elections?
   A. Four
   B. Six
   C. Eight

1020. Many people aren't sure what the difference is between Tennessee and Kentucky, when did they last vote differently for president?
   A. 1924
   B. 1956
   C. 1960

OHIO

1021. In presidential elections from 1804 through 2012 which party carried Ohio the most times?
   A. Democratic Party
   B. Republican Party
   C. Tie

1022. Everyone knows that no Republican has ever won the White House without winning Ohio, since 1832 how many times have Democrats have won the White House without winning Ohio?
   A. Zero
   B. Four
   C. Seven

1023. How many times has a third party candidate carried Ohio? (Any party except the Federalist, Democratic-Republican, National Republican, Democratic, Whig, and Republican Parties)
   A. Zero
   B. One
   C. Two

1024. How many electoral votes is Ohio worth in the 2016 election?
   A. 18
   B. 21
   C. 24

1025. From the 1912 through 2012 how many times has Ohio backed non-winners in presidential elections?
   A. Two
   B. Four
   C. Seven

LOUISIANA

1026. From 1812 through 2012 which party carried Louisiana the most times?
   A. Democratic Party
   B. Republican Party
   C. Tie

1027. How many times has a third party candidate carried Louisiana? (Any party except the Federalist, Democratic-Republican, National Republican, Democratic, Whig, and Republican Parties)
   A. One
   B. Two
   C. Three

1028. How many electoral votes is Louisiana worth in the 2016 election?
   A. Six
   B. Eight
   C. Ten

1029. In presidential elections from 1912 through 2012 how many times has Louisiana backed the non-winners?
   A. Six
   B. Nine
   C. Twelve

INDIANA

1030. From 1816 through 2012 which party carried Indiana the most times?
   A. Democratic Party
   B. Republican Party
   C. Tie

1031. How many times has a third party candidate carried Indiana? (Any party except the Federalist, Democratic-Republican, National Republican, Democratic, Whig, and Republican Parties)
   A. Zero
   B. One
   C. Two

1032. How many electoral votes is Indiana worth in the 2016 election?
   A. 11
   B. 13
   C. 15

1033. In presidential elections from the 1912 through 2012 election how many times has Indiana backed the non-winners?
   A. Six
   B. Nine
   C. Twelve

MISSISSIPPI

1034. In presidential elections from 1820 through 2012 which party carried Mississippi the most times?
   A. Democratic Party
   B. Republican Party
   C. Tie

1035. How many times has a third party candidate carried Mississippi? (Any party except the Federalist, Democratic-Republican, National Republican, Democratic, Whig, and Republican Parties)
   A. One
   B. Two
   C. Three

1036. How many electoral votes is Mississippi worth in the 2016 election?
   A. Six
   B. Eight
   C. Ten

1037. From the 1912 through 2012 election how many times has Mississippi backed the non-winner in the presidential elections?
   A. Six
   B. Eleven
   C. Thirteen

ILLINOIS

1038. From 1820 through 2012 which party carried Illinois the most times?
    A. Democratic Party
    B. Republican Party
    C. Tie

1039. How many times has a third party candidate carried Illinois? (Any party except the Federalist, Democratic-Republican, National Republican, Democratic, Whig, and Republican Parties)
    A. Zero
    B. Two
    C. Three

1040. How many electoral votes is Illinois worth in the 2016 election?
    A. 10
    B. 20
    C. 30

1041. In how many presidential elections from 1912 through 2012 has Illinois backed the non-winners?
    A. Five
    B. Seven
    C. Nine

ALABAMA

1042. In presidential elections from 1820 through 2012 which party carried Alabama the most times?
    A. Democratic Party
    B. Republican Party
    C. Tie

1043. Alabama and Mississippi started voting for president in 1820. For people not from that region the two states might be hard to distinguish. Considering only years in which both states voted for president, when was the last year that they were won by different candidates in the Electoral College?
    A. 1840
    B. 1892
    C. 1912

1044. How many times has a third party candidate carried Alabama? (Any party except the Federalist, Democratic-Republican, National Republican, Democratic, Whig, and Republican Parties)
    A. One
    B. Two
    C. Three

1045. How many electoral votes is Alabama worth in the 2016 election?
    A. Six
    B. Nine
    C. Twelve

1046. From 1912 through 2012 how many times has Alabama backed a non-winner in presidential elections?
    A. Nine
    B. Thirteen
    C. Seventeen

100

MAINE

1047. In presidential elections from 1820 through 2012 which party carried Maine the most times?
    A. Democratic Party
    B. Republican Party
    C. Tie

1048. How many times has a third party candidate carried Maine? (Any party except the Federalist, Democratic-Republican, National Republican, Democratic, Whig, and Republican Parties)
    A. Zero
    B. One
    C. Two

1049. How many electoral votes is Maine worth in the 2016 election?
    A. Three
    B. Four
    C. Five

1050. In presidential elections from 1912 through 2012 how many times did the non-winner carry Maine?
    A. Nine
    B. Eleven
    C. Thirteen

MISSOURI

1051. In presidential elections from 1820 through 2012 which party carried Missouri the most times?
    A. Democratic Party
    B. Republican Party
    C. Tie

1052. How many times has a third party candidate carried Missouri? (Any party except the Federalist, Democratic-Republican, National Republican, Democratic, Whig, and Republican Parties)
    A. Zero
    B. One
    C. Two

1053. How many electoral votes is Missouri worth in the 2016 election?
    A. 10
    B. 20
    C. 30

1054. In presidential elections from the 1912 through 2012 how many times did Missouri back a non-winner?
    A. Two
    B. Three
    C. Four

1055. In the 19th century did Missouri reliably side with the winning candidate?
    A. Yes
    B. No

ARKANSAS

1056. In presidential elections from 1836 through 2012 which party carried Arkansas the most times?
    A. Democratic Party
    B. Republican Party
    C. Tie

1057. How many times has a third party candidate carried Arkansas? (Any party except the Federalist, Democratic-Republican, National Republican, Democratic, Whig, and Republican Parties)
    A. Zero
    B. One
    C. Two

1058. How many electoral votes is Arkansas worth in the 2016 election?
    A. Six
    B. Nine
    C. Twelve

1059. In presidential elections from 1912 through 2012 how many times did Arkansas back a non-winner?
   A. Six
   B. Eight
   C. Ten

MICHIGAN

1060. In presidential elections from 1836 through 2012 which party carried Michigan the most times?
   A. Democratic Party
   B. Republican Party
   C. Tie

1061. How many times has a third party candidate carried Michigan? (Any party except the Federalist, Democratic-Republican, National Republican, Democratic, Whig, and Republican Parties)
   A. Zero
   B. One
   C. Two

1062. How many electoral votes is Michigan worth in the 2016 election?
   A. 16
   B. 21
   C. 26

1063. How many times 1912 through 2012 has Michigan backed a non-winner in the presidential elections?
   A. Eight
   B. Ten
   C. Twelve

FLORIDA

1064. In presidential elections from 1848 through 2012 which party carried Florida the most times?
   A. Democratic Party
   B. Republican Party
   C. Tie

1065. How many times has a third party candidate carried Florida? (Any party except the Federalist, Democratic-Republican, National Republican, Democratic, Whig, and Republican Parties)
   A. Zero
   B. One
   C. Two

1066. How many electoral votes is Florida worth in the 2016 election?
   A. 24
   B. 29
   C. 34

1067. In presidential elections from 1912 through 2012 election how many times has Florida backed a non-winner?
   A. Two
   B. Three
   C. Four

Illinois through Florida:
(More detailed answers at the back of the book)
1038. B. 1039. A. 1040. B. 1041. A.
1042. A. 1043. A. 1044. C. 1045. B.
1046. B. 1047. B. 1048. A. 1049. B.
1050. B. 1051. A. 1052. A. 1053. A.
1054. B. 1055. B. 1056. A. 1057. C.
1058. A. 1059. B. 1060. B. 1061. B.
1062. A. 1063. A. 1064. A. 1065. B.
1066. B. 1067. C.

TEXAS

1068. From 1848 through 2012 which party carried Texas the most times?
   A. Democratic Party
   B. Republican Party
   C. Tie

1069. Who was the first Democrat to be elected president without carrying Texas?
   A. Woodrow Wilson in 1916
   B. Jimmy Carter in 1976
   C. Bill Clinton in 1992

1070. How many times has a third party candidate carried Texas? (Any party except the Federalist, Democratic-Republican, National Republican, Democratic, Whig, and Republican Parties)
   A. Zero
   B. One
   C. Two

1071. How many electoral votes is Texas worth in the 2016 election?
   A. 38
   B. 42
   C. 45

1072. How many times from 1912 through 2012 has Texas backed a non-winner in the presidential elections?
   A. Five
   B. Seven
   C. Nine

IOWA

1073. In presidential elections from 1848 through 2012 election which party carried Iowa the most times?
   A. Democratic Party
   B. Republican Party
   C. Tie

1074. How many times has a third party candidate carried Iowa? (Any party except the Federalist, Democratic-Republican, National Republican, Democratic, Whig, and Republican Parties)
   A. Zero
   B. One
   C. Two

1075. How many electoral votes is Iowa worth in the 2016 election?
   A. Six
   B. Eight
   C. Ten

1076. In presidential elections from 1912 through 2012 how many times has Iowa backed a non-winner?
   A. Five
   B. Seven
   C. Nine

WISCONSIN

1077. In presidential elections from 1852 through 2012 which party carried Wisconsin the most times?
   A. Democratic Party
   B. Republican Party
   C. Tie

1078. How many times has a third party candidate carried Wisconsin? (Any party except the Federalist, Democratic-Republican, National Republican, Democratic, Whig, and Republican Parties)
   A. Zero
   B. One
   C. Three

1079. How many electoral votes is Wisconsin worth in the 2016 election?
   A. Six
   B. Eight
   C. Ten

1080. In presidential elections from 1912 through 2012 how many times has Wisconsin picked a non-winner?
   A. Five
   B. Seven
   C. Nine

CALIFORNIA

1081. In presidential elections from 1852 through 2012 which party carried California the most times?
    A. Democratic Party
    B. Republican Party
    C. Tie

1082. How many times has a third party candidate carried California? (Any party except the Federalist, Democratic-Republican, National Republican, Democratic, Whig, and Republican Parties)
    A. Zero
    B. One
    C. Two

1083. How many electoral votes is California worth in the 2016 election?
    A. 53
    B. 54
    C. 55

1084. In presidential elections from 1912 through 2012 how many times has California backed a non-winner?
    A. Five
    B. Seven
    C. Nine

MINNESOTA

1085. In presidential elections from 1860 through 2012 which party carried Minnesota the most times?
    A. Democratic Party
    B. Republican Party
    C. Tie

1086. How many times has a third party candidate carried Minnesota? (Any party except the Federalist, Democratic-Republican, National Republican, Democratic, Whig, and Republican Parties)
    A. One
    B. Two
    C. Three

1087. How many electoral votes is Minnesota worth in the 2016 election?
    A. Six
    B. Eight
    C. Ten

1088. In presidential elections from 1912 through 2012 how many times has Minnesota backed a non-winner?
    A. Five
    B. Seven
    C. Nine

1089. When was the last year that the Republican candidate won Minnesota?
    A. 2012
    B. 1984
    C. 1972

OREGON

1090. In presidential elections from 1860 through 2012 which party carried Oregon the most times?
    A. Democratic Party
    B. Republican Party
    C. Tie

1091. How many times has a third party candidate carried Oregon? (Any party except the Federalist, Democratic-Republican, National Republican, Democratic, Whig, and Republican Parties)
    A. Zero
    B. One
    C. Two

1092. How many electoral votes is Oregon worth in the 2016 election?
    A. Seven
    B. Nine
    C. Sixteen

1093. In presidential elections from 1912 through 2012 how many times has Oregon backed a non-winner?
    A. Three
    B. Five
    C. Seven

1094. True or False. In Oregon most citizens vote by mail rather than in-person?

1095. Is Oregon really South Washington, and is Washington really North Oregon when was the last year that Oregon and Washington voted for different candidates for president?
    A. 1968
    B. 1988
    C. 1992

KANSAS

1096. In presidential elections from 1864 through 2012 which party carried Kansas the most times?
    A. Democratic Party
    B. Republican Party
    C. Tie

1097. How many times has a third party candidate carried Kansas? (Any party except the Federalist, Democratic-Republican, National Republican, Democratic, Whig, and Republican Parties)
    A. Zero
    B. One
    C. Two

1098. How many electoral votes is Kansas worth in the 2016 election?
    A. Six
    B. Eight
    C. Ten

1099. In presidential elections from 1912 through 2012 how many times has Kansas backed a non-winner?
    A. Five
    B. Seven
    C. Nine

WEST VIRGINIA

1100. In presidential elections from 1864 through 2012 which party carried West Virginia the most times?
    A. Democratic Party
    B. Republican Party
    C. Tie

1101. How many times has a third party candidate carried West Virginia? (Any party except the Federalist, Democratic-Republican, National Republican, Democratic, Whig, and Republican Parties)
    A. Zero
    B. One
    C. Two

1102. How many electoral votes is West Virginia worth in the 2016 election?
    A. Three
    B. Four
    C. Five

1103. In presidential elections from 1912 through 2012 how many times has West Virginia picked a non-winner?
    A. Seven
    B. Nine
    C. Eleven

NEVADA

1104. In presidential elections from 1864 through 2012 which party carried Nevada the most times?
    A. Democratic Party
    B. Republican Party
    C. Tie

1105. How many times has a third party candidate carried Nevada? (Any party except the Federalist, Democratic-Republican, National Republican, Democratic, Whig, and Republican Parties)
    A. Zero
    B. One
    C. Two

1106. How many electoral votes is Nevada worth in the 2016 election?
    A. Six
    B. Eight
    C. Ten

1107. In presidential elections from 1912 through 2012 how many times has Nevada backed a non-winner?
    A. Zero
    B. One
    C. Four

Texas through Nevada:
(More detailed answers are at the back of the book)
1068. A. 1069. C. 1070. B. 1071. A.
1072. B. 1073. B. 1074. A. 1075. A.
1076. B. 1077. B. 1078. B. 1079. C.
1080. B. 1081. B. 1082. B. 1083. C.
1084. B. 1085. B. 1086. A. 1087. C.
1088. B. 1089. C. 1090. B. 1091. A.
1092. A. 1093. C. 1094. T. 1095. A.
1096. B. 1097. B. 1098. A. 1099. C.
1100. C. 1101. A. 1102. C. 1103. A.
1104. B. 1105. B. 1106. A. 1107. B.

NEBRASKA

1108. In presidential elections from 1868 through 2012 which party carried Nebraska the most times?
    A. Democratic Party
    B. Republican Party
    C. Tie

1109. How many times has a third party candidate carried Nebraska? (Any party except the Federalist, Democratic-Republican, National Republican, Democratic, Whig, and Republican Parties)
    A. Zero
    B. Two
    C. Four

1110. How many electoral votes is Nebraska worth in the 2016 election?
    A. Three
    B. Four
    C. Five

1111. In presidential elections from 1912 through 2012 how many times has Nebraska picked a non-winner?
    A. Five
    B. Seven
    C. Nine

1112. When did Nebraska last vote for a different presidential candidate than Kansas (excluding 2008 when Barack Obama won one electoral vote in Nebraska, McCain still won Nebraska and Kansas)?
    A. 1888
    B. 1908
    C. 1924

COLORADO

1113. Who chose the presidential electors in Colorado in 1876?
    A. State legislature
    B. Voters

1114. From 1876 through the 1900 election which party carried Colorado the most times?
   A. Democratic Party
   B. Republican Party
   C. Tie

1115. How many times has a third party candidate carried Colorado? (Any party except the Federalist, Democratic-Republican, National Republican, Democratic, Whig, and Republican Parties)
   A. Zero
   B. One
   C. Two

1116. How many electoral votes is Colorado worth in the 2016 election?
   A. Six
   B. Nine
   C. Twelve

1117. In presidential elections from 1912 through 2012 how many times has Colorado been won by a candidate who lost the White House?
   A. One
   B. Three
   C. Five

NORTH DAKOTA

1118. In presidential elections from 1892 through 2012 which party carried North Dakota the most times?
   A. Democratic Party
   B. Republican Party
   C. Tie

1119. How many times has a third party candidate carried North Dakota? (Any party except the Federalist, Democratic-Republican, National Republican, Democratic, Whig, and Republican Parties)
   A. Zero
   B. One
   C. It depends on how three-way ties are scored

1120. How many electoral votes is North Dakota worth in the 2016 election?
   A. Three
   B. Four
   C. Five

1121. In presidential elections from 1912 through 2012 how many times has North Dakota backed the non-winner?
   A. Five
   B. Seven
   C. Nine

1122. Many people who are not from the Upper Midwest have trouble distinguishing North and South Dakota, what was the last year that North and South Dakota voted for different candidates for president?
   A. 1892
   B. 1916
   C. 1964

SOUTH DAKOTA

1123. In presidential elections from 1892 through 2012 which party carried South Dakota the most times?
   A. Democratic Party
   B. Republican Party
   C. Tie

1124. How many times has a third party candidate carried South Dakota? (Any party except the Federalist, Democratic-Republican, National Republican, Democratic, Whig, and Republican Parties)
   A. Zero
   B. One
   C. Three

1125. How many electoral votes is South Dakota worth in the 2016 election?
   A. Three
   B. Four
   C. Five

1126. In presidential elections from 1912 through 2012 how many times has South Dakota backed the non-winner?
   A. Six
   B. Eight
   C. Ten

MONTANA

1127. In presidential elections from 1892 through 2012 which party carried Montana the most times?
   A. Democratic Party
   B. Republican Party
   C. Tie

1128. How many times has a third party candidate carried Montana? (Any party except the Federalist, Democratic-Republican, National Republican, Democratic, Whig, and Republican Parties)
   A. Zero
   B. One
   C. Two

1129. How many electoral votes is Montana worth in the 2016 election?
   A. Three
   B. Four
   C. Five

1130. In presidential elections from 1912 through 2012 how many times has Montana picked a non-winner?
   A. Five
   B. Seven
   C. Nine

WASHINGTON

1131. In presidential elections from 1892 through 2012 which party carried Washington the most times?
   A. Democratic Party
   B. Republican Party
   C. Tie

1132. How many times has a third party candidate carried Washington? (Any party except the Federalist, Democratic-Republican, National Republican, Democratic, Whig, and Republican Parties)
   A. Zero
   B. One
   C. Two

1133. How many electoral votes is Washington worth in the 2016 election?
   A. Six
   B. Nine
   C. Twelve

1134. In presidential elections from 1912 through 2012 how many times has Washington backed a non-winner?
   A. Five
   B. Seven
   C. Nine

IDAHO

1135. In presidential elections from 1892 through 2012 which party carried Idaho the most times?
   A. Democratic Party
   B. Republican Party
   C. Tie

1136. How many times has a third party candidate carried Idaho? (Any party except the Federalist, Democratic-Republican, National Republican, Democratic, Whig, and Republican Parties)
   A. Zero
   B. One
   C. Two

1137. How many electoral votes is Idaho worth in the 2016 election?
   A. Three
   B. Four
   C. Five

1138. In presidential elections from 1912 through 2012 how many times has Idaho backed a non-winner?
   A. Six
   B. Eight
   C. Ten

1139. Many people have trouble telling Montana and Idaho apart, when was the last time that they voted for different candidates for president?
   A. 1976
   B. 1992
   C. 1996

WYOMING

1140. In presidential elections from 1892 through 2012 which party carried Wyoming the most times?
   A. Democratic Party
   B. Republican Party
   C. Tie

1141. How many times has a third party candidate carried Wyoming? (Any party except the Federalist, Democratic-Republican, National Republican, Democratic, Whig, and Republican Parties)
   A. Zero
   B. One
   C. Two

1142. How many electoral votes is Wyoming worth in the 2016 election?
   A. Three
   B. Four
   C. Five

1143. In presidential elections from 1912 through 2012 how many times has Wyoming backed a non-winner?
   A. Seven
   B. Nine
   C. Eleven

Nebraska through Wyoming:
(More detailed answers are at the back of the book)
1108. B. 1109. A. 1110. C. 1111. C.
1112. B. 1113. A. 1114. B. 1115. B.
1116. B. 1117. C. 1118. B. 1119. C.
1120. A. 1121. C. 1122. B. 1123. B.
1124. B. 1125. A. 1126. C. 1127. B.
1128. A. 1129. A. 1130. A. 1131. A.
1132. B. 1133. C. 1134. B. 1135. B.
1136. B. 1137. B. 1138. A. 1139. B.
1140. B. 1141. A. 1142. A. 1143. C.

UTAH

1144. In presidential elections from 1896 through 2012 which party carried Utah the most times?
   A. Democratic Party
   B. Republican Party
   C. Tie

1145. How many times has a third party candidate carried Utah? (Any party except the Federalist, Democratic-Republican, National Republican, Democratic, Whig, and Republican Parties)
   A. Zero
   B. One
   C. Two

1146. How many electoral votes is Utah worth in the 2016 election?
   A. Six
   B. Eight
   C. Ten

1147. From the 1912 election through the 2012 election how many times has Utah backed the non-winner?
   A. Seven
   B. Nine
   C. Eleven

OKLAHOMA

1148. In presidential elections from 1908 through 2012 which party carried Oklahoma the most times?
   A. Democratic Party
   B. Republican Party
   C. Tie

1149. How many times has a third party candidate carried Oklahoma? (Any party except the Federalist, Democratic-Republican, National Republican, Democratic, Whig, and Republican Parties)
   A. Zero
   B. One
   C. Two

1150. How many electoral votes is Oklahoma worth in the 2016 election?
   A. Seven
   B. Nine
   C. Sixteen

1151. From the 1912 election through the 2012 election how many times has Oklahoma picked a non-winner?
   A. Three
   B. Five
   C. Seven

NEW MEXICO

1152. In presidential elections from 1912 through the 2012 election which party carried New Mexico the most times?
   A. Democratic Party
   B. Republican Party
   C. Tie

1153. How many times has a third party candidate carried New Mexico? (Any party except the Federalist, Democratic-Republican, National Republican, Democratic, Whig, and Republican Parties)
   A. Zero
   B. Two
   C. Three

1154. How many electoral votes is New Mexico worth in the 2016 election?
   A. Three
   B. Four
   C. Five

1155. How many times in presidential elections from 1912 through 2012 has New Mexico backed the non-winner?
   A. Zero
   B. One
   C. Two

ARIZONA

1156. In presidential elections from 1912 through 2012 which party carried Arizona the most times?
   A. Democratic Party
   B. Republican Party
   C. Tie

1157. How many times has a third party candidate carried Arizona? (Any party except the Federalist, Democratic-Republican, National Republican, Democratic, Whig, and Republican Parties)
   A. Zero
   B. One
   C. Two

1158. How many electoral votes is Arizona worth in the 2016 election?
  A. 11
  B. 13
  C. 15

1159. In presidential elections from 1912 through 2012 how many times has Arizona backed a non-winner?
  A. Three
  B. Six
  C. Nine

ALASKA

1160. In presidential elections from 1960 through the 2012 election which party carried Alaska the most times?
  A. Democratic Party
  B. Republican Party
  C. Tie

1161. How many times has a third party candidate carried Alaska? (Any party except the Federalist, Democratic-Republican, National Republican, Democratic, Whig, and Republican Parties)
  A. Zero
  B. One
  C. Two

1162. How many electoral votes is Alaska worth in the 2016 election?
  A. Three
  B. Four
  C. Five

1163. In presidential elections how many times has Alaska backed the non-winner?
  A. Three
  B. Four
  C. Five

HAWAII

1164. In presidential elections from 1960 through the 2012 election which party carried Hawaii the most times?
  A. Democratic Party
  B. Republican Party
  C. Tie

1165. How many times has a third party candidate carried Hawaii? (Any party except the Federalist, Democratic-Republican, National Republican, Democratic, Whig, and Republican Parties)
  A. Zero
  B. One
  C. Two

1166. How many electoral votes is Hawaii worth in the 2016 election?
  A. Three
  B. Four
  C. Five

1167. In presidential elections from the 1960 election through the 2012 election how many times has Hawaii backed a non-winner?
  A. Three
  B. Four
  C. Five

Utah through Hawaii:
(More detailed answers at the back of the book)
1144. B. 1145. A. 1146. A. 1147. A. 1148. B.
1149. A. 1150. A. 1151. C. 1152. A. 1153. A.
1154. C. 1155. C. 1156. B. 1157. A. 1158. A.
1159. B. 1160. B. 1161. A. 1162. A. 1163. C.
1164. A. 1165. A. 1166. B. 1167. C.

POLITICAL PARTY! PARTY! PARTY!

This section includes questions about the different political parties both the major ones and the minor ones

---

1168. Who was the first Federalist president?
   A. George Washington
   B. John Adams
   C. Thomas Jefferson

1169. Who was the last Federalist president?
   A. George Washington
   B. John Adams
   C. Thomas Jefferson

1170. As measured by the first election after the Democratic Party held a national convention, who was the first Democratic Party president?
   A. Andrew Jackson
   B. Martin Van Buren
   C. John Tyler

1171. Who is the most recently elected Democratic President (as of July 2016)?
   A. Barack Obama
   B. Bill Clinton
   C. Jimmy Carter

1172. Who was the first Republican to be elected president?
   A. Abraham Lincoln
   B. John Fremont
   C. Ulysses Grant

1173. Who was the most recent Republican to be elected president (as of July 2016)?
   A. John McCain
   B. George W. Bush
   C. Rudy Giuliani

1174. Who was the first Whig president?
   A. John Tyler
   B. William Harrison
   C. Zachary Taylor

1175. Who was the last Whig to be elected president?
   A. John Tyler
   B. William Harrison
   C. Zachary Taylor

1176. How many Whigs were elected president?
   A. 2
   B. 3
   C. 4

1177. Were there major economic policy differences between the Whigs and the Democrats during the years leading up to the Civil War?
   A. Yes, the two parties had major differences in economic policy
   B. No, the two parties had similar economic policies

1178. Were there major differences in the economic policies between the Republicans and Democrats between 1868 and 1900?
   A. Yes, the two parties had major differences in economic policy
   B. No, with only a few exceptions the two parties had similar economic policies

1179. What geographic shift between the parties began in 1932?
   A. The Democrats moved north and the Republicans moved south
   B. The Democrats moved south and the Republicans moved north
   C. The Democrats moved west and the Republicans moved east

1180. Which party has long enjoyed greater support from recent immigrants?
   A. Generally more recent immigrants have always supported the Democrats
   B. Generally more recent immigrants have always supported the Republicans
   C. Neither, generally recent immigrants have split their support fairly evenly

1181. In 2016 which party gets more support from organized labor?
   A. Democratic Party
   B. Republican Party
   C. Neither

1182. What issue was the Republican Party formed around?
   A. Business expansion
   B. Currency
   C. Slavery

1183. Which party held the first national convention to nominate a presidential candidate?
   A. Anti-Mason Party
   B. Federalist Party
   C. National Republican Party

1184. Who founded the Democratic-Republican Party?
   A. Benjamin Franklin
   B. John Adams
   C. Thomas Jefferson

1185. How many consecutive years did the Democratic-Republican Party control both the White House and Congress?
   A. 10
   B. 16
   C. 24

1186. Where was the main strength of the Democratic-Republican Party?
   A. North
   B. Seacoast
   C. South

1187. In addition to being anti-slavery and pro-westward expansion, what else did the Free Soil Party favor?
   A. Cheap postage
   B. Prohibition
   C. Term limits

1188. What cause is the Green Party most closely associated with?
   A. Currency reform
   B. Drug legalization
   C. Environmentalism

1189. What record did Green Party candidate Ralph Nader set in 2008?
   A. Most campaign events attended in a single day
   B. Most votes for a Green Party candidate
   C. Most times using the word recycle in an acceptance speech

1190. In what state was the Greenback Party founded?
   A. Indiana
   B. New York
   C. Wyoming

1191. Supported by farmers and laborers, what was the main policy goal of the Greenback Party?
    A. Greater harvests
    B. Inflationary monetary policy
    C. Promote ecological working conditions

1192. How many years did the Know-Nothing Party think that immigrants should be forced to wait before becoming U.S. citizens?
    A. 7
    B. 15
    C. 21

1193. Who was the Know Nothing Party candidate for president in 1856?
    A. Henry Marlborough
    B. Millard Fillmore
    C. Thomas Jackson

1194. When was the height of the Liberty Party?
    A. 1840s
    B. 1910s
    C. 1960s

1195. In what state was the Libertarian Party founded?
    A. California
    B. Colorado
    C. Wyoming

1196. What year was the Libertarian Party founded?
    A. 1941
    B. 1971
    C. 1981

1197. How many electoral votes has the Libertarian Party received for president?
    A. 0
    B. 1
    C. 31

1198. When was the heyday of the National Republican Party?
    A. Mid-1820s
    B. Mid-1890s
    C. Mid-1970s

1199. In 1968 which celebrity ran for president under the banner of the People's Party?
    A. Abie Hoffman
    B. Benjamin Spock
    C. Patrick Paulsen

1200. How many states did the Populist Party win in the 1892 presidential election?
    A. 0
    B. 3
    C. 5

1201. True or False. There has been a modern Populist Party that is opposed to the Federal Reserve?

1202. Which Progressive Party candidate won more electoral votes, Robert La Follette in 1924 or Henry Wallace in 1948?
    A. Robert La Follette
    B. Henry Wallace

1203. How many states did the Progressive Party also known as the Bull Moose Party win in 1912?
    A. 5
    B. 6
    C. 7

1204. What political party did American Party candidate George Wallace belong to?
    A. Democratic Party
    B. Republican Party

1205. How many times did Eugene Debs run for president as the candidate of the Socialist Party?
    A. 2
    B. 5
    C. 7

1206. Eugene Debs' best campaign was in 1912, what year was the best year for the Socialist Party in terms of percentage of the popular vote?
- A. 1912
- B. 1932
- C. 1952

1207. To which Soviet political leader does the Socialist Workers Party trace its origins?
- A. Leonid Brezhnev
- B. Leon Trotsky
- C. Nikita Khrushchev

1208. What year was the best year for the Communist Party in terms of electoral support in the United States?
- A. 1856
- B. 1932
- C. 1956

Political Party! Party! Party!

(More detailed answers at the back of the book)

1168. A. 1169. B. 1170. A. 1171. A. 1172. A. 1173. B. 1174. B. 1175. C. 1176. A. 1177. B. 1178. B. 1179. A. 1180. A. 1180. A. 1181. A. 1182. C. 1183. A. 1184. C. 1185. C. 1186. C. 1187. A. 1188. C. 1189. A. 1190. A. 1191. B. 1192. C. 1193. B. 1194. A. 1195. B. 1196. B. 1197. B. 1198. A. 1199. B. 1200. C. 1201. T. 1202. A. 1203. B. 1204. A. 1205. B. 1206. A. 1207. B. 1208. B.

FINALE

1209. One of the hallmarks of campaigning or deciding to run for president is that until fairly recently you were not supposed to want the job or nomination. As a candidate you only accepted the nomination to run for the good of the country. From what famous Roman does the ideal of being a reluctant leader come?

    A. Julius Caesar
    B. Cicero
    C. Cincinnatus

No shortcut here. You have to flip to the back to find out the answer to 1209.

ANSWERS

THE WINNERS!

The answers to the first section are fairly short and just tell who won the election. More detail will be provided about each election in the answers to the more specific questions about each election found in the section about that particular election (e.g. 2004 Election).

1. A. Barack Obama won the 2012 U.S. presidential election.

2. A. Barack Obama won the 2008 U.S. presidential election.

3. A. George W. Bush won the 2004 U.S. presidential election.

4. B. George W. Bush won the 2000 U.S. presidential election.

5. A. Bill Clinton won the 1996 U.S presidential election.

6. A. Bill Clinton won the 1992 U.S presidential election.

7. A. George H.W. Bush won the 1988 U.S presidential election.

8. A. Ronald Reagan won the 1984 U.S presidential election.

9. C. Ronald Reagan won the 1980 U.S presidential election.

10. B. Jimmy Carter won the 1976 U.S presidential election.

11. C. Richard Nixon won the 1972 U.S presidential election.

12. C. Richard Nixon won the 1968 U.S presidential election.

13. B. Lyndon Johnson won the 1964 U.S presidential election.

14. A. John F. Kennedy won the 1960 U.S presidential election.

15. B. Dwight Eisenhower won the 1956 U.S presidential election.

16. B. Dwight Eisenhower won the 1952 U.S presidential election.

17. A. Harry Truman won the 1948 U.S presidential election.

18. A. Franklin D. Roosevelt won the 1944 U.S presidential election.

19. A. Franklin D. Roosevelt won the 1940 U.S presidential election.

20. B. Franklin D. Roosevelt won the 1936 U.S presidential election.

21. A. Franklin D. Roosevelt won 1932 U.S presidential election.

22. B. Herbert Hoover won the 1928 U.S presidential election.

23. A. Calvin Coolidge won the 1924 U.S presidential election.

24. B. Warren Harding won the 1920 U.S presidential election.

25. B. Woodrow Wilson won the 1916 U.S presidential election.

26. C. Woodrow Wilson won the 1912 U.S presidential election.

27. B. William Taft won the 1908 U.S presidential election.

28. C. Teddy Roosevelt won the 1904 U.S presidential election.

29. C. William McKinley won the 1900 U.S presidential election.

30. C. William McKinley won the 1896 U.S presidential election.

31. B. Grover Cleveland won the 1892 U.S presidential election.

32. A. Benjamin Harrison won the 1888 U.S presidential election.

33. B. Grover Cleveland won the 1884 U.S presidential election.

34. A. James Garfield won the 1880 U.S presidential election.

35. A. Rutherford Hayes won the 1876 U.S presidential election.

36. B. Ulysses Grant won the 1872 U.S presidential election.

37. B. Ulysses Grant won the 1868 U.S presidential election.

38. A. Abraham Lincoln won the 1864 U.S presidential election.

39. A. Abraham Lincoln won the 1860 U.S presidential election

40. A. James Buchanan won the 1856 U.S presidential election.

41. A. Franklin Pierce won the 1852 U.S presidential election.

42. C. Zachary Taylor won the 1848 U.S presidential election.

43. B. James Polk won the 1844 U.S presidential election.

44. B. William Harrison won the 1840 U.S presidential election.

45. A. Martin Van Buren won the 1836 U.S presidential election.

46. A. Andrew Jackson won the 1832 U.S presidential election.

47. A. Andrew Jackson won the 1828 U.S presidential election.

48. B. John Q. Adams won the 1824 U.S presidential election.

49. A., C. James Monroe won the 1820 U.S presidential election and he ran unopposed.

50. B. James Monroe won the 1816 U.S presidential election.

51. B. James Madison won the 1812 U.S presidential election.

52. C. James Madison won the 1808 U.S presidential election.

53. C. Thomas Jefferson won the 1804 U.S presidential election.

54. C. Thomas Jefferson won the 1800 U.S presidential election.

55. A. John Adams won the 1796 U.S presidential election.

56. A. George Washington won the 1792 U.S. presidential election.

57. A. George Washington won the 1788-1789 U.S. presidential election.

WHO CAN VOTE FOR THE PRESIDENT AND HOW THE PRESIDENT IS ELECTED

58. A. All of the states had minimum property ownership requirements to vote. These restrictions had disappeared from most states by the end of the first half of the 19th century.

59. B. Former slaves got the guaranteed right to vote in 1870 with the passage of the Fifteenth Amendment. The Fifteenth Amendment also bars discrimination against voters based on race.

60. B. In the 1860s, the political parties supplied ballots to the voters. Voters were responsible for obtaining a ballot and bringing it to the polls. The ballots supplied by the parties typically only listed the preferred candidates of the party that supplied the ballot. To split a ticket the voter would need to cross out the name of a particular candidate and write-in the replacement.

61. A. The Australian ballot was introduced in 1888. This ballot is supplied by the government and lists the candidates from all parties. Prior to the Australian ballot voters had to bring their own ballot to the polls and often brought ballots supplied by political parties. Use of the Australian ballot was widespread in the United States by 1896.

62. C. The Indiana ballot lists all the candidates, sorted by political party. The Massachusetts ballot lists all the candidates sorted by political office. These are both common variations of the Australian ballot.

63. C. Women got the guaranteed right to vote in 1920 with the passage of the Nineteenth Amendment.

64. A. The current minimum voting age is 18 years old. You must be at least 18 years old to vote.

65. A. Convicted felons are generally ineligible to vote. So are the insane and those who are unable to meet residency requirements.

66. C. Election Day is the Tuesday after the first Monday in November.

67. False. The president of the United States is elected by electors. The process of electing the president through electors is referred to as the Electoral College.

68. B. The number of electoral votes that each state gets is the same as the number of Representatives and Senators that the state has in Congress.

69. C. The state legislatures get to determine how electors are appointed. This has historically been by one of three methods, at-large popular vote, district popular vote, and election by state legislature.

70. A. Most states appoint electors based on the winner of the at-large popular vote in the state. A vote for a particular candidate is also a vote for that candidates' slate of electors.

71. True. Until the Twentieth Century most states had the direct election of electors. This could result in electoral vote splits in the state when there was a split in electors with electors who supported opposite candidates winning.

72. B. Each elector would get two votes and the winner would be president and the runner-up would be vice president.

73. B. Incompatible presidents and vice presidents could be elected if they were elected separately and not as a team.

74. False. The Twelfth Amendment penalizes but does not prohibit the vice president and the president from being from the same state. Elector who are also from the same state as the candidates would have to forego voting for either the presidential candidate or the vice presidential candidate. So there is a penalty for having both from the same state but not an absolute prohibition.

75. A. The House of Representatives decides the winner of the presidency.

76. B. Only the top three candidates (as measured by electoral votes won) make it to the next round under the current rules.

77. A. Each state gets one vote in the tie-breaker round. How that vote will be cast is determined by a separate vote by the state delegation in the case of a tie, that state's vote is marked as divided. A divided vote counts as a zero.

78. B. A simple majority of states is needed to win in the House of Representatives so 26 is the correct answer. 26 being the minimum majority share of 50 states.

79. A. Under the Twelfth Amendment, the outgoing vice president becomes president if no new president has been determined in time. The winning vice presidential candidate becomes vice president.

80. C. The vice president-elect becomes acting president if the president-elect dies or a president-elect has not yet been determined. The Twentieth Amendment supersedes parts of the Twelfth Amendment regarding presidential elections.

81. C. According to the un-amended Constitution, March 4 is the start and end date for presidential terms.

82. B. The Twentieth Amendment (ratified in 1933) sets the start and end date for presidential terms as January 20.

83. B. The Senate decides the winner of the vice presidency. The Senate choses between the two highest vote getters among those receiving votes for vice president in the Electoral College.

84. B. One time has the Senate had to decide an election question that only involved the vice presidency. After the 1836 election, all of the Virginia electors refused to vote for Martin Van Buren's vice presidential running mate Richard Johnson even though Van Buren had won Virginia. This loss of votes sent the vice presidential election to the Senate and Richard Johnson's election was confirmed by a vote of the Senate.

85. B. Since 1845 Election Day for presidential elections has been the same for every state. This is changing again as more states are allowing early voting. Election Day remains the deadline to conclude popular voting.

86. B. According to the Twenty-Second Amendment because Jones served for more than two years of Smith's term, Jones can only seek election to the presidency on his own one time. If Jones had served for less than two years of Smith's term, he could seek election twice. The Twenty-Second Amendment was passed during Harry Truman's presidency but did not apply to him. Truman was eligible to run for re-election in 1952 but after testing the waters, opted not to run.

87. B. 270 electoral votes are needed to win. (270 = 50% of the electoral college votes plus 1 vote)

88. A. Six states have exactly three electoral votes.

89. A. 21 states have at least 10 electoral votes.

90. A. Six states have 20 or more electoral votes.

91. B. Two states have 30 or more electoral votes.

92. B. One state has 40 or more electoral votes.

93. B. One state has 50 or more electoral votes.

94. A. Zero states have 60 or more electoral votes.

95. B. Hawaii has four electoral votes, Alaska only has three.

96. C. Currently two states award electoral votes by congressional district rather than winner-take-all statewide. Those two states are Maine and Nebraska. In the past other states have awarded votes based on the winner of congressional district. In early 19th century, Maryland awarded its electoral votes by congressional district winner and frequently awarded split decisions.

THE ELECTIONS (2012 to 1789)

Electoral College Margin Questions: Nearly every election features at least one question about the winning margin in the Electoral College. Remember that the college is a closed universe and there are a finite number of votes available and that if one candidate is getting more votes, another candidate is getting less. The margin is measured not by the absolute margin but by the number of votes needed to change the result. Starting in 1964 the magic number to win has been 270. The margin is how many votes it takes to get the losing candidate's total to 270.

2012 ELECTION

97. A. President Obama ran for re-election with his then-current vice president, Joe Biden.

98. B. Former governor of Massachusetts, Mitt Romney, won the Republican nomination.

99. C. The 2012 Republican convention featured actor/director Clint Eastwood (well-known for his conservative views) lecturing an empty chair.

100. A. Support or opposition for the Affordable Care Act (also known as Obamacare) was made into a major campaign issue in 2012.

101. C. Barack Obama got a slight majority of the popular vote (51%). He received almost 5 million more votes than Mitt Romney. (Approximately 65.9 million votes to 60.9 million votes).

102. C. Obama won by more than 50 electoral votes. He won by 64 electoral votes (332 to 206). If Romney had gotten 64 more electoral votes, Romney would have won.

103. A. Ironically after criticizing the forty-seven percent of Americans who get more in payments from the government than those people pay in taxes, Romney got 47% of the popular vote.

104. B. Obama won about 60% of the Labor vote. This is consistent with other Democratic candidates in recent years. For example John Kerry won about 60% of the Labor vote in 2004.

105. B. Obama carried 26 states and the District of Columbia in 2012.

106. A. Obama received 70% of the popular vote in Hawaii.

107. C. Utah gave Romney his greatest margin of victory in the popular vote in 2012. Romney received 72% of the vote in Utah.

108. A. Obama won 11 out of the 15 largest cities in 2012.

109. B. Romney won more counties than Obama in 2012 (Romney won 77% of counties). Obama clearly had more concentrated urban support and Romney clearly had more rural support.

2008 ELECTION

110. B. In February, 2007, Barack Obama officially announced his candidacy for president at the old statehouse in Springfield, Illinois.

111. A. Obama's win in the Iowa Caucus validated his candidacy and launched him towards winning the nomination.

112. C. Obama ran a very tech-savvy campaign that used cutting edge technology to recruit supporters. His cutting edge campaign very much helped him in his primary battles with Hillary Clinton.

113. C. Obama gave his acceptance speech in front of a crowd of at least 70,000 people at a professional football stadium in Denver, Colorado.

114. A. Barack Obama's slogan in 2008 was "Yes we can!".

115. True. Barack Obama had such a strong donor base that he was able to opt-out of the federal campaign money for the general election campaign and he was the first candidate to do so.

116. A. Senator John McCain from Arizona ran against Obama in the 2008 general election.

117. C. In 2008 for the first time in its history, a woman won the Republican Party nomination for vice president. Governor Sarah Palin of Alaska was nominated for vice president.

118. False. John McCain campaigned heavily in Pennsylvania but was defeated by 10%, 54% to 44%. Obama's 54% was the highest total by a Democratic presidential candidate in Pennsylvania since Lyndon Johnson received almost 65% of the vote in 1964.

119. C. 2008 featured above average turnout and the best voter turnout since the 1968 election. More than 60% of eligible voters voted in 2008. The long-term average turnout between 1960 and 2012 has been in the low 50% range.

120. B. Obama won by a margin of approximately 53% to 46%.

121. C. Obama won by more than 70 electoral votes. He won by 97 electoral votes 365 to 173. (If McCain had received 97 more electoral votes, McCain would have won 270 to 268.)

122. False. In 2008, Obama received an impressive 365 electoral votes. In 1996, Clinton received 379 electoral votes.

123. A. Barack Obama won one electoral vote in Nebraska, carrying the Congressional District in and around Omaha, Nebraska.

124. B. No. McCain and Palin received only 173 electoral votes.

2004 ELECTION

125. C. Howard Dean gave a war cry to rally his supporters after a disappointing finish in the Iowa Caucus. Unfortunately for Dean, the "Dean yell" became a tempting target for mockery.

126. C. Four star general and former NATO commander, Wesley Clark, sought the Democratic Party nomination in 2004.

127. A. Barack Obama gave a major speech at the 2004 convention when he was just a state senator running for U.S. Senate.

128. A. Boston hosted the 2004 Democratic Convention.

129. B. The internet was a major source of fund-raising for the first time in presidential election history during the 2004 campaign.

130. B. New York City hosted the 2004 Republican Convention.

131. A. The group "Swift Boat Veterans for Truth" attacked John Kerry's Vietnam War record. Kerry was slow to respond to the group and that helped sustain the attacks.

132. B. George W. Bush won with a slight majority of the popular vote (51% to 48%).

133. A. If John Kerry had been able to flip Ohio, he would have won. George W. Bush set new records for voter turnout as he won Ohio.

134. B. One of the Democratic electors from Minnesota voted for Kerry's running mate, John Edwards, for both president and vice president.

135. C. There was a procedural challenge to George W. Bush's win. The challenge was defeated by a large margin in the Senate. The challenge centered on the election results in Ohio.

2000 ELECTION

136. A. Senator Bill Bradley from New Jersey was the main challenger to Vice President Al Gore in the 2000 primary season. Bradley was not able to mount a significant challenge to Gore's candidacy.

137. B. John McCain won the New Hampshire Primary and was the main challenger to George W. Bush's candidacy.

138. A. The 2000 Democratic Convention featured a lengthy kiss between Al Gore and his wife Tipper. The kiss was an effort to distance Gore from the Monica Lewinsky scandal.

139. C. The 2000 Republican Convention was held in Philadelphia.

140. A. The popular vote was close in 2000, the top two candidates were within 2% of each other.

141. A. The electoral vote in 2000 was very close. Changing the outcome of just one of a handful of states would have changed the outcome.

142. A. One elector from Washington D.C. abstained to protest the lack of voting representation for Washington D.C. in Congress.

143. True. Al Gore won the popular vote in 2000 by half a million votes.

144. True. The Supreme Court agreed with the arguments of George W. Bush that his Equal Protection and Due Process Rights were violated by arbitrary and inconsistent standards of the recount. Given the deadlines involved of between Election Day and Inauguration Day, close elections involving recounts are difficult.

145. B. A "dimpled chad" is part of a ballot that has been partially marked.

146. B. The 2000 election came down to a dispute over the vote totals in Florida.

147. B. Yes. Green Party Candidate, Ralph Nader, won enough votes in Florida and the vote in Florida was decided by such a narrow margin that he most likely influenced the outcome of the election. Nader also may have helped tip New Hampshire to Bush. If Gore had won New Hampshire, the result in Florida did not decide the election.

148. A. All twenty of the election challenges were rejected by the president of the Senate because none of the challenges had the signature of one senator as required by law.

1996 ELECTION

149. B. Steve Forbes ran for president on a platform featuring a flat tax.

150. B. Pat Buchanan had the second most victories with four wins in the 1996 primary season.

151. C. Bob Dole was 73 years old when he was nominated making him the oldest first-time nominee.

152. B. The 1996 Democratic Convention was held in Chicago.

153. B. Bob Dole was seriously wounded in Italy during World War II.

154. A. No, third party candidates were not a factor in the 1996 election. Ross Perot participated again but only drew 8% of the popular vote.

155. A. Both Bill Clinton and Bob Dole are red-green color blind and needed the same accommodation so that they could distinguish the debate timing lights which are usually red and green.

156. B. Bill Clinton had a big win in the popular vote, defeating Bob Dole 49% to 40%. Bill Clinton won by more than 8 million popular votes (a fairly large margin) but won less than 50% of the popular vote.

157. A. Bill Clinton won the Electoral College 379 to 159. Bob Dole needed 111 more electoral votes to win. This could have been accomplished by shifting about 600,000 votes spread over eight different states.

158. True. Eligible voter participation in 1996 was below 50% which had not been seen since the 1920s.

159. A. Bill Clinton carried Arizona in 1996. He lost it in 1992. Clinton was the first Democrat to win Arizona since Truman in 1948.

160. True. In 1996 Bill Clinton became the first Democratic president to be elected with a Republican Congress. The 1996 election more or less preserved the status quo at a cost of $500 million dollars of campaigning.

1992 ELECTION

161. A. Paul Tsongas won the 1992 Iowa Caucus.

162. B. Winning the New Hampshire Primary earned Bill Clinton the nickname of "comeback kid".

163. True. Bill Clinton made a surprise appearance at the convention in response to delegate cheers. He had been watching on TV from his hotel room in an adjacent hotel and made an impromptu appearance at the convention.

164. A. In his acceptance speech, Bill Clinton called for a set of programs he called a "New Covenant".

165. A. Dan Quayle's new image was that of a family values defender.

166. C. George H.W. Bush focused on making the election about trust.

167. A. Bill Clinton was governor of Arkansas.

168. B. Ross Perot was a billionaire businessman from Texas. He spent $60 million dollars of his own money to run for president.

169. B. The domestic economy was a major issue during the 1992 campaign.

170. B. The popular vote margin was not that close with Clinton winning by about 6% over Bush, 43% to 37%.

171. B. Bush needed about 100 more electoral votes to win. He lost by a score of 370 to 168.

172. True. Clinton only got 43% of the popular vote nationwide which is the fourth lowest total among winning presidents. (Only Adams in 1824, Lincoln in 1860, and Wilson in 1912 got lower percentages of the popular vote and still won the election).

173. True. Ross Perot got about 19% of the popular vote nationwide. Perot probably did not keep Bush from winning but Perot likely brought Bill Clinton's popular vote margin below 50%.

174. A. Generally Perot voters would have voted for George H.W. Bush. The general consensus is that Perot did not cost Bush the election. It would have taken a change of about 300,000 votes over 10 states to flip the outcome.

1988 ELECTION

175. C. Jesse Jackson was Michael Dukakis's most successful competitor.

176. A. Bob Dole won the second most Republican primary contests in 1988.

177. B. Bill Clinton gave an overly lengthy nominating speech at the 1988 Democratic Convention. The speech was widely regarded as being too long and not very good.

178. B. George H.W. Bush promised no new taxes. He broke this promise in 1990 and regretted it during the 1992 campaign.

179. B. Michael Dukakis was governor of Massachusetts.

180. False. Ronald Reagan endorsed George H.W. Bush in 1988.

181. A. Michael Dukakis hurt his election chances by given a poor answer to a tough question on crime. His answer fueled the narrative that the Democratic Party was weak on crime.

182. True. George H.W. Bush trailed by double digits in summer polling taken immediately after the Democratic Convention but rallied to an impressive victory in the fall.

183. C. Bush had a big win in the popular vote winning by about 7.72%.

184. B. Bush won 426 to 111 to 1. One Dukakis elector voted for Lloyd Bentsen for president. Assuming that elector would not have cast such a symbolic vote had victory been possible, Dukakis needed to win 158 more electoral votes to win.

185. B. Bush held Dukakis to 11 states, mostly in the Northeast and Upper Midwest.

186. A. 1988 was the last year that the Republicans carried California.

1984 ELECTION

187. A. Gary Hart was one of Mondale's main rivals for the nomination in1984.

188. C. Mondale did not have the nomination secured until June.

189. B. Mondale selected Geraldine Ferraro as his running mate. It was the first time that a woman was nominated for vice president by a major political party in the United States.

190. A. Hot weather reduced the number of protests at the 1984 Republican Convention.

191. C. Mondale was an emergency substitute candidate for U.S. Senate in 2002. He lost the election to Norm Coleman. (Coleman would lose re-election in 2008 to Al Franken by 312 votes).

192. True. In 1984, Reagan was the oldest candidate to be nominated for re-election.

193. C. Taxes were a major issue in the 1984 election.

194. True. In later interviews, Mondale said that he knew that Reagan was probably going to win the debate after Reagan successfully made a joke about Mondale's age.

195. C. Mondale was never within 10% of Reagan in polls taken during the 1984 campaign.

196. C. Reagan scored a blowout win the in popular vote, getting close to 59% of the popular vote and keeping Mondale to less than 41%.

197. C. Reagan won one of the all-time biggest victories in the history of the Electoral College. He defeated Mondale 525 to 13. Mondale needed 257 more electoral votes to reverse the election result.

198. A. Mondale won his home state of Minnesota by less than 5,000 votes. Had Reagan won Minnesota he would have had the first 50 state sweep.

199. D. All of the above. Reagan dominated Mondale and Reagan held Mondale to Minnesota and the District of Columbia. Reagan won 525 electoral votes and won almost 59% of the popular vote.

1980 ELECTION

200. B. Ted Kennedy was Jimmy Carter's most significant rival for the Democratic nomination.

201. A. George H.W. Bush was Reagan's most successful rival in the Republican primaries.

202. A. The 1980 Democratic Convention was the scene of a bitter struggle over economic platform of the party. Generally Edward Kennedy's proposals prevailed over Jimmy Carter's.

203. B. Gerald Ford was the other finalist to be Reagan's vice presidential running mate.

204. True. Carter's pessimism hurt him in running for re-election.

205. A. Ronald Reagan served two terms as governor of California.

206. B. American prestige particularly as it related to the ongoing Iran-Hostage Crisis was a major issue of the 1980 campaign.

207. True. Reagan's solid debate performance less than one week from Election Day persuaded a large number of undecided voters to vote for Reagan. The margin from these voters solidified his victory.

208. A. Third party candidate John Anderson received six percent of the national popular vote.

209. B. Post-election analysis suggests that most of Anderson's supporters would have otherwise voted for Reagan.

210. C. Ronald Reagan frequently appeared in on campaign buttons and campaign literature wearing a cowboy hat.

211. C. Reagan had a big win in the popular vote, winning by about 9%, 50% to 41%.

212. C. Reagan won the electoral vote 489 to 49. Carter needed 221 more electoral votes to reverse the result.

213. B. Carter only carried six states. He also carried Washington D.C.

214. A. Carter conceded the election before the polls had closed on the West Coast.

1976 ELECTION

215. True. The 1976 Election was the first one to be governed by significant federal oversight into campaign finances.

216. B. Gerald Ford was never elected president or vice president. He became president upon the resignation of Richard Nixon. The other answer choices are false.

217. B. The 1976 Democratic Convention was harmonious, in particular contrast to 1968 and 1972.

218. A. Carter gave his speech at 11 pm local time. This is significant because in many of the preceding Democratic Conventions over the past few decades, most of the acceptance speech were delivered well-after midnight and after most of the TV audience was asleep.

219. C. Prior to becoming vice president, Ford had represented Michigan for more than 20 years in the House of Representatives.

220. A. Carter had served as the governor of Georgia.

221. A. Gerald Ford used the slogan "elephants eat peanuts" in 1976.

222. B. Jimmy Carter used the slogan "the grin will win" in 1976.

223. A. Carter won the presidential debate. It was the first presidential debate since 1960. Ford made a naïve-sounding remark about Soviet domination of Eastern Europe that hurt his debate performance.

224. B. Carter won by slightly more than 2% of the popular vote 50% to 48%.

225. B. Carter won 297 to 240. One Ford elector from Washington voted for Reagan or Ford would have received 241 electoral votes. Ford needed to win about 30 more electoral votes to win.

226. True. Ford almost overcame a significant deficit in the polls. Carter made several gaffes after clinching the nomination and Ford made up much of the deficit only to lose by two points in the end.

227. False. Carter won with the "New Deal Coalition" of African Americans, urban voters, and labor.

228. C. Walter Mondale was Jimmy Carter's running mate.

229. A. Richard Cheney served as Gerald Ford's chief of staff.

230. B. Winning Ohio plus any state worth at least five electoral votes would have tipped the election to Ford. Ford was about 11,000 votes short in Ohio. Ford was about 35,000 votes short in Wisconsin. If he had won those two states he would have won the election.

231. B. Jimmy Carter was from Georgia.

1972 ELECTION

232. A. George Wallace was George McGovern's most significant rival for the nomination.

233. True. Nixon had no serious opposition in the 1972 primaries.

234. True. Both the Democratic and Republican parties adopted planks supporting the Equal Rights Amendment in 1972.

235. False. Although condemning narcotics, marijuana is conspicuously absent from the 1972 Democratic Platform. In contrast, the Republican Platform specifically opposed the legalization of marijuana.

236. B. Eagleton had undergone electric shock treatment for depression.

237. C. Sargent Shriver replaced Eagleton as the Democratic Party vice presidential candidate.

238. A. Dr. Spock received less than 100,000 votes nationwide. About 5/7ths of his votes came from California.

239. B. George McGovern represented South Dakota in the U.S. Senate.

240. True. McGovern knew the procedural rules for winning the nomination backwards and forwards but in the general election he ran a disorganized campaign.

241. C. Richard Nixon set the Republican all-time popular vote record with his 60.67% to 37.52% victory over McGovern. Nixon won nearly 18 million more popular votes than McGovern. This is still the all-time record for margin of victory by number of popular votes.

242. C. Nixon won by more than 500 electoral votes (520 to 17). (One Nixon elector voted for the Libertarian candidate). McGovern needed 253 more electoral votes to reverse the election result.

243. A. The only state that McGovern carried was Massachusetts. He won the Bay State by about 220,000 votes. He also carried the District of Columbia.

244. C. As might be expected given the large defeat that he suffered, McGovern lost 4 states by more than 1 million votes. (He lost 3 more states by more than 800,000 votes).

245. True. The Watergate break-in of the Democratic Headquarters in June of 1972 was totally unnecessary. Nixon had nothing to fear in his quest for re-election. The illegal break-in and cover-up led to Nixon's resignation in August of 1974.

1968 ELECTION

246. A. Eugene McCarthy won the most votes in the 1968 Democratic primaries.

247. A. A strong performance by Eugene McCarthy in the New Hampshire Primary caused Lyndon Johnson to drop out and Robert Kennedy to enter the race.

248. C. Ronald Reagan won the most votes in the Republican Primaries in 1968 but this was based almost entirely on Nixon not competing in California. Nixon had the most total victories and easily secured the nomination.

249. C. Robert Kennedy was fatally shot immediately after giving a victory speech in California after winning the California Primary.

250. A. There were more than 500 (but less than 1,000) convention-related arrests in Chicago.

251. C. The Rev. Phillips was from Washington D.C. He was the first African American nominated for president by either the Democratic or Republican Party.

252. B. Hubert Humphrey won the Democratic nomination for president. He is the last major party candidate for president to have won the nomination without participating in the primaries.

253. B. Richard Nixon won the Republican nomination for president.

254. C. Both Nixon and Humphrey had served as vice presidents. Humphrey was the current vice president.

255. B. The letter M. Edmund Muskie was from Maine and Spiro Agnew was from Maryland.

256. B. Richard Nixon had and lost a large lead in the polls as the election drew near. Humphrey was gaining sharply on Nixon in the polls and if the election had been a week later, Humphrey might have won.

257. B. Nixon outspent Humphrey by a 2 to 1 margin in 1968.

258. B. Hubert Humphrey had advertisements that just said "H H H". The initials of Hubert Horatio Humphrey.

259. A. The election of 1968 was one of the closer ones in the history of the popular vote. Nixon beat Humphrey by less than a percentage point, 43.4% to 42.7%.

260. C. Nixon won roughly 15 percent of the African American vote in 1968. Although 15 percent is not a very large number, no Republican presidential candidate has done better since then.

261. B. Nixon won by little more than 100 electoral votes 301 to 191. Humphrey needed 79 more electoral votes to reach 270. Humphrey needed about 150,000 more votes total to flip Ohio, Illinois, Missouri, and New Jersey and Humphrey would have won.

262. B. Wallace carried two-thirds of the Goldwater states.

263. B. Generally, with some exceptions, Nixon carried the Middle states, Humphrey carried the Northern states and Wallace carried the Southern states.

264. True. Nixon won the popular vote by little more than 500,000 votes out of more than 70 million cast. Nixon won more states than Humphrey and this amounted to a solid victory in the Electoral College.

1964 ELECTION

265. True. Lyndon Johnson had no meaningful competition for the nomination.

266. True. The 1964 Republican Convention was rather quarrelsome with feuding between the conservative and moderate wings of the party.

267. C. There was no roll call of votes at the 1964 Democratic Convention. Most conventions include a roll call of votes.

268. C. William Miller was selected by Goldwater based largely on Miller's ability to annoy Johnson.

269. B. William Miller was the first Roman Catholic to run on the Republican ticket.

270. A. 1964 marked a real divergence in the number of delegates at a given Democratic Convention compared to the Republican Convention of the same year, with the Democrats having significantly more than the Republicans.

271. A. Johnson refused to debate Goldwater and there were no presidential debates in 1964.

272. A. Goldwater was entirely against the New Deal. This position was not popular with voters.

273. B. Lyndon Johnson used the slogan "Let us continue" in 1964. He was asking voters to continue the work that Kennedy has started in 1960.

274. C. Lyndon Johnson set the all-time popular vote share record as he crushed Goldwater 61.0% to 38.5%. Johnson received almost 16 million more votes than Goldwater.

275. C. Johnson won by a score of 486 to 52 in the Electoral College.

276. B. Although not always classified as part of the South (based on the cosmopolitan nature of Miami), from a civil rights standpoint, Florida was akin to other Deep South states in the 1960s. Johnson won Florida. Johnson carried Miami, the Tampa to Gainesville corridor, and the coastal area centered on Daytona Beach. Goldwater carried the panhandle and much of the interior.

277. A. No. Goldwater did not win any states in the Midwest or New England.

278. B. Residents of the District of Columbia could vote for the first time in 1964 due to the passage of the 23rd Amendment.

279. True. 1964 marked the last time that many Great Plains and Mountain West states were carried by a Democratic candidate. Reflecting the weaknesses in Goldwater's candidacy, these states were not competitive in 1964 and were easily carried by Johnson.

1960 ELECTION

280. B. Kennedy won the most votes in the Democratic Primaries.

281. C. Kennedy knew that the West Virginia primary would be very important to show that a Catholic could win a heavily-Protestant state. He prepared for two years in advance in order to win West Virginia primary.

282. C. Nixon won the most votes in the Republican Primaries.

283. True. Delegates from nine Southern states had signed a pledge repudiating the Democratic Party's civil rights plank, the strongest in party history.

284. C. Kennedy chose Lyndon Johnson as his vice presidential running mate.

285. C. Kennedy gave his acceptance speech at a crowded stadium. (The Los Angeles Coliseum)

286. C. Kennedy's program was called the New Frontier.

287. A. Kennedy knew that his Roman Catholic faith would be an issue for some voters. Even though the issue was unreasonable, he confronted the issue and boosted his standing with the voters by doing so.

288. A. Nixon demanded a stronger pro-civil rights plank in the 1960 Republican Platform.

289. B. The 1960 Republican Platform spoke favorably about free enterprise and economic growth. It did not call for a corporate income tax cut.

290. A. 1960 was one of the all-time closest elections in terms of the national popular vote. Kennedy narrowly won 49.7% to 49.5%. There was only an approximately 112,000 vote difference in their respective vote totals.

291. B. Kennedy won 303 to 219 to 15. Nixon would have won if he carried Illinois (lost by about 4,400), Missouri (lost by about 4,900), and New Jersey (lost by about 11,200). Nixon needed only 50 more electoral votes to reach the magic number of 269. If he had won Illinois, Missouri, and New Jersey instead of Kennedy the result would have been a Nixon victory 269 to 247 to 15.

292. True. Kennedy won the urban, the black, and the labor vote, all key components of the New Deal Coalition.

293. A. The youthful and charismatic Kennedy is widely considered to have won the famous 1960 televised debate.

294. B. Nixon made and kept a promise to visit all 50 states while campaigning. This may have helped him with Alaska but cost him valuable time that might have been better spent in Missouri.

295. True. Kennedy promised to resign if there was a conflict between his Roman Catholic beliefs and being president.

296. True. 1960 had the highest voter turnout of the twentieth century. Nationwide 62.8% of eligible voters voted. In 1988 only 50.1% of eligible voters voted.

297. B. Hawaii was the closest state in 1960. Kennedy carried it by barely more than 100 votes. Generally since then, Hawaii has been decidedly in the Democratic column with the only Republican victories in 1972, and 1984.

298. A. Georgia was one of Kennedy's best states and he defeated Nixon 62% to 37% there.

299. A. Nixon underutilized the highly popular Eisenhower on the campaign trail. Choices B and C are false.

300. True. Eisenhower was among those who suggested that Nixon challenge the election results. As was demonstrated in the aftermath of the 2000 election, challenging election results in presidential elections is difficult.

1956 ELECTION

301. A. No Eisenhower was not seriously challenged in the primaries.

302. False. Although Nixon was fairly popular he was controversial enough that some effort was made to get Eisenhower to drop Nixon. The movement quickly fizzled and Nixon retained his place on the ticket.

303. A. Senator Estes Kefauver of Tennessee finished second to Stevenson in the primaries.

304. B. The Democratic Convention was first for the first time since 1888.

305. C. Without warning the presidential nominee passed on choosing a running mate and left the selection to the convention. As a result, neither the delegates nor the candidates felt well-prepared for this selection process.

306. A. Kennedy nominated Stevenson at the convention.

307. A. Adlai Stevenson served memorably as the ambassador to the U.N. He served in this role during the Cuban Missile Crisis in 1962.

308. B. There was one faithless elector from Alabama who voted for Walter Jones (a local judge) for president and Herman Talmadge for vice president. However, there were no significant third party candidates in 1956. 99.4% of the popular vote went to the two major party candidates.

309. C. Eisenhower won by more than 15% defeating Stevenson 57% to 41% in 1956.

310. A. Eisenhower won more states in 1956 than in 1952. Stevenson gained one state and Eisenhower gained three states.

311. A. Surprisingly the Democrats won Congress in 1956, despite Eisenhower posting a larger victory in 1956 than he had in 1952.

312. C. Stevenson carried Missouri in 1956 after losing it in 1952.

313. B. Stevenson lost Kentucky in 1956, he also lost West Virginia and Louisiana as states that he had carried in 1952 but lost in 1956.

1952 ELECTION

314. B. 1952 was the first time in 24 years that there was not an incumbent president on the ballot.

315. C. Dwight Eisenhower had the slogan "I like Ike".

316. B. No. Estes Kefauver got the most votes but he was not popular with party insiders for his sometimes brash antics in the Senate. Truman had entered the primaries but after losing the first two realized that he was not going to win re-election and abandoned his efforts. His early departure from the race opened the door wider for other candidates.

317. C. Robert Taft was Eisenhower's main rival for the nomination. Taft was opposed by members of the Republican Party because he was seen as being too isolationist and out-of-step on foreign policy.

318. A. Eisenhower won key credentials disputes to open the convention and it gave him enough votes to win the nomination. Taft's party machine tactics looked unsavory on television and helped a stampede toward Eisenhower even though Taft had won more primary victories.

319. B. It took Stevenson three ballots to win the nomination. He was the last nominee of either major party (until 2016 and counting) to take more than one ballot to secure the nomination.

320. True. The Democratic Party instituted loyalty rules to prevent a repeat of 1948 when some electors from the South voted for Strom Thurmond instead of Harry Truman.

321. A. Stevenson was the first genuinely reluctant candidate to be drafted into running for president since Garfield in 1880.

322. False. Prior to running for president, Eisenhower had no experience in elected office.

323. A. Corruption in government was a major issue. Generally the two parties agreed on the issues with the Republicans arguing that they could execute the solutions better than the Democrats. Nixon's famous Checkers speech was a big deal because Democratic corruption in government was a major issue in 1952.

324. A. In 1952 Adlai Stevenson was attacked by ads from Eisenhower that made of fun of Stevenson for wearing a shoe with a hole in the bottom of it. "Don't let this happen to you".

325. C. Eisenhower won big in the popular vote and won by about 11% (55% to 44%).

326. C. Eisenhower won by more than 100 electoral votes (442 to 89). Stevenson needed 177 more electoral votes to reverse the result.

327. B. Most of Stevenson's support came from the South.

328. A. The Democratic Party usually carried Florida in the century than spanned 1852 and 1952.

329. B. Stevenson carried two states (Arkansas and Louisiana) that are found west of the Mississippi

330. True. The Democratic Party had also tried to recruit Eisenhower but he opted to run as a Republican.

1948 ELECTION

331. A. Earl Warren won the most votes for president in the 1948 Republican primaries, almost entirely based on his running virtually opposed in the California Primary.

332. A. Harry Truman received the most votes for president in the 1948 Democratic primaries.

333. C. Robert Taft of Ohio (son of William Taft) was the only Republican candidate that did not poll favorably in a hypothetical match-up with Truman.

334. C. Thomas Dewey won on the third ballot. This was the last contested Republican convention of the twentieth century. Although there were rumblings of a convention contest in 2016, nothing happened and Donald Trump won the nomination on the first ballot.

335. A. Harry Truman won on the first ballot.

336. A. Hubert Humphrey gave a powerful speech in favor of civil rights.

337. C. Dewey was the governor of New York.

338. A. Earl Warren was Dewey's running mate. Earl Warren was then the governor of California and later served as Chief Justice of the United States Supreme Court.

339. A. Senator Alben Barkley was nominated by acclamation to serve as Truman's vice presidential running mate.

340. C. Henry Wallace gave his acceptance speech at Shibe Park (a professional baseball stadium) in front of a crowd of 32,000.

341. C. Lowering the voting age to 18 was proposed by the Progressive Party in 1948 and with the passage of the 26th Amendment, became law in 1971.

342. A. The Department of Culture was proposed as a cabinet-level department by the Progressive Party in 1948. That department has yet to come to fruition.

343. C. 13 states were represented at the convention, but the representation was somewhat haphazard. Georgia, Kentucky, and North Carolina had no representation and the representation from Virginia consisted of four students and one traveler.

344. A. The splinter convention was held in Birmingham, Alabama. The convention was pro-segregation.

345. C. The States' Rights Democrats nominated Strom Thurmond for president in 1948.

346. A. The States' Rights Democrats are best described as a faction of the Democratic Party. They generally operated within existing Democratic Party structures whenever possible.

347. B. After it appeared that Dewey had a large lead, many pollsters stopped polling.

348. B. No, Dewey did not campaign effectively in 1948. He campaigned like he thought he had a large lead and that he was going to win.

349. B. Progressive Party candidate Henry Wallace used an image that showed Wallace with FDR's shadow. Wallace had served as FDR's vice president and later in his cabinet. Truman fired Wallace in 1946. After serving as a magazine editor, Wallace ran for president in 1948.

350. C. Wallace may have cost Truman three states: Maryland, Michigan, and New York.

351. A. Truman won in 1948 because he had a plan for how to win and he effectively executed that plan.

352. B. The popular vote was not that close with Truman defeating Dewey by about 4.5% (49.5% to 45.0%).

353. C. A medium win is the best way to characterize Truman's win in 1948. On the one hand Dewey was 77 electoral votes short of winning and lost the popular vote by 4.5%. On the other hand if Dewey had carried California, Illinois, and Ohio (3 states, worth a total of 78 electoral votes, that Truman won by less than 1% each), Dewey would have won. The election was sort of close and sort of not-close.

354. C. Dewey won no states in the South. His electoral strength was in the Northeast, winning most of the states in that region.

355. A. Harry Truman won Ohio in 1948.

1944 ELECTION

356. True. 1944 marked the first "at war" presidential election since 1864.

357. A. Franklin Roosevelt received the most votes in the 1944 Democratic primaries.

358. A. U.S. Army general, Douglas McArthur, who was not a candidate for president, received the most votes for president in the 1944 Republican primaries.

359. A. Dewey was the first Republican candidate to accept the nomination in person.

360. False. Thomas Dewey's running mate was John Bricker of Ohio. Obviously their first names are different.

361. C. Henry Wallace was dropped from the ticket in favor of Harry Truman.

362. C. Dewey in 1944 was well-funded and spent heavily.

363. C. Franklin Roosevelt won by about 7.5% roughly 53.3%/45.8%.

364. B. Dewey carried the Central Great Plains states such as the Dakotas, Kansas, and Nebraska in 1944.

365. C. In his worst election, Roosevelt still managed to get 432 electoral votes.

366. B. No. Dewey was held to 99 electoral votes in 1944.

367. C. Roosevelt never carried Vermont. Maine is the only other state that he never carried.

1940 ELECTION

368. B. Franklin Roosevelt received the most votes in the 1940 Democratic primaries.

369. B. Thomas Dewey received the highest vote share in the 1940 Republican primaries.

370. True. Roosevelt issued a statement that was read to the delegates that he was not a candidate but that they could vote for anyone. After sitting in stunned silence, the delegates began chanting "We want Roosevelt" and nominated him for a third term.

371. C. Wendell Willkie was a rare presidential nominee who had no political experience and no significant military experience. He had served in the infantry during World War I but had not seen combat.

372. C. Prior to running for president, Willkie had served as an executive with a private utility.

373. True. Henry Wallace was not popular and was reluctantly approved by the convention as Roosevelt's running mate.

374. B. Roosevelt's "court-packing scheme" where he proposed to stack the Supreme Court in his favor under the pretext of helping out elderly justices hurt his popularity. Roosevelt abandoned the idea but it hurt his image.

375. B. Wendell Willkie featured many advertisements with keys. Often the key was used as part of his name.

376. True. In 1940 FDR used the slogan "Willkie for the Millionaires Roosevelt for the Millions".

377. C. Roosevelt won by about 10% in the popular vote (54.7% to 44.7%). This was the closest popular vote margin since 1916.

378. C. The Electoral College result in 1940 was another big win for Roosevelt, he won 449 electoral votes to Willkie's 82. Willkie needed 184 more electoral votes to win.

379. B. Willkie won Iowa. His electoral strength was in the Great Plains and to a lesser extent some of the Great Lakes states.

380. A. Roosevelt won New York. It was worth 47 electoral votes in 1940.

381. B. Franklin Roosevelt was the first candidate to actually win a third term. Grant had actively sought the nomination for a third term in 1876 but had lost to Hayes.

1936 ELECTION

382. B. Franklin Roosevelt received the most votes for president in the 1936 Democratic primaries.

383. C. William Borah won about twice as many votes as the eventual nominee, Alf Landon. The party leadership almost uniformly supported Landon. Borah was 70 years old and his age may have hurt his candidacy.

384. A. In a bit of publicity genius, Franklin Roosevelt accepted his nomination at Franklin Field at the University of Pennsylvania.

385. A. The two-thirds rule for nominating a candidate was abolished in 1936.

386. B. Alf Landon was the governor of Kansas prior to running for president.

387. C. Franklin Roosevelt had served in the Department of the Navy during the Wilson Administration.

388. B. Father Coughlin ran for president as a member of the Union Party. He was a priest with his own radio show and he had a national audience for his populist message.

389. A. Landon aggressively attacked all of the New Deal during the 1936 campaign. Judging by the response of voters this was not a popular argument.

390. C. Landon's campaign was well-funded so his defeat was not due to a lack of money.

391. A. Starting with 1936 the Democratic Party has won a majority of the African American vote. In 1932 Roosevelt won 35% of the black vote. In 1936 he won 70%.

392. A. More than two-thirds of poor voters supported Roosevelt. 1936 marks the year when class became a reliable predictor of voting habits.

393. C. Franklin Roosevelt won a major victory winning the popular vote by a margin of 60.80% to 36.54%. He received more than 10 million more votes than Landon.

394. C. Roosevelt won a big win in the Electoral College in 1936, winning 523 out of a possible 531 electoral votes. 266 electoral votes were needed for victory. It stands as the biggest win by percentage of the electoral vote share in the Electoral College since 1820. Landon needed 258 more electoral votes to win, this is the all-time largest margin of defeat as measured by total electoral votes needed to change the result.

395. C. Roosevelt won 46 out of the 48 states.

396. C. Landon lost New Hampshire by less than 2% of the vote. Otherwise it was not close as Roosevelt generally won the other states by at least 10% of the vote.

1932 ELECTION

397. A. Franklin Roosevelt won the most votes in the Democratic primaries of 1932.

398. A. Herbert Hoover received the most votes in the Republican primaries of 1932.

399. C. Franklin Roosevelt had nominated Alfred Smith three times for the presidency.

400. A. No is the best answer. The 1928 Republican platform praised Hoover and blamed the Depression as being caused by forces outside of Hoover's control.

401. A. No. The Socialist Party candidate for president in 1932 was Norman Thomas.

402. A. 1932 was the best election for the Socialist Party in 20 years.

403. C. One of the slogans used by Franklin Roosevelt in 1932 was "Roosevelt or Ruin".

404. C. Roosevelt smiled on the campaign trail and conveyed optimism that was missing from Hoover who did not smile.

405. C. In a precursor to his popular "Fireside Chats" Roosevelt made effective use of the radio while campaigning for president.

406. C. Despite his physical limitations from polio, Roosevelt campaigned vigorously, traveling more than 23,000 miles, and visiting forty-one states.

407. True. Roosevelt campaigned on a platform that included the repeal of Prohibition and one of the slogans that he used was "Roosevelt and Garner = Beer". When Roosevelt was elected he quickly made good on his promise to repeal Prohibition.

408. C. Roosevelt greatly improved the Democratic Party's showing with urban voters. From the 1870s to the 1930s this demographic had largely been a Republican constituency.

409. C. Roosevelt was elected by an impressive margin, defeating Hoover approximately 57% to 40% in the popular vote.

410. C. Roosevelt scored a big win in the Electoral College in 1932, defeating Hoover 472 to 59. Hoover was 207 electoral votes short of the 266 needed to win.

411. A. Franklin Roosevelt dominated the Western states in the 1932 election.

412. C. Although he did not sweep New England, most of the states won by Hoover were located in New England.

413. A. Roosevelt received approximately 58% of the popular vote in 1932.

1928 ELECTION

414. C. Herbert Hoover won the most votes in the Republican primaries of 1928. Herbert Hoover was the first candidate to spend lots of money on winning the nomination, spending $400,000.

415. A. Al Smith won the most votes for president in the 1928 Democratic primaries.

416. A. Hoover was easily nominated on the first ballot.

417. A. Smith was also easily nominated on the first ballot.

418. A. Houston was the first Southern city to host a major party convention since 1860.

419. B. Hoover's vice presidential running mate, Charles Curtis, was of mixed Native American and white ancestry. Curtis downplayed his heritage but in a different era it would have been looked at as a diversity milestone.

420. C. Joseph Robinson was the first Southerner on a major party ticket since the Civil War.

421. B. A major figure in the Democratic Party for decades, William Jennings Bryan had passed away shortly after the famous "Scopes Monkey Trial" in 1926.

422. C. Although Hoover would be on the losing side of such a result in 1932, in 1928 he was on the winning side as he defeated Smith by a margin of about 58% to 41% in the popular vote.

423. C. The Electoral College vote result was a big win for Hoover in 1928, defeating Smith 444 to 87. Smith needed 179 more electoral votes to get to the winning number of 266.

424. B. All of Hoover's losses came in the South.

425. A. Smith won Alabama 51% to 48%, all of his other wins in the South were by comfortable or very comfortable margins.

1924 ELECTION

426. A. Calvin Coolidge won the most votes in the 1924 Republican presidential primaries.

427. C. William McAdoo won the most votes in the 1924 Democratic presidential primaries.

428. A. Calvin Coolidge was easily nominated for president in 1924.

429. C. In stark contrast to the Republican Convention, the Democratic Convention was locked into a bitter struggle between the urban and rural factions of the party. It took 103 ballots to select a nominee, John W. Davis of West Virginia. The two factions also feuded about the party platform.

430. B. The controversial League of Nations and whether or not the United States should support it was also debated at the 1924 conventions.

431. C. 1924 marked the first live radio broadcast from a convention.

432. C. Coolidge beat Davis by barely more than 15%, making D the best answer. (54.03% to 28.82%)

433. C. Third party candidate Robert La Follette received close to 17% of the vote (16.67%).

434. B. The Progressive Party favored the nationalization of certain industries.

435. True. In 1924, the Socialist Party endorsed Progressive Party candidate Robert La Follette.

436. C. Coolidge scored a big win in the Electoral College in 1924, winning 382 to 136 to 13. Davis needed 130 of Coolidge's 382 electoral votes in order to change the election result.

437. A. Davis generally only won states of the former Confederacy. He also carried Oklahoma.

438. C. Coolidge did very well in Vermont, winning the popular vote 78% to 15%.

439. B. Keep Cool with Coolidge was Coolidge's slogan in 1924.

440. C. Robert La Follette won his home state of Wisconsin.

1920 ELECTION

441. A. Hiram Johnson won the most votes for president in the 1920 Republican primaries.

442. C. Unpledged delegates won the most votes for president in the 1920 Democratic primaries.

443. True. There was no clear front runner when the Republican Convention convened.

444. B. Harding won on the 10th ballot after backroom deals were made. Harding was viewed as a good compromise or unity candidate.

445. True. There was no clear front runner when the Democratic Convention convened.

446. C. The 1920 Democratic Convention was held in San Francisco. It was the first major party convention to be held west of the Rockies.

447. B. Cox was leading and then he was trailing. He came back to win on the 44th ballot.

448. True. Calvin Coolidge and Franklin Roosevelt would both go on to win election to the presidency.

449. C. When Eugene Debs received his fifth nomination to run for president he was currently serving time in federal prison relating to his protesting World War I. Debs was later pardoned.

450. C. Although seeking legal protections for migrant workers and recognition of the U.S.S.R., the Socialist Party did not seek tax cuts for factory owners.

451. A. Eugene Debs had campaign buttons endorsing "For President Convict No. 9653" and featuring pictures of Debs in prison garb.

452. C. Harding had an impressive in the popular vote, winning 60.35% to 34.12%. Harding was the first candidate since the popular vote began to be tallied in 1824 to win 60% of the popular vote.

453. C. Harding won a big win in the Electoral College in 1920, winning 404 to 127. Cox needed 139 more electoral votes to win.

454. False. Harding won the White House and the Republicans captured large margins in Congress.

455. C. The Republican, Warren Harding, edged out a 51% to 48% win in Tennessee. Four years later it was won by the Democratic candidate, John Davis.

456. A. Of the choices, California is the best answer. Harding received 66% of the popular vote there. California was not his best state. He received more than 70% of the vote in Iowa, Minnesota, North Dakota, and Vermont.

457. C. Harding was the first candidate since 1824, when the popular vote began to be counted, to win 60% of the popular vote.

458. A. With the passage of the Nineteenth Amendment women could vote in presidential elections for the first time in 1920.

459. C. Franklin Roosevelt lost as a vice presidential candidate in 1920.

1916 ELECTION

460. C. Woodrow Wilson won the most votes in the 1916 Democratic Primaries. He ran virtually unopposed.

461. C. Unpledged delegates won the most votes for president in the 1916 Republican primaries.

462. C. William J. Bryan gave the keynote speech at the 1916 Democratic Convention.

463. B. Warren Harding chaired the 1916 Republican Convention.

464. False. The 1916 Democratic Convention was marked by the calm that usually prevails when an incumbent president is seeking re-election.

465. B. Charles Hughes served as a member of the Supreme Court. He resigned and ran for president. He was later reappointed to the Supreme Court. Hughes was not a very dynamic candidate but he had the full support of both the liberal and conservative wings of the Republican Party.

466. True. Both members of the Republican ticket had the first name of Charles.

467. True. The tariff disappeared as an issue in 1916 after being an enduring issue for decades. The legalization of the income tax with the passage of the Sixteenth Amendment in 1913 was a major reason for the import tariff disappearing as a political issue.

468. C. Wilson's support for women's voting rights helped him win in the West.

469. A. As might be expected from someone of his intelligence, Wilson made very good tactical and strategic decisions about where to campaign in 1916 and focused heavily on the "swing states" like Ohio. He conceded that he would lose Illinois early and focused on other states.

470. B. Eugene Debs did not use the slogan "America First" in 1916. Both Hughes and Wilson used that slogan or a close variation of it in 1916. Wilson: "America First" and Hughes: "American First and Efficient".

471. B. Wilson won the popular vote by about 3% in 1916, 49% to 46%.

472. A. 1916 was one of the closest elections of the twentieth century and is best characterized as a small win. Wilson won 277 to 254. (266 electoral votes needed to win). Hughes needed 12 more electoral votes to win.

473. C. Due to the direct election of electors, there was a split electoral vote in West Virginia. Eight Republican electors won election and one Democratic elector won. This was the last time that a state split electoral votes based on the outcome of voting for individual electors.

474. C. Wilson won the South and the West. Hughes won the Midwest and New England.

475. A. California's 13 electoral votes would have changed the outcome of the election. Alternatively if Hughes had received 16,500 more votes in Washington (7) and 2,000 more votes in North Dakota (5), he also would have won the election. As stated in the question, the other states that were worth 12 or more electoral votes that Wilson won were probably out of reach for Hughes as Wilson generally won these by at least 10% of the popular vote. Most of these states were located in the South.

1912 ELECTION

476. C. Woodrow Wilson won the most votes in the 1912 Democratic primaries.

477. A. Roosevelt won the most votes in the 1912 Republican Primaries.

478. A. Wilson is the first and so far the only president to have a Ph.D. Several presidents have had law degrees. No medical doctors have been elected president. Medical school drop-out William Harrison was elected president in 1840. Medical doctor Howard Dean unsuccessfully sought the Democratic Party nomination in 2004.

479. B. The Socialist Party Platform in 1912 included support for a minimum wage.

480. B. James "Champ" Clark was Wilson's major rival for the nomination.

481. C. It took Wilson 46 ballots to win the nomination. This is the 20th century record for most ballots to nominate a candidate who later went on to win the election.

482. True. The 1912 Democratic Platform included support for a graduated income tax.

483. C. The 1912 Republican Convention was a tumultuous one with noisy feuding between the Taft and Roosevelt supporters.

484. C. In a performance art display of poor sportsmanship, the Roosevelt supporters made loud noises with sandpaper and horns to protest Taft winning the procedural vote that effectively guaranteed him the nomination.

485. B. There were no delegates from South Carolina present at the 1912 Progressive Party convention.

486. B. The Progressive Party nominated Teddy Roosevelt for president.

487. B. Theodore Roosevelt ran in 1912 with a slogan calling for "social and industrial justice".

488. C. As measured by margin of victory, Wilson had a big win in the popular vote getting about 14.5% more of the popular vote than his next closest competitor. Wilson received 41.8% to Roosevelt's 27.4% to Taft's 23.2% to Debs's 6.0%.

489. C. Whatever is said about the popular vote, Wilson scored a decisive win in the Electoral College, winning 435 to 88 to 8. Roosevelt would have needed 178 from Wilson in order to win. Although the record would not last long, Wilson's win in 1912 set a record for greatest margin of victory by number of Electoral College votes.

490. B. No the Democratic Party controlled Congress in the 63rd Congress. The Democratic Party gained control of the Senate in the Election of 1912 and gained seats in the House.

491. A. Although competitive in many states in the Mountain West and in New England, Taft only won Vermont and Utah.

492. B. New states Arizona and New Mexico participated in their first presidential election in 1912.

493. B. Roosevelt's 88 electoral votes are the most by a third party candidate in a single election.

494. C. Wilson was the first candidate to win more than 40 states and more than 400 electoral votes in a single election.

1908 ELECTION

495. True. In 1908, the Socialist Party nominated Eugene Debs for president.

496. B. Ending child labor was an idea first advocated by the Socialist Party.

497. A. William Taft won on the first ballot in 1908.

498. False. The Republican Platform of 1908 was basically the same platform as in 1904.

499. A. The 1908 Democratic convention was in Denver. It was the first major party convention to be held in a Western state.

500. A. William Bryan won easily on the first ballot.

501. True. The major differences between the Democratic and Republican parties in 1908 revolved around foreign policy and foreign trade. The Republicans favored expansionism and protectionism whereas the Democratic Party was more isolationist yet more in favor of free trade.

502. C. Taft secured a big win in the popular vote in 1908. He defeated Bryan 52% to 43%.

503. C. Taft secured a big win in the Electoral College, defeating Bryan 321 to 162. Bryan needed 80 more electoral votes to get to the minimum number needed for a win.

504. C. 1908 was the first year that Oklahoma voted in presidential elections.

505. A. Taft generally won the North.

1904 ELECTION

506. A. Eugene Debs made his first run for president in 1904.

507. B. Theodore Roosevelt was personally conservative but as president he often supported liberal policies. He was what might be described today as a "big government conservative".

508. B. The most contentious issue at the 1904 Republican Convention was whether Hawaii territory had six votes or two votes.

509. C. A telegram about a military rescue mission in Morocco was read to the delegates after the platform had been adopted. The telegram was read with the purpose of getting the delegates excited and it was successful in that purpose.

510. B. Newspaper publisher William Hearst was Alton Parker's major rival for the Democratic Party nomination.

511. B. At 80 years old Henry Davis was the oldest vice presidential nominee of a major party.

512. A. The Democratic Party was opposed to federal subsidies for American shipping firms. The Republican Party supported such subsidies.

513. C. Teddy Roosevelt won a landslide of the popular vote, drawing 56.4% to Parker's 37.6%.

514. C. Teddy Roosevelt won a landslide in the electoral college as well, 336 to 140. Parker needed 99 more electoral votes to win.

515. B. Generally speaking, Parker's wins were confined to the South.

516. B. Roosevelt carried New York.

517. C. Roosevelt was the first candidate to win more than 30 states.

1900 ELECTION

518. A. William McKinley was nominated on the first ballot.

519. A. William J. Bryan was nominated on the first ballot.

520. True. Both McKinley and Bryan ran unopposed for the nomination. This made it easy to win on the first ballot.

521. A. In 1900 the Democratic Party first proposed creating a Department of Labor.

522. A. Teddy Roosevelt won the vice presidential nomination on the first ballot.

523. A. Adlai Stevenson won the Democratic Party nomination for vice president. Adlai Stevenson was the grandfather of 1950s Democratic presidential candidate Adlai Stevenson.

524. False. The Democratic Party favored a route through present-day Nicaragua, and the Republican Party favored a route through present-day Panama.

525. B. McKinley won the popular vote by about 6% (52% to 46%).

526. C. McKinley won big over Bryan by an Electoral College score of 292 to 155 (224 needed to win). Bryan needed 69 more electoral votes to win.

527. B. Favorite son, William J. Bryan, failed to carry his home state of Nebraska in 1900. Bryan underperformed with farmers in 1900. 1900 was a more prosperous year for farmers and they may have hurt his message.

528. A. Populous New York was Eugene Debs best state in 1900 in terms of total votes won.

529. B. McKinley was the first candidate to win more than 290 electoral votes.

1896 ELECTION

530. A. William McKinley won the nomination of the first ballot.

531. C. William Jennings Bryan won the nomination on the fifth ballot.

532. A. Bryan's famous "Cross of Gold" speech during the debate on currency raised his standing among the delegates and propelled him to the nomination.

533. B. Long associated with banking interests, the Republican Party favored a gold standard. This policy favors lenders over debtors. The 1896 shift of the Democratic platform away from the gold standard angered conservative Democrats, and some subsequently withheld support for the populist Bryan.

534. B. The Republican Party Platform took at strong stand against lynching in 1896.

535. A. In 1896 the Democratic Party Platform favored presidential term limits of two terms.

536. B. William McKinley was from Ohio.

537. A. William J. Bryan was from Nebraska.

538. C. In 1896 the Republican Party had more strength in urban areas. McKinley won urban areas in the South and West even while losing some of those states to Bryan.

539. C. Bryan tried to get the support of labor but failed. His efforts may have helped lay the groundwork for future success. By the 1930s, labor had become an important Democratic Party constituency.

540. True. By 1896 the end of Reconstruction had clearly taken hold in voting patterns with the Republican being stronger in the North and Democrats being stronger in the South.

541. B. The Election of 1896 featured gold or silver beetle-shaped lapel pins. Gold beetles supported McKinley.

542. A. The Election of 1896 featured gold or silver beetle-shaped lapel pins. Silver beetles supported William Jennings Bryan.

543. B. William Jennings Bryan had a clock showing the time 12:44. That time cloud be said as "sixteen minutes to one". Bryan advocated the coinage of silver in the ratio of 16 to 1. In 1908 when Bryan ran against Taft, Taft ran an ad calling Bryan "the Nebraska cuckcoo clock – will run every four years if properly wound".

544. A. William McKinley won the popular vote by about 4% (51% to 47%).

545. B. William McKinley won a medium size victory in the Electoral College winning by a score of 271 to 176. 224 votes were needed to win, so Bryan was 48 electoral votes short.

546. A. McKinley and Bryan split the electoral votes of California and Kentucky in 1896.

547. C. 1896 was the first year that Utah participated in presidential elections.

1892 ELECTION

548. B. The 1892 Republican Convention was held in Minneapolis, Minnesota.

549. A. Future president William McKinley was chair of the convention. An active convention presence has helped many on the path to the White House.

550. A. Not surprisingly, sitting president, Benjamin Harrison was nominated on the first ballot.

551. A. The 1892 Democratic Convention was held in Chicago, Illinois.

552. A. The hall used for the 1892 Democratic Convention had a very leaky roof that caused problems during the convention.

553. A. Despite some resistance to his candidacy, Grover Cleveland prevailed on the first ballot in 1892.

554. A. Both Harrison and Cleveland had reputations for honesty.

555. B. The Republican Party favored prohibition. The Democratic Party was always opposed to prohibition.

556. B. For the 1892 election, Michigan awarded electoral votes by congressional district with the result in a 9 to 5 split of electoral votes in the state. (This move was designed to aid Democrat Cleveland, otherwise all 14 votes would have gone to Harrison). Before the 1896 election, Michigan switched back to a winner-take-all method of awarding electoral votes.

557. False. Third party candidates did fairly well in 1892, getting about 10% of the vote. With both the Democrats and Republicans being overtly pro-business at this time, there was an opening for more populist parties.

558. A. Adlai Stevenson was the grandfather of future presidential candidate Adlai Stevenson.

559. A. The corrupt bosses of Tammany Hall were opposed to Grover Cleveland.

560. A. The goose was the symbol of the Populist Party in the 1890s.

561. B. The popular vote split 46.1% to 43.0% with Populist candidate James Weaver getting 8.5%, and John Bidwell of the Prohibition Party getting 2.2%

562. C. Cleveland scored a big win in the rematch with Harrison, notching a 277 to 145 to 22 win. 223 electoral votes was the minimum number needed to win, so Harrison was 78 votes short.

563. C. Six new states voted in the 1892 election for the first time. (North Dakota, South Dakota, Montana, Idaho, Wyoming, and Washington).

564. A. North Dakota had three electoral votes in 1892, and the Democratic and Populists electors ran together under a fusion ticket. Two fusion electors and one Republican elector won. One fusion elector voted for the Democrat, one voted for the Populist and the Republican elector voted for the Republican. The result was a three-way split.

565. True. Harrison became the first sitting president to lose an election to an ex-president.

1888 ELECTION

566. True. Incumbent president Grover Cleveland ran unopposed for the Democratic Party nomination.

567. B. It took four days to conduct eight ballots including taking Sunday off from balloting.

568. A. Allen Thurman was 75 years old.

569. A. Allen Thurman's symbol was a red bandana.

570. A. The Democratic Party favored a reduction in the import tariff in 1888.

571. B. The Prohibition Party was also opposed to polygamy.

572. B. A core constituency of the Republican Party in 1888 was Civil War veterans and the Republican Party supported pensions for veterans.

573. A. The popular vote in 1888 was very close with the winning candidate actually losing the popular vote by slightly less than one percentage point. (47.8% to 48.6%)

574. B. The election of 1888 was a close one in the Electoral College, with a single state deciding the outcome of the election. Harrison won 233 to 168. 201 electoral votes were needed to win so Cleveland needed 33 more votes to win. New York with 36 electoral votes would have provided that margin. Harrison won New York by less than 15,000 votes.

575. B. Harrison flipped Indiana and New York to win the election.

1884 ELECTION

576. A. The first African American to be elected as a temporary chair of a major party convention, John Lynch, was elected in 1884.

577. B. Grover Cleveland won on the second ballot.

578. C. Grover Cleveland was the first urban progressive candidate. He supported programs to use government power to help the poor get a better education.

579. B. James Blaine was from Maine. Blaine was known as the "plumed knight".

580. A. For whatever reason the two respective major party platforms were fairly similar. Both were expansionist and pro-business.

581. A. 1884 was a close election. The candidates were less than a percentage point apart in the popular vote 48.5% to 48.2%.

582. A. The electoral vote was close in 1884 with just a single state deciding the election. Cleveland won 219 to 182 (201 votes to win). If Blaine had won 19 more electoral votes he would have won.

583. True. Blaine insulted party boss Roscoe Conkling by comparing him to a strutting turkey; he failed to disavow an anti-Catholic remark spoken in his (Blaine's) presence at a campaign event; and he attended a millionaire's dinner which was contrary to his image.

584. A. Cleveland won New York (and with it the presidency) by less than 2,000 votes.

585. A. Although he never won the state by more than 6,000 votes in a given election, Cleveland carried Connecticut in all three of his campaigns for president.

1880 ELECTION

586. True. Ulysses Grant did seek to run for president in 1880. His candidacy had little support.

587. A. No. In a rare occurrence, Garfield did not run for president but was drafted by the convention. He was a compromise candidate that Republicans could unite behind.

588. C. Garfield won the nomination after 35 ballots. Garfield is the record holder for most ballots taken to secure the Republican Party nomination.

589. A. It only took two days to cast the 35 ballots necessary to determine the nominee.

590. A. Chester Arthur was put on the Republican ticket to help win New York.

591. B. Previously the Republican Conventions had been open to all, 1880 was the first year that only Republicans could participate.

592. B. Although in the 21st Century the Democratic Party is known as a strong supporter of the federal government, in the latter half of the 19th and first part of the 20th century it was a supporter of states' rights.

593. A. Winfield Hancock won the nomination on the second ballot.

594. A. In addition to two very similar candidates, the two parties had fairly similar platforms other than that the Democrats were (understandably) bitter about the 1876 election and the Republicans were not.

595. B. The Greenback Party favored an inflationary monetary policy. Such a policy favored small farmers and debtors at the expense of big banks.

596. A. The popular vote in 1880 was a virtual tie at 48.3% to 48.3%. Both candidates received 4.44 million votes. Garfield only won the popular vote by about 20,000 votes nationwide.

597. B. The election of 1880 was a close one. 214 to 155 was the score with 185 needed to win. Hancock needed 30 more electoral votes to win.

598. A. New York was decided by about 21,000 votes.

1876 ELECTION

599. A. Frederick Douglas spoke at the 1876 Republican Convention.

600. C. Tories was not the name of one of the three factions of the Republican Party in 1876.

601. B. An electrical power failure interrupted the speech nominating James Blaine.

602. B. Rutherford Hayes won the nomination of the seventh ballot.

603. C. The 1876 Democratic Convention took place in St. Louis. It was the first major party convention to be held west of the Mississippi River.

604. A. Samuel Tilden won the nomination on the second ballot.

605. True. Samuel Tilden was a reformer known for fighting political corruption.

606. B. Samuel Tilden won the popular vote 51% to 48% but he lost the Electoral College. His 51% is the highest share of the popular vote achieved by a non-winning candidate.

607. A. Hayes won the closest decision since 1824. He won 185 to 184 with 185 being the minimum number needed to win. If Tilden had gotten one more vote the result would have flipped.

608. B. The election returns in Florida, Louisiana, Oregon, and South Carolina were disputed in 1876. All four states sent two sets of results to Congress, one claiming that Hayes had won the state and the other that Tilden had prevailed.

609. C. In four separate, partisan, 8 to 7 decisions, the 15 member commission awarded all four of the disputed states to Hayes, resulting in his 185 to 184 victory in the Electoral College. The 15 member commission had five members each from the U.S. House of Representatives, the U.S. Senate, and the U.S. Supreme Court.

610. A. Hayes agreed to end Reconstruction and the federal occupation in exchange for the Southern states' promises to respect the rights of African Americans. The states did not live up to their end of the bargain.

1872 ELECTION

611. False. Grant was nominated again for president but he was not challenged for the nomination.

612. A. The 1872 Republican Party Platform strengthened its position on civil rights.

613. B. A major issue that brought together the Liberal Republican Party was corruption in the Grant Administration.

614. B. The Credit Mobilier scandal tarnished Grant's re-election bid. It cost vice president Schuyler Colfax his spot on the ticket. Colfax was replaced by Henry Wilson.

615. A. It took six ballots for Horace Greeley to win the Liberal Republican nomination.

616. True. In 1872 the Democratic Party did not run its own candidate but endorsed the Liberal Republican candidate, Horace Greeley.

617. B. No, Greeley was not able to capitalize on the scandal that cost Grant his first vice president. Grant was re-elected by a larger margin in 1872 than his initial victory in 1868.

618. B. Ulysses Grant had campaign literature referring to him as the "Galena Tanner" to emphasize his working class ties.

619. B. Grant defeated Greeley 56% to 44% in the popular vote.

620. C. Grant won big in the Electoral College, gaining 286 electoral votes and holding Greeley to less than 85. Greeley needed to win about 115 more electoral votes to win. Grant's win in 1872 was one of the most lopsided wins in the Electoral College in the 19th century.

621. C. Two states had balloting issues due to Reconstruction and the votes from Arkansas and Louisiana were not counted.

622. A. The most allegations of voting irregularities came from Southern states undergoing reconstruction.

623. A. Greeley died before the electoral votes were counted and most of his votes went to Thomas Hendricks, governor-elect of Indiana. Hendricks would later serve as Cleveland's vice president. Greeley's death did not change the result that Grant had won an overwhelming victory.

1868 ELECTION

624. True. The former confederate states were represented at both major party conventions.

625. A. Ulysses Grant was the only Republican candidate for president at the Republican Convention in 1868. Earlier in the year a convention of soldiers and sailors had nominated him for president.

626. C. Eleven candidates received at least one vote for vice president at the Republican Convention.

627. B. In an odd contradiction, the 1868 Republican Platform only sought voting rights for former slaves in the South but not in the North. This weak stance on civil rights would be corrected in the 1872 platform.

628. True. The Democratic Party voted in 1868 to renew the two-thirds rule. In 1912 this rule would impact who the Democratic Party nominated for president. James "Champ" Clark would get a majority but not two-thirds, without the two-thirds rule, Clark would have been the nominee in 1912 instead of eventual nominee Woodrow Wilson.

629. True. The Democratic Party sought Grant much the same way that Eisenhower would be sought about 85 years later.

630. B. To break the deadlock, the chair of the convention, Horatio Seymour, was reluctantly nominated in 1868.

631. A. Ulysses Grant won the popular vote 53% to 47%.

632. True. New black voters voted for Grant in significant numbers that helped him win the popular vote. Several former Confederacy states narrowly voted Republican in 1868 and black voters may have helped tip those states into the Republican column.

633. C. Ulysses Grant won a big win in the Electoral College, 214 to 80. Horatio Seymour needed to flip about 70 electoral votes to change the outcome of the election.

634. A. Three states did not vote in the 1868 presidential election due to the Reconstruction, Mississippi, Texas, and Virginia.

635. C. Nebraska voted for the first time in 1868.

1864 ELECTION

636. True, The Republicans invited Democrats to the 1864 Republican Convention.

637. C. Delegates from Tennessee and South Carolina were allowed to vote at the 1864 Republican Convention.

638. A. Lincoln let the convention choose his vice president in 1864. The move was to promote unity and the convention picked Lincoln's preferred candidate, Andrew Johnson.

639. False. There were no delegates from the Confederate States at the Democratic Convention.

640. True. George McClellan and George Pendleton were the Democratic Party candidates for president and vice president. In 1916 the Republicans accomplished the same name feat by nominating a ticket with two men named Charles.

641. B. The Republican Party supported unconditional surrender as a term for ending the Civil War.

642. B. Lincoln won big in the popular vote, winning 55% to 45%.

643. C. Without the confederate states supporting the Democratic candidate, Lincoln won the largest victory in the Electoral College (by percent of the vote) since Monroe. Lincoln won 212 to 21, capturing more than 90% of the electoral vote. McClellan needed to win about 100 more electoral votes to flip the election result by getting to the 118 electoral votes needed for victory in 1864.

644. A. McClellan only carried three states although he narrowly lost New York and Pennsylvania.

645. B. Yes, Lincoln carried Maryland in 1864. He won the state 55% to 44%, winning by roughly 8,000 votes.

646. C. Three new states (West Virginia, Kansas and Nevada) voted for the first time in 1864.

647. C. Both Louisiana and Tennessee were under federal occupation by the Election of 1864 but neither state participated in that election.

648. B. The Election of 1864 marked the first time that a man fired by a president ran against his former boss. So far Chester Arthur is the only man to have been fired by a president to become president. Chester Arthur was fired for corruption by President Hayes from Arthur's federal post overseeing the New York Harbor. Arthur was later Garfield's vice president and became president when Garfield was assassinated by a deranged man. Despite his past, Chester Arthur ran an upright administration that was remarkably corruption-free. Henry Wallace, fired as Truman's Secretary of Commerce in 1946, ran against Truman in 1948 as the Progressive Party candidate. In another case of a man fired by a president later seeking to become president, Gen. Douglas McArthur, fired by Truman, unsuccessfully sought the nomination in 1952.

1860 ELECTION

649. B. The Democratic Convention was held in Charleston, South Carolina.

650. A. Part two of the Democratic Convention was held more than one month later, in Baltimore, Maryland.

651. C. Stephen Douglas was finally selected as the nominee.

652. A. The strongly pro-slavery faction of the Democratic Party, the Southern Democrats, nominated John Breckenridge.

653. A. The Constitutional Union Party ran with a goal of trying to preserve the Union.

654. C. At the time of the Civil War, immigration was not a major issue (it had been before, and it would be again). To the extent that immigration was an issue both parties supported unlimited immigration.

655. True. Both the Democrats and the Republicans favored federal subsidies for a transcontinental railroad.

656. B. Only the Republican Party supported federal spending for harbor improvements, the Democratic Party was opposed.

657. B. The Republicans campaigned with the promise of the Homestead Act and "vote yourself a home". The Homestead Act granted large parcels of land in exchange for the promise to work those lands for a few years. The Homestead Act promoted westward expansion.

658. True. Lincoln used slavery as a wedge issue to split the Democrats. Lincoln campaigned against slavery in a way that would appeal to poor whites. Later Lincoln would free slaves and become known as the Great Emancipator.

659. A. Abraham Lincoln gave out a rail splitters badge to supporters. The badge was equivalent to a modern campaign button. It showed that the wearer supported Lincoln.

660. C. Lincoln benefitted from the split in the Democratic Party and drew the largest plurality of the vote, winning 40% to 30% (Southern Democrats) to 18% (Democrats) to 12% (Constitutional Unionists).

661. C. Lincoln won 180 to 72 to 39 to 12 (152 needed to win). His opponents needed to win 29 electoral votes that Lincoln instead won to deny Lincoln an outright win and send the election to the House of Representatives. The Democratic Party controlled Congress at the time and likely would have chosen someone other than Lincoln. Lincoln's divided opposition helped him win California, Indiana, Illinois, and Oregon (worth a total of 31 electoral votes). California, Indiana, and Illinois had been won by the Democrats in 1856.

662. C. Two new states participated in 1860 (Oregon and Minnesota).

663. B. Breckenridge received the second highest electoral vote total, carrying 9 future confederate states and winning 72 electoral votes.

664. A. Lincoln won the election despite only receiving about 40% of the popular vote.

665. B. Douglas was on the ballot in 32 of 33 states. (At this time South Carolina's legislature still chose presidential electors rather than the voters. South Carolina switched methods after the Civil War). Breckenridge and Bell were not on the ballot in New Jersey, New York and Rhode Island. Lincoln was not on the ballot in Alabama, Arkansas, Florida, Georgia, Louisiana, Mississippi, North Carolina, Tennessee, and Texas. Generally in the North Douglas ran against Lincoln, Breckenridge, and Bell and in the South he ran against Breckenridge, and Bell but not Lincoln. This contributed to Douglas getting 30% of the popular vote but only winning 12 electoral votes. (Missouri and part of New Jersey)

1856 ELECTION

666. C. The first national Republican Convention was held in Philadelphia.

667. A. A simple majority was required to win the nomination at the Republican Convention.

668. B. Opposition to slavery was the issue that unified the Republican Party.

669. A. The Whig American Party was unified by its members' opposition to immigration.

670. C. Former president, Millard Fillmore, was the candidate of the Know Nothing Party.

671. C. James Buchanan won the nomination on the 17th ballot.

672. A. In 1856 the Democratic Party supported an expansionist foreign policy.

673. C. Buchan won by about 12% in a three-way race 45% to 33% to 22%.

674. B. Buchan won a three-way race 174 to 114 to 8 (149 to win). Fremont needed to take 34 electoral votes from Buchanan to change the result.

675. A. Buchanan won California with a plurality of the vote in 1856 (48% to 19% to 33%).

676. B. New England is the best answer, Fremont also won some of the states that border the Great Lakes but his best region was New England. This reflected the Republicans "Northern Strategy" in 1856 that concentrated on sweeping the North in order to win. Although the strategy failed in 1856, it worked in 1860.

677. B. Fillmore carried Maryland in 1856.

1852 ELECTION

678. True. The first permanent chairman of the Democratic National Committee was selected in 1852. (Benjamin F. Hallett of Massachusetts was selected).

679. B. Each state delegation was limited based on the number of electoral votes that each given state possessed.

680. False. Another member of the fairly short list of people who became president (or major party presidential nominee) without really trying is Franklin Pierce. Franklin Pierce, Horatio Seymour, James Garfield, and Adlai Stevenson were all genuinely reluctant nominees who got "drafted" into the role at their respective conventions. All were seen as compromise candidates that could unite the party.

681. A. The 49 ballots were conducted efficiently and the balloting only took two days.

682. C. Winfield Scott won the nomination on the 53rd ballot.

683. True. The Whig Party had difficulty finding a willing vice presidential candidate in 1852 and the eventual selection was declared to be unanimous without an actual vote.

684. True. The anti-slavery Free Soil Party opposed the Compromise of 1850.

685. B. The Whig Party favored greater spending on internal improvements that might only benefit a few states.

686. False. In 1852 both the Whig and Democratic Parties still supported the Compromise of 1850.

687. B. Pierce beat Scott by a margin of 6.9% in the popular vote 50.8% to 43.9%. John Hale of the Free Soil Party got 4.9% of the popular vote.

688. C. Pierce won big in the Electoral College in 1852. He won 254 to 42 to 0 (149 to win). Scott needed to win more than 100 additional electoral votes to change the outcome of the election.

689. A. New York was the biggest electoral prize in 1852 with 35 electoral votes. The next largest state was Pennsylvania with 27 electoral votes.

690. C. California had only 4 electoral votes in 1852. By 1940 it would have 22 electoral votes.

691. C. Scott won only 4 states in 1852 (Kentucky, Tennessee, Vermont and Massachusetts).

1848 ELECTION

692. C. New York had two rival groups present at the 1848 Democratic Convention and neither delegation ended up voting. One group left and other refused to vote as a protest.

693. A. James Buchanan was Lewis Cass's main rival for the nomination.

694. B. In 1848 the Democratic Party position on slavery had not yet hardened and it supported allowing individual states and territories to choose whether they allowed slavery. The Democrats had more room within their party than the Whigs to compromise on slavery.

695. A. The Democrats had a stronger and more cohesive base than the Whigs. The Democratic base was supported by agrarian, populist-leaning voters.

696. True. In 1848 Texas let Louisiana vote on behalf of Texas at the Whig Convention.

697. B. Democrat John Calhoun was not a major rival to Zachary Taylor in Taylor's attempts to secure the Whig Party nomination.

698. B. The Whig Party did not have an official platform in 1848. The Whigs were divided over slavery and attempted to bridge or at least minimize those differences by not having an official platform. The Whigs had more hardcore abolitionists than the Democrats and were hurt politically sooner than the Democrats by the slavery issue. The Whigs were unable to confront the issue of slavery and it eventually destroyed them.

699. B. The Free Soil Party nominated former president Martin Van Buren.

700. B. The Free Soil Party was also in favor of cheap postage.

701. B. Taylor won the popular vote by about 4% (47% to 43% to 10%)

702. A. The election of 1848 was a close one with Taylor winning 163 to 127 to 0 (146 needed to win).

703. B. Taylor won Pennsylvania by about 18,000 votes. Van Buren received about 11,000 votes in Pennsylvania.

704. C. Free Soil Party candidate, former Democratic president, New Yorker, Martin Van Buren received 120,000 votes in New York, a state won by Taylor by about 100,000 votes. Had Cass been able to win New York instead of Taylor, Cass would have won the election.

705. B. Two new states participated in presidential elections for the first time (Florida and Texas).

706. A. Taylor carried most of the states that bordered the ocean. Cass did better with interior states.

1844 ELECTION

707. True. Both the Whig and Democratic Party Platforms could have fit onto their own postcard in 1844. The Whig Platform was less than 100 words long.

708. A. The Whig Party wanted to remit the revenue to the states that came from the sale of federal lands.

709. A. The main focus of the Liberty Party was the abolition of slavery.

710. A. Henry Clay was the Whig nominee for president in 1844.

711. B. James Polk was the Democratic nominee for president in 1844.

712. C. The convention nominee telegraphed his refusal to serve as vice president and so James Polk chose his own running mate.

713. A. The annexation of Texas and Oregon proved to be a significant campaign issue.

714. A. Henry Clay attempted to appear folksier by using a folksy raccoon character in 1844. By this time Clay had already served in the Kentucky Legislature, as Speaker of the U.S. House of Representatives, as Secretary of State, and in the U.S. Senate. There may have been a limit to how folksy he could become.

715. A. Polk won the popular vote 50% to 48%. (The Liberty Party candidate got 2%).

716. A. Polk won a close victory in the Electoral College 170 to 105 (138 to win). Clay needed to win 33 more electoral votes to change the outcome.

717. B. The largest margin of victory in any given state was less than 15,000 votes. (For comparison in 1840 the largest margin of victory was more than 25,000 votes and in 1848 it was more 98,000 votes).

718. True. New York was only won by Polk by about 5,000 votes out of 485,000. The Liberty Party candidate received more than 15,000 votes. It is possible that if the Liberty Party candidate, James Birney, were not in the race that Clay would have won New York and with it the presidency.

719. A. Looking at the map of the 1844 election results there is not much of a pattern. As might be expected with such close margins in the popular vote in each state, the candidates generally split the states in a given region.

1840 ELECTION

720. False. There was no Whig Party Platform in 1840.

721. True. Secret ballot rules made it possible for people to vote for the less distinguished Harrison without any social stigma.

722. False. In 1840 the Democratic Party Platform favored limited government and was pro-slavery.

723. B. The popular vote was not that close with Harrison defeating Van Buren 53% to 47%.

724. C. Harrison won big in the Electoral College in 1840. He won 234 to 60 (148 needed to win). Van Buren needed 88 more electoral votes to change the result.

725. A. There is not an obvious pattern to the 1840 map. Most states were fairly close as the candidates were competitive with each other in all of the states. Most states had a genuine two party system.

726. A. No new states participated in the 1840 election.

727. B. William Harrison had the slogan "Tippecanoe and Tyler Too".

728. True. William Harrison's "Log Cabin and Hard Cider" campaign captivated the imagination of the electorate. Well into the future campaigns would be imitating his 1840 campaign hoping to recapture some of the same success.

1836 ELECTION

729. B. The first credential dispute involved rival delegations from Pennsylvania.

730. A. Martin Van Buren was Andrew Jackson's hand-picked successor and he won the nomination with 100% of the first ballot.

731. B. The Democratic Convention for the 1836 election was held in May of 1835, more than a year earlier than conventions are usually held. Most conventions are held in the summer of the year of the election.

732. B. No. The Democratic Party did not have a platform in 1836. However, Martin Van Buren did publish the equivalent of a letter to the editor whereby he promised to follow in Andrew Jackson's footsteps.

733. B. No the Whig Party did not have a platform in 1836. The Whig Party was still organizing and did not have platform or a convention in 1836.

734. C. Martin Van Buren won about 51% of the popular vote, his next closest opponent received about 37%.

735. A. Martin Van Buren won a close election in 1836. The Whigs needed only to win 23 more electoral votes to cause a tie.

736. A. Martin Van Buren accomplished the rare feat of being a sitting vice president and being elected president. The next sitting vice president to accomplish this feat was George H.W. Bush in 1988.

737. B. Martin Van Buren clinched the election by winning Pennsylvania. If Van Buren had not won Pennsylvania's 30 electoral votes the election would have gone to the House of Representatives. Van Buren won Pennsylvania by less than 5,000 votes.

738. B. One new state (Arkansas) participated in the 1836 election.

1832 ELECTION

739. A. The first presidential nominating convention took place in Baltimore.

740. C. William Wirt was the first candidate to be nominated for president by a political convention. Political conventions had previously been used to nominate candidates for local office.

741. B. Martin Van Buren was the first candidate nominated by the Democratic Party for vice president.

742. True. The Democratic Party in 1832 stood for continuing the policies of Andrew Jackson. The other parties were opposed to Andrew Jackson or opposed to the Freemasons.

743. A. The National Republicans were a branch of the Democratic Party and they opposed Andrew Jackson.

744. C. Andrew Jackson won big in the popular vote in 1832, 54% to 37% to 8%

745. C. Andrew Jackson won big in the Electoral College 219 to 49 to 11 to 7. Henry Clay needed to win about 100 more electoral votes (from Jackson) to get to the winning number of 145.

746. B. William Wirt won a single state, Vermont, in 1832.

747. C. Clay did not do that well in terms of winning states but outside of Kentucky his best region was New England where he won a few states.

1828 ELECTION

748. C. Andrew Jackson was nominated by the Tennessee legislature in 1825. His nomination was endorsed by other legislatures and gatherings of supporters.

749. C. John Q. Adams was nominated by the Pennsylvania legislature. His nomination was also endorsed by other legislatures and gatherings of supporters.

750. B. Jackson won the popular vote over Adams by about 56% to 44%.

751. B. Jackson won the electoral vote over Adams 178 to 83 (131 needed to win). Adams needed 48 more electoral votes to win.

752. A. The electoral votes/states won by Crawford and Clay in 1824 generally went to Jackson in 1828.

753. B. Three states awarded split electoral votes by congressional district in 1828 (Maine, Maryland, and New York). Tennessee also awarded votes by congressional district but Jackson decisively swept the state, winning about 95% of the vote statewide. In contrast Jackson won 40% of the vote in Maine but only came up with one electoral vote whereas Adams won eight. Maryland and New York were split fairly evenly in terms of both popular and electoral vote totals.

1824 ELECTION

754. C. William Crawford received the nomination of the Democratic-Republican Congressional Caucus in 1824. Crawford's candidacy was weakened by a stroke he had suffered in 1823.

755. A. The Congressional Caucus became known as King Caucus because of its role as "king-maker". There had been growing opposition to the caucus and 1824 was the last time that the caucus nominated anyone. The nomination of Crawford was rejected leading to a new era in the presidential nominee selection process.

756. True. In 1824 there was effectively only one national political party, the Democratic-Republicans, but there were factions within that party.

757. C. John Calhoun received the most electoral votes – for vice president. He was the undisputed winner of the election for vice president. Four years later he would be elected as Andrew Jackson's vice president, making him only the second vice president to serve two different presidents. No one has done so since.

758. C. Jackson won a plurality of the popular vote winning 41% to 31% to 13% to 11% to 3% but because he failed to win a majority in the Electoral College (and no one else did) the election was determined in the House of Representatives and Adams won.

759. D. The electoral vote of 1824 is best described as a tie as no candidate got the required majority of the electoral vote.

760. True. 1824 was the first year that the popular vote for president was counted.

761. B. Generally John Q. Adams electoral strength was in New England.

762. B. The U.S. House of Representatives decided the winner in 1824.

763. A. John Q. Adams won with the minimum number of states needed for victory.

764. C. Andrew Jackson won a plurality of the popular vote in 1824. He won 41% of the popular vote to John Q. Adams 31%.

765. True. Andrew Jackson was upset because he won the plurality of the popular vote and he felt that Henry Clay had made a deal with John Q. Adams to give Adams the victory in Congress whereby Clay supported Adams in exchange for Clay being made Secretary of State.

766. A. In 1824 it is estimated that 3.8% of the U.S. population participated in the election. Women, blacks, some religious groups, and poor people were disenfranchised in some or all states at the time. This was changing slowly as religious restrictions and property owning requirements gradually fell by the wayside.

1820 ELECTION

767. True. James Monroe was highly popular when he ran for re-election in 1820. That his presidency is known as the "era of good feelings" reflects on his popularity.

768. True. Everyone knew that James Monroe was going to serve another term and so he was not formally nominated. The Electoral College still met and voted.

769. B. Five new states voted for the first time in 1820 (Maine, Alabama, Mississippi, Missouri, and Illinois).

770. True. James Monroe ran unopposed for re-election.

771. True. An elector from New Hampshire felt that only George Washington should have the honor of a unanimous win in the Electoral College and so voted for John Q. Adams to deny James Monroe a unanimous victory. Monroe beat Adams by 117 electoral votes, an absolute margin of victory that would not be surpassed for almost 100 years.

1816 ELECTION

772. C. William Crawford of Georgia was James Monroe's major rival for the Democratic-Republican presidential nomination.

773. A. The attendance at the first caucus was low enough that another caucus was scheduled for a few days later with the hopes of improving attendance. The second caucus had much better attendance.

774. C. Supporters of William Crawford made up the majority of those at the first caucus. If a nominating vote had been held at the caucus, Crawford would have likely won the nomination. At the second caucus Monroe only narrowly defeated Crawford 65 to 54.

775. False. Madison and Monroe were longtime friends and Madison heartily endorsed Monroe for the presidency.

776. A. Rufus King was the Federalist Party candidate from New York.

777. True. Monroe had a long and successful career of serving in important posts for the Washington, Jefferson, and Madison administrations prior to running for president. His service included time as a diplomat, Secretary of State, and time serving simultaneously as both the Secretary of State and the Secretary of War. Monroe had also fought in the Revolutionary War and was seriously wounded in battle.

778. A. King won three states in 1816.

779. B. One new state (Indiana) voted for the first time in 1816.

780. False. James Monroe was not hurt politically by the sacking of Washington D.C. in the War of 1812. In contrast the anti-war Federalists were hurt politically by their opposition to the war.

1812 ELECTION

781. False. The Federalists did not nominate their own candidate to run against Madison, instead endorsing the candidacy of a rival Democratic-Republican, DeWitt Clinton.

782. A. DeWitt Clinton from the anti-Madison branch of the Democratic-Republican Party ran against him. DeWitt Clinton was the nephew of George Clinton. Neither George nor DeWitt is related to Bill or Hillary Clinton. Later as governor of New York, DeWitt Clinton was politically responsible for the creation of the Erie Canal.

783. A. John Langdon thought himself to be too old (he was 70). Elbridge Gerry of Massachusetts was nominated instead.

784. B. Yes, the war made Madison less popular, particularly in New England, but he still won re-election.

785. C. Madison's support was strongest in the South.

786. A. One new state (Louisiana) voted in the 1812 election.

787. True. The War of 1812 cost Madison electoral votes in New England in 1812. Generally New England was opposed to the war, whereas other parts of the country were more bellicose.

1808 ELECTION

788. B. James Madison was nominated by Congress. This was not without controversy as many members of Congress felt that it was wrong for Congress to nominate any presidential candidates.

789. C. Charles C. Pinckney was nominated by a secret meeting of Federalist politicians in New York City.

790. B. Although Madison did not get along with George Clinton, George Clinton was his vice presidential running mate. George Clinton is a rare vice president to have served under two different presidents. Clinton also received 6 presidential votes from New York's electors.

791. B. Both Madison and Charles C. Pinckney were major participants at the Constitutional Convention. Both contributed important ideas that made it into the Constitution.

792. False. Jefferson endorsed his political protégé, Madison, and Madison won the nomination of the Democratic-Republican Party.

793. B. Madison had served as Jefferson's Secretary of State for all eight years prior to running for president. It used to be common for a Secretary of State to become president.

794. A. Zero new states voted in 1808.

795. A. The electors of Delaware only chose Federalist candidates while the Federalist Party existed.

1804 ELECTION

796. A. Both political parties used a caucus of their respective members of Congress to determine who was running for president and vice president. The Democratic-Republican caucus was publicly reported. The Federalist one was not.

797. True. Jefferson was at the height of his popularity in 1804 and was easily re-elected. Aaron Burr was dropped from the ticket and replaced with George Clinton.

798. A. Charles C. Pinckney ran against Jefferson in 1804.

799. C. Jefferson scored a big win in the electoral college in 1804 when he defeated Charles Pinckney 162 to 14 (89 votes required to win). Pinckney needed 75 more electoral votes to win the election.

800. B. One new state (Ohio) voted for the first time in 1804.

1800 ELECTION

801. A. Both political parties used a caucus of their respective members of Congress to determine who was running for president and vice president. Neither caucus was publicly reported.

802. C. From 1800 to 1820, four out of five presidents from Virginia with vice presidents from New York were elected.

803. True. The way that the election of 1800 transpired triggered a constitutional amendment that required electors to distinguish between votes for president and vice president.

804. B. John Adams electoral strength was in New England.

805. A. Thomas Jefferson's electoral strength was on the frontier.

806. C. Burr and Jefferson tied in the Electoral College.

807. B. Jefferson carried New York in 1800. He failed to carry it in 1796.

808. B. The result of the tie election was that the election was sent to the House of Representatives to determine a winner. The Federalist Party had a majority in Congress but eventually they did the right thing and chose the better man, Thomas Jefferson, to be the third president of the United States.

1796 ELECTION

809. B. One new state (Tennessee) voted for the first time in 1796.

810. C. Thomas Jefferson finished second in 1796.

811. B. Thomas Jefferson was nominated by a caucus of the members of his political party in Congress. The caucus was unable to reach an agreement on a vice presidential candidate.

812. B. The Democratic-Republicans were unable to decide whether Aaron Burr or Pierce Butler should run for vice president with Jefferson and so Thomas Jefferson never had a running mate in the 1796 campaign.

813. B. A caucus of Federalist politicians met in Philadelphia and chose John Adams to run for president and Thomas Pinckney to run for vice president.

814. C. Because Jefferson finished second, under the Constitution he was elected vice president. Jefferson and Adams belonged to different political parties. The strife from this situation and the tie in 1800 led to the passage of the Twelfth Amendment.

815. A. Alexander Hamilton did not like John Adams and tried to sabotage the Adams/Pinckney ticket in order to create a tie. The result of Hamilton's whisper campaign was that Adams was elected president and Jefferson was elected vice president.

1792 ELECTION

816. B. In 1792 Congress changed the election laws to give the states a 34 day window in which to choose electors rather than requiring every state to choose electors on the same date. The law also started the practice of the states counting their own electoral votes in December and reporting those votes to Congress in February. A national election day was not set until 1845 and from time to time Congress has slightly altered the timeline for when the election results are due to be certified in Congress.

817. A. In the early 1790s the Anti-Federalists were slowly becoming the Democratic-Republicans. George Clinton received the endorsement of the Democratic-Republicans in October, 1792. It marked the first step towards the nominating conventions of today. George Clinton was the governor of New York during the Revolutionary War. He opposed the Constitution but supported the Bill of Rights.

818. B. No. George Washington was not formally nominated for president in 1792.

819. B. No. Thomas Jefferson was abroad serving as the U.S. ambassador to France and did not run for president in 1792.

820. True. George Washington was unanimously re-elected in 1792.

821. False. John Adams was not formally nominated for vice president in 1792.

822. B. Vermont and Kentucky joined the United States in time for the 1792 election.

1789 ELECTION

823. C. The election and the inauguration were held in the same year in 1789. Starting in 1792 the election was held earlier than the inauguration.

824. False. The compound nature of the question makes the answer false. Congress intended for the states to vote on the same day but the states did not cooperate. The states voted over a period of several months spanning 1788 and 1789. In September of 1788 Congress set a date in January of 1789 for the states to elect electors and a date in February for the electors to elect a president. Many states chose electors prior to the January election date set by Congress.

825. A. George Washington received the most votes for president.

826. C. George Washington received 69 electoral votes in 1789.

827. True. George Washington was unanimously elected.

828. True. Rhode Island and North Carolina did not participate in the first presidential election because they had not yet ratified the Constitution. New York did not participate because it failed to choose electors by the required January 1789 deadline.

829. B. Although there were not yet political parties, James Madison became the leader of the members of Congress who were most likely to oppose the policies of the Washington Administration. This group was known as the Anti-Federalists and they later became the Democratic-Republicans.

CLINTON, TRUMP, AND 2016

830. C. Hillary Clinton's birthday is October 26. (President Teddy Roosevelt was born on October 27).

831. B. Hillary Clinton was born in 1947.

832. A. Donald Trump was born on June 14 (Flag Day).

833. B. Donald Trump was born in 1946.

834. A. Hillary Clinton grew up in the Chicago area (Park Ridge) and lived there until college.

835. B. Donald Trump grew up in the New York City area (Queens) and has always maintained a residence there.

836. C. Hillary Clinton's father worked in the textile industry; he sold fabric in downtown Chicago.

837. A. Donald Trump's father worked in the construction industry; he built large apartment buildings in Brooklyn.

838. C. Hillary Clinton's ancestors include Welsh coal miners.

839. B. Donald Trump's ancestors include Scottish farmers.

840. B. Hillary Clinton's paternal grandmother intervened when her father (as a young boy) was involved in a serious accident involving an ice delivery truck. The doctors wanted to amputate. Clinton's grandmother prevented the doctors from amputating and forced them to get a second opinion and Clinton's father's leg was saved.

841. A. Donald Trump's paternal grandfather emigrated from Germany and moved west to the Cascades (Idaho/Washington territory) and later to the Yukon gold rush. Trump's grandfather became wealthy operating a saloon that was always open in the Alaskan gold fields. He later sold his business and moved back to New York City. He died in the Spanish Flu epidemic of 1918-1919.

842. C. Hillary Clinton attended Wellesley College.

843. C. Donald Trump attended the University of Pennsylvania, Wharton School of Business.

844. C. In her autobiography, Clinton speaks favorably of her youth pastor, that he had taught her important lessons.

845. A. Trump attended a church in New York City that was run by celebrity pastor Norman Vincent Peale. Peale wrote a book called "The Power of Positive Thinking". Trump believes that Peale had a positive influence on him.

846. A. Clinton has been married once.

847. B. Trump has been married three times.

848. A. Marla is the name of Trump's second wife. Trump's first wife is named Ivanka and his third wife is named Melania.

849. True. Clinton attended Donald Trump's third wedding.

850. A. Clinton has one daughter.

851. C. Trump has five children, three sons and two daughters.

852. C. Clinton received her law degree from Yale. She met her future husband, Bill Clinton, at Yale.

853. B. Bill and Hillary Clinton are not related to 18th and 19th century presidential candidates George and DeWitt Clinton.

854. A. Clinton specialized in children and the law while at Yale.

855. A. Trump successfully renovated The Commodore hotel. His work involved juggling several complex deals simultaneously.

856. B. Hillary Clinton participated in an unsuccessful effort at healthcare reform effort during her husband's first term.

857. A. Donald Trump's casinos have had trouble turning a profit and have been one of his less successful business ventures. His hotels and merchandizing efforts have been far more profitable.

858. C. There were 17 Republican candidates at the start of the contest, making it one of the most crowded fields in the history of presidential elections.

859. True. States have complicated rules for winning delegates and sometimes winning a state can be a fairly hollow victory that nets a very small advantage and in other contests it can be a winner-take-all matter.

860. A. The Democratic Party has around 4700 convention delegates compared with around 2400 delegates for the Republicans.

861. C. Donald Trump won 37 states (plus 3 territorial contests) in the Republican Primaries.

862. C. Ted Cruz finished second to Donald Trump in the Republican Primaries. He won 11 states and no territories. John Kasich tied with Trump in Vermont and won Ohio. Marco Rubio won Minnesota and Puerto Rico.

863. A. In contrast there were only four candidates at the first Democratic Party debate.

864. C. Hillary Clinton won 33 states and five territories. Bernie Sanders won 17 states.

865. C. Disgruntled members of both parties complained about superdelegates in 2016. Democrats who thought that the superdelegates gave Clinton an unfair advantage over Sanders complained about them. Meanwhile the Republicans who do not have superdelegates complained that they did not have any because superdelegates could have been used to stop Trump from winning the nomination.

866. B. Knowing the winner of Florida and Pennsylvania would be most helpful in terms of predicting the outcome of 2016. Likely Trump has to win both to win the White House. If Clinton has won both or split, likely Clinton is the winner.

867. A. Trump made a series of controversial statements during the primary campaign. His standing in the polls generally went up in the aftermath of his controversial statements.

868. B. Trump made immigration into a signature issue of his campaign. Likely the election will be seen as a referendum on U.S. immigration policy.

869. A. 2016 voters are likely to set a record for gender imbalance in support between candidates; with considerably more than half of all female voters projected to vote for Clinton and considerably more than half of all male voters projected vote for Trump. We shall see what happens.

870. C. The Equal Rights Party nominated Victoria Claflin Woodhull for president and Frederick Douglas for vice president. Woodhull was not technically eligible to be president because she would not be 35 on Inauguration Day. Woodhull was also not on the ballot in any states. Some argue that based on this ineligibility that the honor of being first should go to Belva Ann Lockwood of the National Equal Rights Party. Lockwood was old enough, was on the ballot in six states and received about 4,100 votes for president in 1884.

871. A. 1872 was the first year that a woman was nominated for president for the United States.

872. B. In 1964 Margaret Chase Smith was nominated for president by the Republican Party. She was the first woman to be formally nominated by a major political party.

873. C. Shirley Chisholm, an African-American woman was the first woman to be nominated for president by the Democratic Party.

874. C. Hillary Clinton was elected to the Senate in the year 2000. She was re-elected in 2006.

875. C. Hillary Clinton was elected from New York.

876. B. In 2000 Donald Trump ran for a few weeks for the presidency, seeking the nomination of the Reform Party. He had fun and his campaign appeared to be more of a promotional tour for his latest book than a serious one. When Trump dropped out he said that "the Reform Party is a mess".

877. C. Barack Obama appointed Hillary Clinton as Secretary of State. She served in that role for his entire first term.

878. False. Hillary Clinton travelled extensively as Secretary of State and travelled more than 100,000 miles and visited more than 100 different countries.

879. A. At the White House Correspondents Dinner in 2011, Barack Obama roasted Donald Trump. Obama made no jokes about Bin Laden at the Dinner.

880. C. In the famous picture of the White House Situation Room with several White House officials including Obama, Clinton is covering her mouth to stifle an allergic sneeze.

881. C. Hillary Clinton chose Senator Tim Kaine of Virginia as her running mate.

882. A. Donald Trump chose Governor Mike Pence of Indiana as his running mate.

883. B. Obama won 23 states by at least 5% of the popular vote. He also won the District of Columbia by more than 5% of the vote.

884. B. Romney won 23 states by at least 5% of the popular vote.

885. A. Only four states were won by less than 5% of the popular vote (Florida, North Carolina, Ohio, and Virginia). Most lists of swing states include around 10 or 12 states but many of these states are swing states based on a tendency to pick the winner rather than their more ideologically rigid neighbors. Many states that are listed as swing states in longer lists of swing states have consistently voted for the same party over the last two decades. Will 2016 redraw the electoral map or will it be a rerun of 2012?

886. C. Based on the August polling, the election results may resemble Bill Clinton's victory in 1996, with Hillary Clinton winning states like Arizona and Georgia, winning the popular vote by a significant margin but still getting less than 50% of the popular vote.

U.S. PRESIDENTIAL ELECTIONS' GREATEST HITS

887. True. No presidential election map has ever duplicated another one with candidates from the same parties winning the exact same states. 2012 came the closest with only two states and one electoral vote changing from the previous election. 1972 and 1984 are also only two states and one electoral vote different from each other.

888. A. Franklin D. Roosevelt was elected to four terms. No other president has been elected to more than two terms. The 22nd Amendment establishes presidential term limits at two terms.

889. B. Lyndon Johnson received the largest percentage of the popular vote (61%).

890. C. John Quincy Adams received the smallest share of the popular vote by a winning candidate (31%).

891. A. George Washington won a unanimous election in the Electoral College. George Washington was unanimously elected both times. He is the only president to have been unanimously elected.

892. A. James Garfield won the popular vote by the fewest votes. In 1880 he won by only about 20,000 votes nationwide.

893. C. 18 elections (1824, 1844, 1848, 1856, 1860, 1876, 1880, 1884, 1888, 1892, 1912, 1916, 1948, 1960, 1968, 1992, 1996, and 2000) were won by candidates who received less than 50% of the popular vote.

894. A. Franklin Roosevelt received 60.80% of the popular vote in 1936, the second best percentage all-time. Richard Nixon received 60.67% of the popular vote in 1972 for third best percentage.

895. B. Richard Nixon beat George McGovern by almost 18 million votes in 1972. This is the largest margin of victory by raw vote total. (FDR won by 11.1 million, Johnson by 15.9 million, and Reagan by 16.8 million votes in their respective landslide wins)

896. C. Ronald Reagan won the popular vote by the second largest raw vote total, winning by 16.8 million votes in 1984.

897. A. Lyndon Johnson won the popular vote by the third greatest margin in terms of number of votes. Johnson won by 15.9 million votes in 1964.

898. C. In the last election of the 19th century, William McKinley had the largest margin of victory in terms of total number of votes. McKinley defeated Bryan by about 860,000 votes.

899. B. In 1872 Grant defeated Greeley by about 763,000 votes. This was the second largest margin in the 19th century.

900. C. In 1856 James Buchanan defeated John Fremont by about 494,000 votes. This was the third largest margin of victory in the 19th century.

901. A. In 1828, Andrew Jackson won 56% of the popular vote. This mark would not be eclipsed until 1904 when Teddy Roosevelt received 56.4% of the popular vote.

902. B. In 1872, Ulysses Grant received 55.6% of the popular vote for the second best percentage of the 19th century.

903. A. In 1864, Abraham Lincoln received 55% of the popular vote for the third best percentage of the 19th century.

904. C. Both Richard Nixon and Ronald Reagan won 49 states in their respective reelection victories.

905. A. In 1936 Franklin Roosevelt carried 46 out of 48 states.

906. C. In 1964 and in 1980 both Lyndon Johnson and Ronald Reagan won 44 out of 50 states.

907. A. In 1932 Franklin Roosevelt carried 42 out of 48 states.

908. A. In 1956 Dwight Eisenhower carried 41 out of 50 states.

909. C. In 1960 John F. Kennedy won despite carrying only 22 out of 50 states. (In 1916 Hughes just missed winning with only 19 states which would have set the modern record. As it was he lost only winning 18 states.)

910. B. In 1976 Jimmy Carter won despite only carrying 23 out of 50 states. Carter and Kennedy are the only presidents to win fewer than half of the states and win the election outright.

911. B. In 1824 John Quincy Adams only won seven states out of 24. He received electoral votes from a total of 11 states. No candidate won the majority and the election was sent to the House of Representatives to resolve. There Adams won 13 states out of 24. (The bare minimum needed for victory). (Jefferson and Burr had each won 8 states in the 1800 election that also required the House of Representatives to resolve a tie). John Adams also won 8 out 16 states in 1796.

912. B. Grant in 1872 won 29 states (out of 37), the most in a 19th century election. McKinley won 28 states (out of 45), and Lincoln won 22 states (out of 25) in their respective victories. In 1852 Franklin Pierce won 27 states out of 31.

913. B. Four times have both candidates won the same number of states. Two of those times occurred prior to the 12th Amendment (1796 and 1800) and two of them (1848 and 1880) occurred after. In 1796 and 1800 both candidates won 8 states. In 1848 both candidates won 15 states and in 1880 both candidates won 19 states. Not surprisingly these were all close elections.

914. A. "In gold we trust" was a slogan for McKinley and gold-backed currency.

915. C. In 1852 Winfield Scott ran under the slogan "hero of many battles".

916. B. In 1932 the Republicans tried the slogan "it's an elephant's job no time for donkey business" in response to the Great Depression.

917. B. 1988 was the last year that a candidate won 40 or more states.

918. B. Ten times a candidate has won 40 or more states. (1912, 1928, 1932, 1936, 1956, 1964, 1972, 1980, 1984, and 1988)

919. A. 1880 was the last year that a winning candidate won fewer than 20 states. (Garfield won 19 out of 38 that year).

920. B. 34 states is the largest number of states that flipped from Republican to Democratic in a single election. (This flip happened in 1932).

921. A. 26 states is the greatest number of states that flipped in a single election from Democratic to Republican. (This flip happened in 1968).

922. C. George W. Bush won the closest election that did not go to the House of Representatives to resolve. (His election did take a ruling by the U.S. Supreme Court to resolve).

923. C. Only four times has the winner of the popular vote not won the presidency.

924. A. The election of 1916 was also close.

925. C. In 13 elections if the winner of a single state is reversed, the winner of the election is reversed or a tie is created that would send the election to the House of Representatives. (1812, 1836, 1844, 1848, 1860, 1876, 1880, 1884, 1888, 1916, 1976, 2000, and 2004 are the 13 close elections decided by a single state).

926. B. Four elections (1800, 1824, 1876, and 2000) have required additional action by another branch of government to resolve the election.

927. B. In 1800, Thomas Jefferson and Aaron Burr both received 99 electoral votes.

928. B. In 1836 the U.S. Senate had to decide the vice presidential winner. Van Buren's running mate, Richard Johnson was unpopular in the South. Virginia refused to vote for him for vice president which resulted in his being one vote short of the minimum number needed in the Electoral College. The full Senate confirmed his election as vice president. That is the only time the U.S. Senate has had to break a vice presidential tie.

929. A. In 1824 both John Q. Adams and Andrew Jackson ran with John C. Calhoun as their respective vice presidential running mate. (There was only one political party at the time but with distinct factions within that party). When Adams and Jackson tied, it became necessary for the U.S. House of Representatives to resolve the presidential election. The vice presidential winner was clearly John C. Calhoun.

930. C. The election of 1876 most resembled the election of 2000 in terms of disputed election results.

931. B. Barack Obama has received more votes for president than any other candidate.

932. C. Three times the loser has won the rematch. Jackson in 1828, Harrison in 1840, and Cleveland in 1892 all won rematches after losing to the same opponent four years earlier.

933. B. Bryan in 1900 and Stevenson in 1956 both lost rematches after losing to the same opponent four years earlier.

934. B. Three presidents (Franklin D. Roosevelt in 1936, Richard Nixon in 1972, and Ronald Reagan in 1984) all received more than 500 electoral votes in a single election.

935. A. William Taft in 1912 received 23.2% of the vote. This is the worst that a Republican has done in a single election. Taft was hurt by the presence of Theodore Roosevelt in the race.

936. A. John Davis received only 28.8% of the vote in 1924. This is the worst that a Democrat has done in a single election. Davis was hurt by the presence of third party candidate Robert La Follette and also by a deeply divided Democratic Party that had shredded itself at the party convention that year.

937. B. Minnesota has not been carried by the Republican candidate since Nixon won the state in 1972. Since Hoover won the state in 1928, Republicans have only carried it in 1952, 1956, and 1972.

938. C. Nine states have not been won by the Democratic candidate since Johnson's big win in 1964. The nine states are Alaska, Idaho, Wyoming, Utah, North Dakota, South Dakota, Nebraska, Kansas, and Oklahoma. (Barack Obama did win one of Nebraska's electoral votes in 2008 but overall the state was carried by John McCain).

939. B. A state since 1912, New Mexico has only backed the loser of the popular vote a single time. In 1976 New Mexico went for Ford.

940. A. Of the choices given, Alabama has done the worst with 13 times picking a non-winner. Mississippi has also picked on non-winners 13 times (1912 through 2012 election). During the same span, Maine, Vermont, South Dakota, South Carolina, and Georgia all picked non-winners 11 times.

941. C. 15 states (New Mexico, Nevada, Missouri, Ohio, New Hampshire, Tennessee, Florida, Maryland, California, Montana, Illinois, Kentucky, New Jersey, Delaware, and Colorado) have been fairly good at choosing the winner and have each backed the non-winner five or fewer times in the last hundred years of presidential elections (1912 through 2012).

FIFTY STATE CHALLENGE

DELAWARE

942. A. In presidential elections from 1789 through 2012 the Democratic Party has carried Delaware 22 times and the Republican Party has carried Delaware 18 times.

943. C. Not surprisingly the Federalist Party won the First State eight times.

944. B. A third party has carried Delaware once. In 1860 Delaware was won by the Southern Democrats.

945. A. Delaware is worth three electoral votes in 2016.

946. B. Delaware backed a loser five times (in 1916, 1932, 1948, 2000, and 2004).

PENNSYLVANIA

947. B. From 1789 through 2012 the Republican candidate won Pennsylvania 25 times compared with 18 times for the Democratic candidate.

948. B. The only third party to carry Pennsylvania was the Bull Moose Party in 1912.

949. B. The Keystone State is worth 20 electoral votes in 2016.

950. C. Pennsylvania backed a loser seven times (1912, 1916, 1932, 1948, 1968, 2000, and 2004).

NEW JERSEY

951. A. In presidential elections from 1789 through 2012 the Democratic candidate carried New Jersey 23 times compared to 19 Republican victories.

952. B. The Whig Party won the Garden State four times.

953. A. A third party candidate has never carried New Jersey.

954. B. New Jersey is worth 14 electoral votes in 2016.

955. B. New Jersey was carried by a losing candidate five times (1916, 1948, 1976, 2000, and 2004).

GEORGIA

956. A. In presidential elections from 1789 through 2012 the Democratic Party candidates carried Georgia 31 times compared with 9 Republican victories.

957. C. A third party candidate has carried Georgia twice, in 1860 and in 1968.

958. A. Georgia is worth 16 electoral votes in 2016.

959. A. Yes. The Democratic candidates have won the Peach State 31 times. Georgia has been one of the best states for Democrats over the years.

960. B. Between 1912 and 2012 Georgia did not back the winner in all but three or fewer elections. Georgia was won by the loser of the election 11 times (1920, 1924, 1928, 1952, 1956, 1964, 1968, 1980, 1996, 2008, and 2012).

CONNECTICUT

961. B. The Republican Party has 23 presidential election wins in Connecticut compared to 19 Democratic Party wins.

962. C. The Federalist Party won Connecticut eight times.

963. A. No third party candidates have ever won Connecticut.

964. B. Connecticut is worth seven electoral votes in 2016.

965. B. No, the Nutmeg State has not backed the winner in all but three or fewer elections. Connecticut has backed a non-winner seven times including 1916, 1932, 1948, 1968, 1976, 2000, and 2004.

MASSACHUSETTS

966. B. In presidential elections through 2012 the Republicans have won Massachusetts 21 times compared to 19 wins for the Democrats.

967. A. No third party candidates have won Massachusetts.

968. A. Massachusetts is worth 11 electoral votes in 2016.

969. B. Massachusetts has not backed a winner in all but three or fewer elections between 1912 and 2012. The Bay State has backed non-winners seven times including 1916, 1928, 1968, 1972, 1988, 2000, and 2004.

MARYLAND

970. A. Overall the Democratic Party has won Maryland 27 times compared to 12 Republican wins.

971. B. Third Party candidates have won Maryland twice, in 1856 and 1860. The 1856 winner was an anti-immigrant offshoot of the Whig Party. The winner in 1860 was the pro-slavery faction of the Democratic Party.

972. C. Maryland is worth ten electoral votes in 2016.

973. B. No, Maryland has not backed the winner in all but three or fewer elections. The Old Line State has backed non-winners five times between 1912 and 2012 including 1948, 1968, 1980, 2000, and 2004.

SOUTH CAROLINA

974. A. The Democratic Party has won South Carolina 26 times overall compared to 15 wins for the Republican Party.

975. C. South Carolina has been won by a third party candidate four times. In 1832 and in 1836, local "favorite son" candidates won South Carolina. In 1860 the pro-slavery faction of the Democratic Party (Southern Democratic Party) won and in 1948, the States' Rights Democratic Party won.

976. B. South Carolina is worth nine electoral votes in 2016.

977. B. No, South Carolina has not backed the winner in all but three or fewer elections since 1912. The Palmetto State has backed non-winners 11 times including 1920, 1924, 1928, 1948, 1952, 1956, 1964, 1992, 1996, 2008, and 2012.

978. B. South Carolina was the last state to adopt the direct election of presidential electors, doing so in time for the 1868 Election. From 1789 to 1860 the South Carolina Legislature had chosen the presidential electors.

NEW HAMPSHIRE

979. B. The Republicans have won New Hampshire 29 times overall compared to 17 Democratic Party wins.

980. A. A third party candidate has never carried New Hampshire.

981. B. New Hampshire is worth four electoral votes in 2016.

982. A. In 1916 Woodrow Wilson set the all-time record for closest margin of victory in a state when he carried the state by 56 votes over Charles Hughes.

983. A. Between 1912 and 2012, the Granite State has remained firm for non-winners four times (1944, 1948, 1976, and 2004).

VIRGINIA

984. A. Historically Virginia has been won by the Democratic Party. The current score is 28 wins for the Democrats and 15 wins for the Republicans.

985. C. From 1904 through 2012, the Democratic and Republican Parties have each won Virginia 14 times.

986. B. A third party candidate has won Virginia once. The Constitutional Union Party carried Virginia in 1860.

987. B. The Old Dominion is worth 11 electoral votes in 2016.

988. C. Between 1912 and 2012 Virginia backed the non-winner six times (1920, 1924, 1960, 1976, 1992, and 1996).

989. C. In 2012 Virginia and West Virginia backed different candidates with Obama winning Virginia and Romney winning West Virginia.

NEW YORK

990. A. From 1789 through 2012 the Democratic Party has 24 wins compared with 20 Republican wins.

991. A. No third party candidate has ever conquered the Empire State.

992. A. New York is worth 29 electoral votes in 2016.

993. A. New York backed the non-winner six times (1916, 1948, 1968, 1988, 2000, and 2004).

NORTH CAROLINA

994. A. Overall the Democratic Party has the most wins in North Carolina with 28 compared with 13 Republican wins.

995. B. A third party candidate won the Tar Heel State only once. In 1860 it was won by the Southern Democratic Party.

996. C. North Carolina is worth 15 electoral votes in 2016.

997. B. North Carolina backed the non-winner seven times (1920, 1924, 1952, 1956, 1992, 1996, and 2012).

998. C. In 2008 North Carolina voted for Barack Obama and South Carolina voted for John McCain.

RHODE ISLAND

999. C. Overall the Republicans and Democrats have tied and have each won Rhode Island 21 times. Prior to the Civil War Rhode Island also split fairly evenly among the various political parties.

1000. A. No third party candidate has won the Ocean State yet.

1001. B. Rhode Island is worth four electoral votes in 2016.

1002. C. From 1912 through 2012 Rhode Island backed the non-winner seven times (1916, 1928, 1968, 1980, 1988, 2000, and 2004).

1003. A. Rhode Island and Delaware have been voting together since 1988 when Dukakis won Rhode Island and the elder Bush won Delaware.

VERMONT

1004. B. Overall the Republican Party has won Vermont 33 times compared to only 7 wins for Democratic candidates.

1005. C. Prior to 1992, the only Democrat to win the Green Mountain State was Lyndon Johnson in 1964.

1006. B. A third party candidate has won Vermont once. In 1832 the Anti-Mason Party won Vermont.

1007. A. Vermont is worth three electoral votes in 2016.

1008. C. Vermont has been won by the Republicans 33 times. This is the most wins for either party in any state.

1009. C. Starting with the 1912 Vermont has backed the non-winning candidate 11 times including 1912, 1916, 1932, 1936, 1940, 1944, 1948, 1960, 1976, 2000 and 2004.

1010. B. Vermont and New Hampshire: these two states most recently "disagreed" in 2000 when Gore won Vermont and Bush won New Hampshire.

KENTUCKY

1011. A. Overall the Democrats have won the Bluegrass State 25 times compared to 14 Republican wins.

1012. A. The Constitutional Union Party won Kentucky in 1860; the only time that a third party candidate has won the state.

1013. B. Kentucky is worth eight electoral votes in 2016.

1014. B. Kentucky has backed the non-winner five times including 1920, 1952, 1960, 2008, and 2012.

TENNESSEE

1015. A. Overall the Democrats have 24 victories compared to 15 wins for the Republicans in Tennessee.

1016. B. Prior to Harding's win in 1920, Grant's win in 1868 was the only time that the Republicans had won Tennessee.

1017. B. The only third party to win the Volunteer State was the Constitutional Union Party in 1860.

1018. A. Tennessee is worth 11 electoral votes in 2016.

1019. B. From 1912 through 2012, Tennessee has backed only four non-winners (1924, 1960, 2008, 2012).

1020. B. In 1952, Kentucky went narrowly for Illinois governor Adlai Stevenson over Dwight Eisenhower. This is the most recent time that Tennessee and Kentucky backed different candidates.

OHIO

1021. B. Overall the Republicans have 28 wins in Ohio compared with 15 wins for the Democrats.

1022. C. Since 1832, seven times have the Democrats, (Van Buren in 1836, Polk in 1844, Buchanan in 1856, Cleveland in 1884 and 1892, Roosevelt in 1944, and Kennedy in 1960) won the White House despite losing Ohio. No Republican has ever won the White House while losing Ohio.

1023. A. A third party candidate has never won the Buckeye State.

1024. A. Ohio is worth 18 electoral votes in 2016.

1025. A. From 1912 through 2012 the Buckeye State has only backed non-winners twice (1944 and 1960).

LOUISIANA

1026. A. Overall (through 2012) the Democratic Party has 28 wins in Louisiana compared with 11 wins for the Republicans.

1027. C. A third party candidate has won the Pelican State three times (1860, 1948, and 1968).

1028. B. Louisiana is worth eight electoral votes in 2016.

1029. B. From 1912 to 2012 Louisiana backed the non-winner nine times including 1920, 1924, 1928, 1948, 1952, 1964, 1968, 2008, and 2012.

INDIANA

1030. B. Overall through 2012 the Republicans have 31 wins compared with 13 for the Democrats in the Hoosier State.

1031. A. Third party candidates have never won Indiana.

1032. A. Indiana is worth 11 electoral votes in 2016.

1033. B. Starting in 1912, Indiana has backed the non-winner nine times including 1916, 1940, 1944, 1948, 1960, 1976, 1992, 1996, and 2012.

MISSISSIPPI

1034. A. Through 2012 the Democratic Party has the most wins of any political party in Mississippi with 27. The Republicans have only 13 wins.

1035. C. A third party candidate has won Mississippi 3 times (1860, 1948, and 1968). Additionally Robert F. Byrd of West Virginia won the state's electoral votes in 1960.

1036. A. Mississippi is worth six electoral votes in 2016.

1037. C. Starting with 1912 the Magnolia State has backed the non-winner 13 times including 1920, 1924, 1928, 1948, 1952, 1956, 1960, 1964, 1968, 1992, 1996, 2008, and 2012.

ILLINOIS

1038. B. In the Land of Lincoln the Republicans narrowly edge the Democrats for most victories with 24 versus 22.

1039. A. No third party candidates have ever won Illinois.

1040. B. Illinois is worth 20 electoral votes in 2016.

1041. A. Starting with 1912 Illinois has picked a non-winner five times including 1916, 1968, 1976, 2000, and 2004.

ALABAMA

1042. A. The Democrats have won Alabama 29 times compared to only 13 wins for the Republicans.

1043. A. 1840 is the last and only year that Mississippi and Alabama have been won by a different candidate in the Electoral College. In 1840 Harrison won Mississippi and Van Buren won Alabama. In 1868, Mississippi did not vote due to Reconstruction. In 1960 both states gave a majority of their electoral votes to Robert Byrd. Alabama also gave five electoral votes to Kennedy that year but gave a majority to Byrd.

1044. C. A third party candidate has won the Cotton State three times (1860, 1948, and 1968). Additionally Robert F. Byrd of West Virginia won a majority of the unpledged Alabama electors in 1960.

1045. B. Alabama is worth nine electoral votes in 2016.

1046. B. Starting in 1912 Alabama has backed a non-winning candidate thirteen times including 1920, 1924, 1928, 1948, 1952, 1956, 1960, 1964, 1968, 1992, 1996, 2008, and 2012.

MAINE

1047. B. Overall Maine has been won by the Republicans 31 times compared with 14 wins for the Democrats. It is one of a handful of states that have been won by either party more than 30 times.

1048. A. The Pine Tree State has never been won by a third party candidate.

1049. B. Maine is worth four electoral votes in 2016.

1050. B. Starting in 1912 Maine has backed the non-winner eleven times including 1916, 1932, 1936, 1940, 1944, 1948, 1960, 1968, 1976, 2000, and 2004.

MISSOURI

1051. A. Overall the Democrats have posted 29 wins in Missouri compared with 17 wins for the Republicans.

1052. A. A third party candidate has never won the Show-Me State.

1053. A. Missouri is worth 10 electoral votes in 2016.

1054. B. Missouri has only backed the non-winner three times and two of those times were really close. Stevenson narrowly carried Missouri in 1956 and McCain narrowly won Missouri in 2008. Missouri also backed Romney in 2012 but that was not by a close margin.

1055. B. In the elections from 1820 through 1900, Missouri backed the non-winner ten times. It was far from the bellwether state that it proved to be in the 20th century elections.

ARKANSAS

1056. A. Overall through 2012 the Democrats have won Arkansas 32 times compared with 9 Republican wins. Although this may change in 2016, Arkansas is among the last of the states where one of the two major parties has fewer than double digit wins in presidential elections.

1057. C. Arkansas has been carried twice by third party candidates, in 1860 and again in 1968.

1058. A. Naturally the Nature State is worth six electoral votes in 2016.

1059. B. Starting in 1912 Arkansas has backed the non-winner eight times including 1920, 1924, 1928, 1952, 1956, 1968, 2008, and 2012.

MICHIGAN

1060. B. The Republicans have won Michigan 27 times compared to 17 wins for the Democrats.

1061. B. Michigan has been won by a third party candidate one time. In 1912 the Bull Moose Party won the Wolverine State.

1062. A. Michigan is worth 16 electoral votes in 2016.

1063. A. Starting in 1912, Michigan has backed a non-winner eight times including 1912, 1916, 1940, 1948, 1968, 1976, 2000, and 2004.

FLORIDA

1064. A. Overall the Democratic Party has 24 wins in Florida compared with 15 for the Republicans.

1065. B. Florida was carried once by a third party (in 1860).

1066. B. It will be a bright day for the winner of the Sunshine State's 29 electoral votes in 2016.

1067. C. Since 1912 Florida has backed the non-winning candidate only four times including 1920, 1924, 1960, and 1992.

TEXAS

1068. A. Overall the Democrats have 26 wins in Texas compared with 13 for the Republicans.

1069. C. Prior to Bill Clinton winning the presidency in 1992 without Texas, no Democrat had been elected president without winning the Lone Star State.

1070. B. Texas was won by a third party candidate once, in 1860.

1071. A. Texas is worth 38 electoral votes in 2016.

1072. B. Starting with the 1912 election, Texas has backed the non-winner seven times including 1920, 1924, 1968, 1992, 1996, 2008 and 2012.

IOWA

1073. B. Overall the Republicans have 29 wins in Iowa compared to 13 wins for the Democrats.

1074. A. No third party candidate has ever won the Hawkeye State.

1075. A. Iowa is worth six electoral votes in 2016.

1076. B. Starting with 1912, Iowa has backed the non-winner seven times including 1916, 1940, 1944, 1960, 1976, 1988, and 2000.

WISCONSIN

1077. B. Overall the Republicans have 24 victories in the Badger State compared with 16 for the Democrats.

1078. B. Wisconsin has been won once by a third party candidate, native son Robert La Follette won the state in 1924 as a Progressive Party candidate.

1079. C. Wisconsin is worth ten electoral votes in 2016.

1080. B. Beginning the tally in 1912, Wisconsin has backed a non-winner seven times including 1916, 1924, 1940, 1960, 1984, 2000, and 2004.

CALIFORNIA

1081. B. Overall the Republicans have the most wins in California with 24, the Democrats have won 16 times.

1082. B. Third party candidates have shined once in the Golden State. (Teddy Roosevelt in 1912).

1083. C. California is worth 55 electoral votes in 2016.

1084. B. California has picked a non-winner five times including 1912, 1960, 1976, 2000 and 2004.

MINNESOTA

1085. B. The Republicans have won Minnesota 20 times overall, the Democrats have 18 wins.

1086. A. A third party candidate has won once in the North Star State (Again, Teddy Roosevelt in 1912).

1087. C. Minnesota is worth ten electoral votes in 2016.

1088. B. Starting in 1912 the North Star State has backed a non-winning candidate in seven elections including 1912, 1968, 1980, 1984, 1988, 2000, and 2004.

1089. C. The Republican candidate last won Minnesota in 1972. (Reagan came close to winning but didn't carry the state in 1984). This is the longest current streak among states won by consecutive Democratic candidates.

OREGON

1090. B. In presidential elections in Oregon the Republicans have 25 wins, and the Democrats have 14 wins.

1091. A. No third party candidate has ever won the Beaver State.

1092. A. Oregon is worth seven electoral votes in 2016.

1093. C. Starting in 1912 Oregon has backed a non-winning candidate seven times including 1916, 1948, 1960, 1976, 1988, 2000, and 2004.

1094. True. Most citizens in Oregon vote by mail rather than in-person. This system has been in place since being adopted by referendum in 1998 and is credited with boosting voter turnout in the state.

1095. A. In 1968, Humphrey won Washington while Nixon carried Oregon. Since then the two states have matched each other in picking presidential candidates.

KANSAS

1096. B. The Republicans have won Kansas 31 times, compared with only 6 victories for the Democrats.

1097. B. In 1892, the Populist Party won Kansas. Otherwise, no other third party has carried Kansas in a presidential election.

1098. A. The Sunflower State is worth six electoral votes in 2016.

1099. C. Kansas has picked a non-winner nine times (starting the analysis in 1912) including 1940, 1944, 1948, 1960, 1976, 1992, 1996, 2008, and 2012.

WEST VIRGINIA

1100. C. The Democrats have won West Virginia 18 times and the Republicans have won 18 times.

1101. A. No third party candidates have won the Mountaineer State.

1102. C. West Virginia is worth five electoral votes in 2016.

1103. A. Starting in 1912 West Virginia has picked a non-winner seven times in presidential elections including 1916, 1952, 1968, 1980, 1988, 2000 and 2004.

NEVADA

1104. B. The Republicans have won Nevada 20 times overall compared with 17 wins for the Democrats.

1105. B. A third party candidate has won Nevada once. The Populist Party won in 1892.

1106. A. Nevada is worth six electoral votes in 2016.

1107. B. Perhaps it is not surprising in a state that features a city known for gambling that the residents of the Silver State are good at picking a winner, Nevada has only missed once in the elections from 1912 through 2012. In 1976, Nevada was carried by the non-winner, Gerald Ford. (However, in the 12 elections from Nevada statehood in 1864 through 1908, Nevada only picked a winner six out of twelve times).

NEBRASKA

1108. B. Nebraska has been won by the Republicans 30 times and the Democrats have only won 7 times there.

1109. A. The Cornhusker State has never been carried by a third party candidate.

1110. C. Nebraska is worth five electoral votes in 2016.

1111. C. Over the last hundred years of elections, Nebraska has chosen a non-winner nine times including 1940, 1944, 1948, 1960, 1976, 1992, 1996, 2008, and 2012. (Obama did win an electoral vote in Nebraska in 2008 but McCain still won the state).

1112. B. In 1908, Nebraska went for native son William Jennings Bryan while Kansas went for William Taft.

COLORADO

1113. A. The state legislature chose the electors in 1876 to avoid the expense of an election so soon after new statehood. After the 1876 election, Colorado went to the direct election of electors by statewide vote.

1114. B. Overall the Republicans have 22 wins and the Democrats have 12 wins in Colorado.

1115. B. Colorado was also carried by the Populist Party in 1892, the only time a third party candidate has won the Centennial State.

1116. B. Colorado is worth nine electoral votes in 2016.

1117. C. From 1912 through 2012 Colorado has picked a non-winner five times including 1940, 1944, 1960, 1976, and 1996.

NORTH DAKOTA

1118. B. The Republicans have won North Dakota 25 times compared to 5 wins for the Democrats.

1119. C. In 1892 the Democrats and Populists ran on a combined ticket. The only names on the ballot were the Republican and the Populist. The Populist won the popular vote. Two Populist electors and one Republican elector were elected. The Populist electors split with one voting for the Democrat and one voting for the Populist. The result in the Electoral College was a 1 to 1 to 1 tie in terms of electoral votes won in North Dakota. Other than this unusual result in 1892, no third party candidate has won North Dakota.

1120. A. The Peace Garden State is worth three electoral votes in 2016.

1121. C. Since 1912 North Dakota has picked a non-winner nine times including 1940, 1944, 1948, 1960, 1976, 1992, 1996, 2008, and 2012.

1122. B. 1916 is the last year that North and South Dakota were won by different candidates. The Democrat, Wilson, won North Dakota and the Republican, Hughes, won South Dakota.

SOUTH DAKOTA

1123. B. Overall the Republicans have won South Dakota 26 times and the Democrats have four wins.

1124. B. In 1912, Bull Moose candidate Teddy Roosevelt won the Mount Rushmore State. In the 1930s a likeness of his face would be carved into Mount Rushmore.

1125. A. South Dakota is worth three electoral votes in 2016.

1126. C. Since 1912 South Dakota has picked a non-winner 11 times, all other states that have been wrong 10 or more times are in the South or New England. South Dakota picked non-winners in 1912, 1916, 1940, 1944, 1948, 1960, 1976, 1992, 1996, 2008, and 2012.

MONTANA

1127. B. Overall the Republicans have 20 wins and the Democrats have 11 wins in Montana.

1128. A. No third party candidate has found electoral treasure in the Treasure State.

1129. A. Montana is worth three electoral votes in 2016.

1130. A. Since 1912 Montana has backed a non-winner five times including 1960, 1976, 1996, 2008, and 2012.

WASHINGTON

1131. A. Overall the Democrats have 16 wins and the Republicans have 14 wins in Washington.

1132. B. Washington was one of six states that third party candidate Roosevelt won in 1912. That is the only time so far that a third party candidate has carried the Evergreen State.

1133. C. Washington is worth twelve electoral votes in 2016.

1134. B. Since 1912 Washington has picked a non-winner seven times including 1912, 1960, 1968, 1976, 1988, 2000, and 2004.

IDAHO

1135. B. The Republicans have won Idaho 20 times compare with only 10 wins for the Democrats.

1136. B. The Populist Party won Idaho in 1892, the only time so far that a third party candidate has sparkled in the Gem State.

1137. B. Idaho is worth four electoral votes in 2016.

1138. A. Since 1912 Idaho has backed a non-winner six times including 1960, 1976, 1992, 1996, 2008, and 2012.

1139. B. In 1992 Clinton won Montana while the elder Bush carried Idaho.

WYOMING

1140. B. Overall the Republicans have 23 victories in Wyoming and the Democrats have only eight.

1141. A. Third party candidate wins have equaled zero in the Equality State. (Wyoming was the first state to allow women to vote in statewide elections).

1142. A. Wyoming is worth three electoral votes in 2016.

1143. C. Starting with 1912 Wyoming has picked a non-winner seven times including 1944, 1960, 1976, 1992, 1996, 2008, and 2012.

UTAH

1144. B. Overall the Republicans have won Utah 22 times compared with 8 wins for the Democrats.

1145. A. Third party candidates have gotten stung in the Beehive State and have no wins there.

1146. A. Utah is worth six electoral votes in 2016.

1147. A. Starting in 1912, Utah has picked a non-winner seven times including 1912, 1960, 1976, 1992, 1996, 2008, and 2012.

OKLAHOMA

1148. B. From 1908 through 2012, the Republicans won Oklahoma 17 times and the Democrats have won 10 times.

1149. A. No third party candidates have carried the Sooner State. In 1960, one Oklahoma elector voted for Byrd instead of Nixon.

1150. A. Oklahoma is worth seven electoral votes in 2016.

1151. C. Oklahoma has been wrong seven times about which candidate would win. Non-winners won Oklahoma in 1924, 1960, 1976, 1992, 1996, 2008, and 2012.

NEW MEXICO

1152. A. The Democrats have won 14 of the 26 presidential elections that New Mexico has participated in.

1153. A. Third party candidates have never won New Mexico. The 2016 Libertarian Party candidate is from New Mexico (former governor Gary Johnson). The Republicans have won New Mexico 12 times.

1154. C. New Mexico is worth five electoral votes in 2016.

1155. C. The Land of Enchantment has only been wrong twice, backing Electoral College non-winners Ford in 1976, and Gore in 2000.

ARIZONA

1156. B. The Republicans have won Arizona 18 times, the Democrats have won Arizona eight times.

1157. A. No third party candidates have won the Grand Canyon State.

1158. A. Arizona is worth 11 electoral votes in 2016.

1159. B. Arizona has backed a non-winner six times including 1960, 1964, 1976, 1992, 2008, and 2012.

ALASKA

1160. B. The Republican Party has won Alaska 13 times, the Democrats only have one victory in the Last Frontier.

1161. A. No third party candidates have won the Last Frontier.

1162. A. Alaska is worth three electoral votes in 2016.

1163. C. Alaska has picked non-winners five times including 1976, 1992, 1996, 2008, and 2012.

HAWAII

1164. A. The Democratic Party has won Hawaii 12 times. The Republicans have won twice.

1165. A. A third party candidate has never carried the Aloha State.

1166. B. Hawaii is worth four electoral votes in 2016.

1167. C. Hawaii has picked non-winners five times including in 1968, 1980, 1988, 2000, and 2004.

POLITICAL PARTY! PARTY! PARTY!

1168. A. Although George Washington was not fond of political parties and associated labels, it is accurate to label him as the first Federalist president.

1169. B. John Adams was the last Federalist to be elected president.

1170. A. The first Democratic Party Convention was in advance of the 1832 election. Andrew Jackson was the first Democratic Party president. Jackson's presidency spans the creation of the Democratic Party. The party was still coalescing in 1828, it was not solidly formed until 1831. This book measures the beginning of the Democratic Party from 1832, other authors simplify things and start at 1828, this starting point is reasonable but less historically accurate. The reality is that it was not an overnight process for the Democratic-Republican Party to split into new parties and there are not easy dividing lines.

1171. A. As of July 2016, Barack Obama is the most recently elected Democratic Party president (also the current president).

1172. A. Abraham Lincoln was the first Republican to be elected president.

1173. B. As of July 2016 George W. Bush (2001-2009) is the most recent Republican president.

1174. B. William Harrison (1841) was the first Whig president.

1175. C. Zachary Taylor (1849-1850) was the last Whig to be elected president. Taylor died in office and his successor, Millard Fillmore (1851-1853), was never elected.

1176. A. Two Whigs were elected president.

1177. B. The Whigs and the Democrats had fairly similar economic policies.

1178. B. Between 1868 and 1900 there were few differences in economic policy between the Republicans and Democrats. Overall both parties had conservative economic policies. In 1896 the establishment of the Democratic Party turned on its own candidate (William Jennings Bryan) because it thought that his monetary policies were too radical.

1179. A. Starting in 1932 the base of support of the parties began to switch with Democrats performing better in the North and the Republicans performing better in the South.

1180. A. Historically and at the present most recent immigrants tend to support the Democratic Party. It certainly possible to find exceptions.

1181. A. Since the 1930s, organized labor has been a core constituency of the Democratic Party.

1182. C. The Republican Party was founded in the mid-1850s around the issue of slavery. Both Ripon, Wisconsin and Jackson, Michigan lay claim to hosting important early gatherings of the Republican Party.

1183. A. In 1831 the Anti Mason Party was the first party to hold a national convention to nominate a presidential candidate. Conventions had previously been used to nominate candidates at the local level.

1184. C. Thomas Jefferson founded the Democratic-Republican Party. This party was sometimes referred to as the Jeffersonian-Republican Party.

1185. C. The Democratic-Republican Party controlled both the White House and Congress for 24 consecutive years (1801-1825).

1186. C. Generally the strength of the Democratic-Republican Party was in the South. The party favored individualism and agrarian interests.

1187. A. The Free Soil Party was mostly an anti-slavery party. One of the few planks in its platform that did not deal with slavery, called for cheap postage.

1188. C. The Green Party is most closely associated with the cause of environmentalism and protecting natural lands from human encroachment.

1189. A. On October 26, 2008, Nader attended 21 campaign events in 21 different Massachusetts towns, setting an unofficial record for most campaign events in a single day.

1190. A. The Greenback Party was founded in Indianapolis, Indiana, in 1874.

1191. B. The Greenback Party promoted an inflationary monetary policy that was beneficial to poor people with high debts. In 1878 it elected 14 members to the U.S. House of Representatives. It was a forerunner of the Populist Party.

1192. C. An anti-immigrant offshoot of the Whig Party, (also known as the Whig American Party) the Know Nothing Party favored a 21 year waiting period for naturalization. At its height of popularity in 1854 and 1855 the party elected a total of seven governors, five senators, and 43 congressmen.

1193. B. Millard Fillmore was the Whig American/Know Nothing Party candidate for president in 1856. He carried the state of Maryland. The Know Nothings split on the slavery issue and generally either became Republicans or members of the Constitutional Union Party.

1194. A. The Liberty Party was a New York-based anti-slavery party. Its height was in the 1840s. Most abolitionists remained Whigs or Democrats rather than joining the Liberty Party.

1195. B. The Libertarian Party was founded in Colorado.

1196. B. The Libertarian Party was founded in 1971.

1197. B. The Libertarian Party has received one electoral vote in its history. In 1972 a faithless elector from Virginia voted for the Libertarian candidate instead of the Republican one. Generally the Libertarian Party receives about 1% of the popular vote in presidential elections. (Will 2016 be different?)

1198. A. An offshoot of the Democratic-Republican Party, the heyday of the National Republican Party was in the mid-1820s when from 1825 to 1827 it controlled Congress.

1199. B. Celebrity doctor, Benjamin Spock, was the presidential candidate of the People's Party in 1968. On the ballot in several states, most of his support came from voters in California.

1200. C. The farmer/laborer party of the West, the Populists won 5 states in 1892. In the 1894 elections the Populists elected six senators and seven congressmen.

1201. True. The Populist Party made a comeback of sorts in the 1980s featuring a platform that was opposed to the Federal Reserve Bank. The modern Populists have had controversial white nationalist candidates.

1202. A. Robert La Follette won Wisconsin in 1924. Henry Wallace did not carry any states in 1948.

1203. B. The Bull Moose Party won six states and 88 electoral votes in 1912.

1204. A. After the Democratic Party supported an end to segregation, George Wallace broke ranks with the party and campaigned for president as a member of the American Party. Later in life Wallace apologized for his pro-segregation views that he had held earlier.

1205. B. Eugene Debs ran for president five times as a member of the Socialist Party. One of Debs' campaigns was run from prison. He had been jailed for protesting World War I. He was later pardoned.

1206. A. The Socialist Party's best year running for president was 1912 when it got more than 900,000 votes and almost 6% of the popular vote. In 1932 the Socialists received about 800,000 votes but that was only 2.3% of the popular vote.

1207. B. The Socialist Workers' Party traces its origins to Leon Trotsky in the 1930s.

1208. B. The Communist Party's best year in the U.S. was 1932 when William Z. Foster got more than 100,000 votes.

FINALE

1209. C. The ideal of being a reluctant president comes from Cincinnatus.

BIBLIOGRAPHY

Adler, David A. *Heroes of the Revolution.* New York : Holiday House, 2003.

Allen, Jonathan and Parnes, Amie. *H R C : State secrets and the rebirth of Hillary Clinton.* New York : Crown Publishers, 2014.

Bausum, Ann. *Our Country's Presidents.* Washington D.C. : National Geographic Society, 2005.

Bernstein, Carl. *A Woman in Charge.* New York : Alfred Knopf, 2007.

Beschloss, Michael R. *Presidential Courage : brave leaders and how they changed America.* New York : Simon and Schuster, 2007.

Blair, Gwenda. *Donald Trump : Master Apprentice.* New York : Simon and Schuster, 2005.

Boeller, Paul F. *Presidential Diversions.* New York : Harcourt Inc., 2007.

Brands, H.W. *T.R. : The Last Romantic.* New York : Basic Books, 1997.

Bush, George W. *Decision Points.* New York : Crown Publishers, 2010.

Chuck, Todd and Gawiser, Sheldon. *How Barack Obama Won.* New York : Random House Inc., 2009.

Clinton, Hillary Rodham, *Living History.* New York : Simon and Schuster, 2003.

    Hard Choices. New York : Simon and Schuster, 2014.

Clinton, William J. *My Life.* New York : Alfred A. Knopf, 2004.

D'Antonio, Michael. *Never Enough : Donald Trump and the pursuit of success.* New York : Thomas Dunne Books, 2015.

Davis, Kenneth C. *Don't know much about the Presidents.* New York : Harper Children's, 2002.

    Don't know much about the American Presidents. New York : Hyperion, 2012.

Lisa Demauro and Time, Inc. *Time for Kids Special Edition: Presidents of the United States.* New York : HarperCollins, 2006.

Draper, Robert. *Dead Certain : the presidency of George W. Bush.* New York : Free Press, 2007.

Englar, Mary. *An illustrated timeline of U.S. Presidents.* North Mankato, MN : Picture Window Books, 2012.

Fischer, Roger. *Tippecanoe and Trinkets Too: The material culture of American presidential campaigns 1828-1984.* Chicago : University of Illinois Press, 1988.

Frey, Mark and Davis, Todd. *The New Big Book of U.S. Presidents.* Philadelphia : Running Press, 2009.

Garraty, John A. *1001 Things Everyone Should Know about American History.* New York : Doubleday, 1992.

Germond, Jack. *Fat man fed up: how American politics went bad.* New York : Random House, 2004.

Grant, Ulysses S. *Memoirs and Selected Letters.* New York : Library of America, 1990.

Green, Dan. *Basher History: U.S. Presidents: The Oval Office All-Stars*. New York : Kingfisher, 2013.

Halbert, Patricia A., editor. *I wish I knew that: U.S. Presidents*. New York : Reader's Digest Association Inc., 2012.

Halperin, Mark and Heilemann, John. *Double down : game change 2012*. New York : Penguin Press, 2013.

Heilemann, John and Halperin, Mark. *Game change : Obama and the Clintons, McCain and Palin, and the race of a lifetime*. New York : Harper, 2010.

Krull, Kathleen. *Lives of the Presidents: Fame, Shame, (and what the neighbors thought)*. New York : Harcourt Children's Books Houghton Mifflin Harcourt, 2011.

Lehrer, Jim. *Tension City: Inside the Presidential Debates from Kennedy-Nixon to Obama-McCain*. New York : Random House, 2011.

McCullough, David G. *Truman*. New York : Simon and Schuster, 1992.

Melanson, Phillip. *The Secret Service : The hidden history of an enigmatic agency*. New York : Basic Books, 2005.

Moore, James. *Bush's brain : how Karl Rove made George W. Bush presidential*. New York : Wiley, 2003.

Obama, Barack H. *The Audacity of Hope : Thoughts on Reclaiming the American Dream*. New York : Crown Publishers, 2006.

O'Connor, Jane. *If the walls could talk : Family life at the White House*. New York : Simon and Schuster, 2004.

Plouffe, David. *The Audacity to Win : The inside story and lessons on Barack Obama's historic victory*. New York : Viking, 2009.

Popkin, Samuel L. *The Candidate : What it takes to win and hold the White House*. New York : Oxford University Press, 2012.

Ringstad, Arnold. *Weird-but-true facts about the U.S. Presidents*. Mankato, MN : The Child's World 2013.

Rove, Karl. *Courage and Consequence : my life as a conservative in the fight*. New York : Threshold Editions, 2010.

Shenkman, Richard. *Legends, Lies & Cherished Myths of American History*. New York : William Morrow and Co., 1988.

Smith, Carter. *Presidency : every question answered*. San Diego : Thunder Bay Press, 2014.

Trump, Donald J. *Crippled America*. New York : Threshold Editions, 2015.

Vecchione, Glen. *The Little Giant Book of American Presidents*. New York : Sterling Publishing Co., 2007.

Whitney, David C. and Whitney, Robin Vaughn. *The American Presidents, 11th Ed.* New York : Reader's Digest Association Inc., 2009.

Young, Beverly. *Presidential Cookies: Cookie Recipes of the Presidents of the United States*. Sacramento : Presidential Publishing, 2005.

Woodward, Bob and Bernstein, Carl. *All the President's Men*. New York : Simon and Schuster, 1974.

Woodward, Bob. *Shadow : five presidents and the legacy of Watergate*. New York : Simon and Schuster, 1999.

Woodward, Bob. *Bush at War*. New York : Simon and Schuster, 2002.

The World Book of America's Presidents. Chicago : World Book Inc., 2001.

Presidential Elections 1789-2008. Washington D.C. : Congressional Quarterly Press, 2010.

The Presidency A to Z 4th edition. Washington D.C. : Congressional Quarterly Press, 2008.

Presidential Elections 1789-1992. Washington D.C. : Congressional Quarterly Inc., 1995.

National Party Conventions 1831-1992. Washington D.C. : Congressional Quarterly Inc., 1995.

Music:

Oscar Brand, *Presidential Campaign Songs*, Copyright 1999 by Smithsonian Folkways Recordings, iTunes.

Oscar Brand, *Elections Songs of the United States*, Copyright 2004 by Smithsonian Folkways Recordings/Folkways Records, iTunes.

Television:

"The Presidents" (2005) History Channel, Mini-series

Websites:

270 to Win: http://www.270towin.com/historical-presidential-elections/ (Last checked August 4, 2016)

Dave Leip's Election Atlas: http://uselectionatlas.org (Last checked September 2, 2016)

ABOUT THE AUTHOR

The author is a lawyer who lives with his family near St. Paul, Minnesota. He has a B.A. in history/political science from the University of Jamestown, Jamestown, North Dakota. He has written several trivia quiz books.

http://triviachallengebooks.webs.com/